Ship Radiogram

(49

CW01024898

The filing time shown in the date line on telegrams and day letters is STANDARD TIME at point of origin.   Time of receipt is STANDARD TIME at point of destination

AC62

WN97 W.WMUA291 44 GOVT= WUX WASHINGTON DC 1945 JAN 11 PM 6 06

CLARENCE R CARPENTER=

410 EAST SWON AVENUE WEBSTER GROVES MO=

THE   SECRETARY OF WAR DESIRES ME TO EXPRESS HIS DEEP REGRE

THAT YOUR SON PRIVATE FIRST CLASS PAUL L CARPENTER HAS BEE

REPORTED MISSING IN ACTION SINCE SIXTEEN DECEMBER IN GERMANY

IF FURTHER DETAILS OR OTHER INFORMATION ARE RECEIVED YOU

WILL BE PROMPTLY NOTIFIED=

DUNLOP ACTING THE ADJUTANT GENERAL

BATTLE OF THE BULGE
THROUGH THE LENS

PHILIP MICHAEL VORWALD

Credits

ISBN: 1 870067 23 1
© Philip Vorwald/*After the Battle*   Photographed and designed by Philip M. Vorwald.

PUBLISHERS
Battle of Britain International Limited, Church House, Church Street, London E15 3JA.

PRINTERS
Printed in Great Britain by Heronsgate Ltd, Basildon, Essex.

PHOTOGRAPHS
All photographs are accredited to the US Signal Corps, US Army or USAAF save for the following:
BFZ, Stuttgart 219. **W. Cavanagh** 48, 52, 80, 81 (both), 141, 143 (both), 144, 145 (both) 146 (top). **Jean Collignon** 91, 179. **E. Courtejoie** 245 bottom, 246 bottom, 248 top right. **A. Crouquet** 55, 230 top, 231 top right. **J. Deblau** 182 top. **P. Drösch** 146 bottom. **Roland Gaul** 71. **La Gleize Museum** 14, 47, 58, 150 top, 151 bottom, 152 top right and bottom left, 153 all, 154 bottom, 155, 156, 163, 216, 257 top. **G. Grégoire** 96. **Photo Hemmer** 129 top. **Imperial War Museum** 18, 19, 20. **J. Jacob** 220 bottom right, 246 top. **Tony Krier** 113, 124, **Photo Luma** 152 top left, 176. **S. de Meyer** 54, 248 bottom left and right. **H. Ritgen** 208. **Jean Schickes** 72 (both). **R. F. Vorwald** dustjacket photo of author. Headlines: Copyright 2000 by the *New York Times* Company. Reprinted by permission. All present day comparisons are copyright of the author.

COVER
Clockwise: **Panzers on the move in Lanzerath (page 165); the 101st Airborne Division march out of Bastogne (page 30); The 'End of a Dream' in Rochefort (page 232), and the end of the road for a Panther in Grandmenil (page 103).** *Centre:* **An award ceremony in Born (page 48).**

ENDPAPERS
Front left: **American prisoners shuffle through the slush to the rear as the panzers roll westwards. A scene on Rollbahn D near Lanzerath as a Tiger II of schwere SS-Panzer-Abteilung 501, Kampfgruppe Peiper, 1. SS-Panzer-Division, passes prisoners of the US 99th Infantry Division.**

Front right: **The telegram which every mother and father dreaded receiving: their son, missing in action. The date: December 16, 1944. The Battle of the Bulge had just begun.**

Rear left: **Four months later and still no word of Pfc Paul L. Carpentier.**

Rear right: **The Victory Day present beyond any price: Paul Carpentier . . . safe and well.**

FRONTISPIECE
The camera does not lie . . . or does it? This is a stunning example of Philip Vorwald's painstaking work to recreate the scenes of yesterday. This is in fact two pictures, the Tiger II now 'digitally restored'; once commanded by Obersturmführer Rudolf Dollinger of the 1. SS-Panzer-Division 'Leibstandarte Adolf Hitler' and now on display at La Gleize Belgium. A snowy field east of Nisramont pictured by Philip today forms the backdrop as it might have been, the marriage of the two images being accomplished through the computerised facilities of Adobe Photoshop (see page 292).

REAR COVER
Under the protective watch of a US Army M4 Sherman, American soldiers of the US 75th Infantry Division (VII Corps) march eastwards through the village of Forzée, Belgium, in the footsteps of the US 2nd Armored Division. *Inset:* **The soldiers having marched into history, the exact location is captured 50 years later. A long shadowed afternoon in December finds the scene virtually identical to that which once was. In the peaceful village of Forzée today, the only mechanised sounds come from farm machinery.**

Acknowledgements

Across the many years it took to photograph, compile, write and design this book, the author was supported by many people, both friends and professionals. This book could not have been made without their sincere and enthusiastic help and the author hereby wishes to acknowledge and credit their fine contributions. First, to the people of Belgium and Luxembourg, whose outgoing, friendly manner towards a total stranger knocking on their doors made my endeavour always enjoyable. Their coffee invitations, property trespassing permission and deep sense of respect for post-war studies were most cordial. They are true ambassadors for their beautiful countries.

To all of my friends and well-wishers who contributed photographs for inclusion in the book, my heartfelt appreciation and thanks. Particular appreciation is paid to William Cavanagh (Durham, England) as well as Simon Pugh-Jones and David Donavan (both of South Wales), all of whom provided a treasure of unpublished photographs, telegrams and vintage photo montages. Additional acknowledgements to Gilles Luciani (Limax Communications, Alzette, Luxembourg) and Wim Verheije (Standaard Uitgeverij, Antwerp, Belgium) for permission to reproduce maps. My special gratitude is paid to US Army veterans of the Battle of the Bulge who contributed their unique and priceless original photographs. It is difficult to describe the feeling of reviewing these relics for the first time, new windows and angles to a timeless conflict. Your work and struggle will never be forgotten.

Two native Frenchmen were likewise supportive of this book. First, the world-renowned military historian Jean Paul Pallud, whose prior work on the Battle of the Bulge set the standard against which all are measured. His encouragement was greatly appreciated. I hope this work measures up to his historic expectations, and serves to 'carry the torch' for this battle, as he so aptly described the effort. Second, my close friend and confidante, Francois Hasbroucq. Besides serving with distinction as my financial controller in our European business headquarters, he accompanied me on several trips to the Ardennes, linguistically unlocking doors and buildings when entry was paramount to the comparison. Always enthusiastic and chain-smoking, he argued over many a Michelin map in the middle of nowhere, as snowfall slowly covered our car. It was a pleasure to work with the gentleman. Likewise thanks to all of my former business associates in Belgium; your encouragement and support was vital to the cause.

For publication and production, the team at *After the Battle* in London performed their usual superb job. Many thanks to Winston Ramsey, Editor-in-Chief, who believed in the quality of my photo set enough to bring it to press. His patience with my computers, laptops and CDs was exceeded only by his Herculean efforts at editing my tortured photo captions. To Rob Green as well, who endured my endless explanations on how things should be laid out, only to improve upon them later. Editor Karel Margry likewise contributed his considerable expertise during the editing process. To my parents, Richard and Patricia, who were constantly perplexed by their son's behaviour in a far-off foreign country, your continuing support and love for a work-obsessed son is greatly felt and appreciated. A special and heartfelt thanks to my wife Catherine who spent many a Sunday alone with our daughters while her husband tramped through the snow with his camera. Your love and support served to keep the entire monstrous project moving. I am deeply in debt to your patience and understanding.

And last, to my two precious daughters, Charlotte and Gabrielle. You grew up in Belgium, and watched as daddy worked on the 'big war book' on his Macintosh. May the historic photographs you reviewed with your father on the kitchen table, and the nature of human conflict they represent, remain just that — forever history.

PHILIP VORWALD, NOVEMBER 2000

CONTENTS

Preface   5

Introduction   7

LOCATIONS ILLUSTRATED

The New York Times.

Copyright, 1944, by The New York Times Company.

NEW YORK, WEDNESDAY, DECEMBER 20, 1944.

Temperatures Yesterday—Max., 26; Min.,
Sunrise, 8:16 A. M.; Sunset, 5:32 P. M.

THREE CENTS IN NEW YORK CITY

Entered as Second-Class Matter,
Postoffice, New York, N. Y.

NAZIS GAIN IN BELGIUM IN GREAT BATTLE;
FORTRESSES CALLED UPON TO STEM PUSH;
B-29'S BOMB JAPAN AND CHINA CENTERS

res
Hand

Times.
c. 19—The
as expired
ening with
die of the
ight mem-
final quo-

had lacked
t few days,
e o'clock with
presentatives

s the Rivers
d through in-
ate to muster
he conference

r the first rise
l employes who
was also

KYUSHU HIT AGAIN

Osaka Aircraft Factory
Raked—Shanghai and
Nanking Also Scored

FOE IN LEYTE TRAP

Americans Cut Ormoc
Corridor in 2 Places,
Take Strongpoint

ATTEMPTED LANDING BEHIND OUR LINES FAILS

OUR MEN CONFIDENT

Americans Fight Their
Biggest Battle to
Check Foe's Drive

Down this road, the soldiers came.

They stayed only a few hours.

When they had gone, a community which had lived

for over a thousand years . . . was dead.

SIR LAURENCE OLIVIER, *THE WORLD AT WAR*

It stands along a street of a small Belgian town, facing a modest square. Two stories tall, the century-old house maintains an air of quiet distinction amongst the adjoining row houses. The architecture is turn-of-the-century French, with a Belgian influence. Expert lattice and masonry joints speak of quality workmanship. Stately windows march in orderly fashion across its front, each trimmed with fine stone accents and adorned with Belgian lace. Careful selection of a two-tone stonework pattern highlight the corners of the house, while an ornate door with subtle brass fittings greets its visitors. With flowers blooming on the window sills, the house is an architectural site to behold.

An architectural site to behold indeed, for its proud stone façade is multilated and scarred. Gaping holes and pock marks splash across its face in a deliberate swath. The effect is jarring; it violates the face of the house. Yet such a pattern, deep and ruinous, is not random. It speaks of an unnatural event which took place long ago. Today, the house silently bears such scars with dignity.

In front of the house, an old lady on the street pauses to speak to an elderly man. Both are old enough to have seen and experienced the events which occurred in their town of Bourcy in Belgium on December 20, 1944. Their childhood memories sleep with images of sudden destruction . . . soldiers in the streets . . . tremendous concussions . . . screams of men . . . rumble of German armour . . . shouts in American English.

The house today, meticulously maintained, could have been repaired and restored, along with the others in the town. The scars could have been carefully reworked in the style of the era, the house given a new façade to match the rest of its elegance.

But it deliberately was not. The reason is simple and profound. An unofficial monument, found on no map, celebrated with no plaque, it speaks for the ages. Its proprietors intended the house to look down upon the inhabitants and visitors of Bourcy with a visual message and an untold warning: *Remember. Peace is fragile. Complacency and apathy invite disaster. The proof stands before you.* The elders of the village understand. They once watched through terrified teenage eyes as their town was ripped asunder by two opposing forces. The house today, in the brilliant sunshine, speaks for them, and will continue to do so when they have passed on.

Long ago, it happened here. They came this way.

Silent testimony in Bourcy, Belgium

The New York Times

"All the News That's Fit to Print"

Copyright, 1944, by The New York Times Company.

NEW YORK, SATURDAY, DECEMBER 23, 1944.

THREE CENTS

VOL. XCIV...No. 31,745.

Entered as Second-Class Matter.
Postoffice, New York, N. Y.

GERMANS SWEEP WEST THROUGH LUXEMBOUR[G]
REPORT PATTON ATTACKING ON SOUTH FLAN[K]
EISENHOWER URGES GREATEST ALLIED EFF[ORT]

GERMAN TOWN REDUCED TO RUBBLE AFTER SHELLING BY BOTH SIDES

MAYOR DEMANDS U. S. ACT AT ONCE ON MEAT CRISIS

...st a Temporary

President Accepts Just One Columnist

Special to The New York Times.
WASHINGTON, Dec. 22—President Roosevelt called columnists today an unnecessary excrescence on our civilization.

ROOSEVELT URGES HOMEFOLKS TO BACK SOLDIERS AT FRONT

RAIL H[...]

Panzers[...]
Past Ba[...]
Slo[...]

INTRODUCTION

As an American expatriate who lived in Belgium for nine years, working as Vice-President of European Operations for a large multi-national health care company, I came to know and enjoy the country. My family and I (my wife Catherine and two children) benefited a great deal from living and working in Europe. It offered a rich cultural lifestyle and a diverse environment for raising children. The town which we called home, Waterloo, is steeped in cultural and military history. Having studied military history for some time, the timing was indeed fortuitous when I first arrived in Europe in September 1990, coinciding with the beginning of the 50-year anniversaries of the major battles and events of the European Theater in World War II. I looked forward to 'retracing' such historic moments on the actual fields of battle. I could not have possibly known at the time that such an interest would set in motion a four-year project. Begun on a snowy day in La Gleize, Belgium, on December 28, 1994, it would end precisely four years later, high atop the abbey château in Stavelot, Belgium, on December 28, 1998.

Upon arriving in Europe my first impression of many small towns and villages was one of vague amusement. Recalling the grainy black and white US Army Signal Corps photographs of American forces advancing across Europe, it all looked rather like an elaborate Hollywood war movie set, albeit now rendered in colour. Walking the brick-lined back streets of a Belgian village or town, I seemed to be waiting for the tanks to rumble down the next cross street, followed by American GIs ducking for cover as they dashed from doorway to doorway. One expected at any moment to hear a director yell 'Cut!', and all the inhabitants to settle in off the streets, relaxing at the studio sandwich truck that was surely parked behind me.

But it never happened that way, and gradually it sank in that this was indeed the real set. This was first brought home by the scattered memorial plaques placed on the sides of buildings and on stone plinths in town squares. All proclaimed in French the sacrifice, bravery or atrocity which had occurred at each location; here a Resistance fighter shot for partisan activity, there a dozen citizens massacred by the 'German invaders'. Reading French in a rudimentary way, my eyes always sought out the dates on such memorials, and I was never disappointed. In the towns of northern Belgium, '1940'; in central Belgium, '1942'.

And then, in countless villages, towns and cities in south-eastern Belgium and Luxembourg, the years marked on memorials ran together into one, and the past began to be measured in weeks and days of a single fateful period of conflict. Now the memorials became stone roll-calls, listing the honoured dead of each village in alphabetical order. As one approached the German border deep inside southern Belgium, the dates marched into the past, all seeming to coalesce in a particular moment in time: December 1944. Around each village and town, the dwellings held further clues. Close inspection of the houses, farms and town halls by a discerning eye now revealed brickwork that did not match, walls that were pockmarked with strange patterns, or buildings bearing

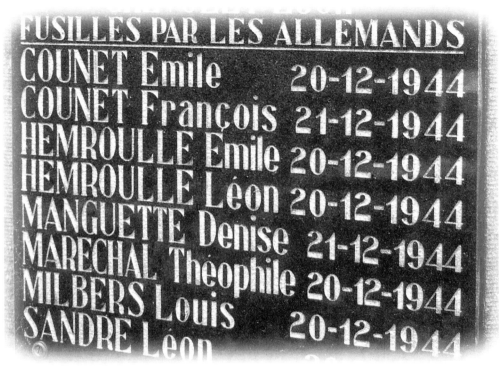

Roll-call in stone around a fateful date in Waimes, Belgium.

grotesque scars. More disconcerting still, the strange juxtaposition of modern steel and glass buildings standing directly opposite much older structures, in odd patterns and locations. The most unusual sight was the occasional American flag, snapping proudly in the middle of a Belgian town square.

Of all the World War II battles in Europe, the one series or campaign which has always captured my imagination has been La Bataille des Ardennes; the battle for the Ardennes. Remaining to this day the largest sustained battle ever fought by the US Army (including that of Desert Storm), its ferocity and strategic drama were matched only by the appalling conditions under which it was fought. As the year 1994 drew to a close, I found myself setting out to visit some historic battle locations to be marked by 50 year anniversaries in Belgian villages, towns and cemeteries. My initial intent was to simply capture a few of the somber remembrances with a close friend, using Jean-Paul Pallud's renowned 1984 publication *The Battle of the Bulge Then and Now* as an historic background guide. Having visited Normandy in the summer of the same year for the D-Day remembrances, it then dawned on me that the photographic record of the Battle of the Bulge itself should likewise be captured on a 50-year anniversary time scale. Being an interested photographer, and living 'on-site' to these locations, I set about documenting the historical photo record of the Battle of the Bulge.

As readers of the premier military publication series *After the Battle* are well aware, the 'then and now' photo comparison technique, beyond the historical value of scene location and identification, can be an emotionally powerful one. Historic wartime images of extreme destruction, suffering, and gallantry, when viewed in the context of the mundane, banal, present-day locations, can often invoke complex feelings. To research, visit and photograph these sites often led to feelings of isolation and mortality, heightened by those locations which hadn't changed at all over half a century later.

As the project began to unfold, I realised that many of the complex feelings associated with photo sets in the 'then and now' format were in fact closely linked to the technical accuracy of the comparisons themselves. Since provoking these feelings is what the 'then and now' format is indeed all about, I studied the photographic comparisons I had taken early on in my project for clues as to why some comparisons seemed to be more powerful than others.

Apart from the obvious influence of the photo's content itself, three characteristics became readily apparent. First, a photographic comparison seemed to have the maximum 'impact' when the comparison was rendered as accurately and as perfectly as possible, in terms of image alignment, angle and composition. Such accuracy tended to 'free the eyes' to focus on what had occurred at the site itself, without visually seeking to 'adjust' the photo alignment. Second, the impact was greatest when either the location hadn't changed at all, or had changed substantially. The latter could be tragic (a children's playground on the site of a massacre), ironic (a hair salon where soldiers once bivouacked) or majestic (flowers blooming in a field where a destroyed tank once sat burning).

The third and final comparison aspect, which in fact links the previous two for the best visual impact, was something that jumped out of the wartime photos when compared 50 years later: the weather. To provide the best possible timeless comparison, you had to match the weather. When all of these criteria were met, the impact was greatest; objects and people simply vanished from the historic location, and the gravity of the site was revealed. Often I would stand in the freezing cold and fog of the Ardennes, photographing a particular farmhouse from a certain angle, and pause . . . recalling the devastation which once lay about the site. The farmhouse in front of me was absolutely identical to its state 50 years ago . . . the scars in the stone wall still there . . . the exact number and shape of the fence posts . . . and all framed in a similar snow and fog as long ago. I seemed to be standing there, waiting . . . waiting for someone to drag the shattered soldiers away before my eyes . . . so I could take the exact comparison picture without them; 50 years had melted away.

Following in the footsteps of one of the greatest *After the Battle* researchers of all, Jean-Paul Pallud, I vowed to do the job as perfectly as possible, and document the present-day locations of these sites as well, so that others could easily locate and experience them. This was a key, important element driving the layout of this publication; the combination of historical, photographic documentation of military activity in the Ardennes with site location maps and data, to make history accessible and alive to the interested reader. When presented in the proper format, and supported by additional digital techniques, history can in a literal sense be revisited – viewed 'through the lens' of war photographers of long ago, both German and American. These places still exist. The scenes and locations where once the fate of nations was decided can be visited and experienced today.

To fully support such activity, I have organised the main body of the book alphabetically by village and town. This is the easiest way for the interested, knowledgeable reader to find, review and revisit the action in a particular location. Since the battle for the Ardennes was fought along a wide front and contained many sectors of simultaneous engagements, attempts to capture the photographic sequences chronologically were difficult and ulti-

mately distracting to this book's intention. Therefore, I left this aspect to previously published volumes on the order of battle itself. The entire scope of each village's contributions was then arranged with photographic comparisons in the 'then and now' format which, as indicated earlier, were rigorously aligned and matched for maximum effect. Digital photography allowed for optimal comparison accuracy, including photo light levels, sharpening and enhancement. Supporting each photo are historically accurate, informative captions. Indeed, one of the most time-consuming tasks of the project was caption writing. A wartime photograph carries little meaning to the non-historian if the caption simply reads 'US soldiers walking by a German tank'. I've tried to give each photo comparison in each village some historical meaning; which unit the tank belonged to, why they were attacking what, how the tank was disabled, what happened in the village itself. This at least enables the reader to mentally frame the photo and become more involved. The same applies to the modern-day comparison photo. I'll share any interesting items to search for or examine, and perhaps give a few anecdotes about the site today. This is all in support of what I believe to be the emotional and historical power of the 'then and now' format, what many people quickly pick up on and realise; we live in the history books themselves.

Further to the photos and captions, I then employed a series of three map sequences, each progressively more detailed than the previous, and each having its own purpose. I have used the first of a set of three maps to position each site within both the maximum extent of the 'bulge' of the battle as well as the site's proximity to the planned German attack routes west (Rollbahns). In the first map, one can see at a glance the relative location of each site in context to the entire salient of battle activity. A second map then pinpoints the precise cartographic location of the site itself in relationship to major thoroughfares and roads, along with longitude/latitude and instructions on how to reach the site(s) by car. A third and final map documents the site in the greatest detail. The exact location of every photo comparison is identified, by street name and house number, including visual tips, clues and comments. This third level of detail is most important – find it and document it, so that others may experience it.

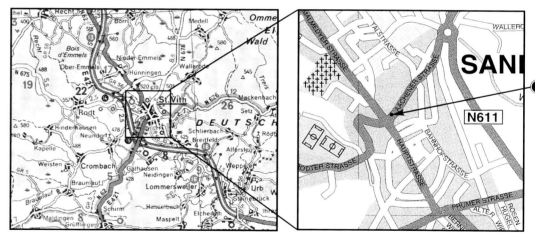

Left: **Geographic overview of the Battle of the Bulge salient places each town or village action in perspective. A relief overlay of the maximum 'bulge at high tide' shows the furthest extent of German penetration into Belgium and Luxembourg. Intended operational sectors of three German armies on the right are indicated by horizontal grey lines. Black arrows denote planned 'Rollbahn' attack routes as assigned to major German divisions. Finally, the location of each photo comparison site is indicated by a target square on the map.** *Centre:* **Each town or village's cartographic location is then viewed at a thoroughfare resolution, including latitude/longitude and directions by car.** *Right:* **Further detailed map enhancement reveals the precise location of the photo comparison(s) at a street and road level resolution. Numbered circles pinpoint each photo location and match those given to each photo comparison.**

Additional sections of the book highlight the digital techniques used (Photoshop Goes to War) and the intriguing visual possibilities that digital imaging can bring to military history (In the Field: Then Meets Now) in which elements of the past once again assume their rightful place in time today. Finally, all of the photo comparisons in the book are also available on a separate cross-platform CD-ROM for content review, key word searches and enhanced viewing on computers. An on-disc media browser for both PC and Macintosh makes searching and viewing quick and easy.

Therefore, for the last four years, my 'other office' has been the vast expanse of south-eastern Belgium and Luxembourg known as the region of the Ardennes. It is at once beautiful, majestic, and prone to rapid weather changes. The conditions under which these pictures were taken ran the gamut of meteorological states. However, when going after weather-matches beyond a standard comparison, operating in winter conditions became the norm for Battle of the Bulge research. And this meant two challenges, both of which were faced by the military forces of 50 years ago; short daylight hours, and the cold. Though both were seasonal facts of life, the second was intimidating and onerous. The Ardennes is a very, very cold place in December and January. It is a type of wet, damp, bottomless cold, hanging heavy in the air. The geography of the Ardennes, with its deep valleys, rushing streams and heavily forested landscapes, seems to somehow concentrate the cold in a deep freeze. When surrounded by breathtaking landscapes in the cold, dull grey mornings of an Ardennes winter, the effect is complete. The swollen Amblève river rushing through the frozen farmland amidst towering pines sends out a siren's song, whispering a frigid message. I recalled the perfect description of such a deadly cold once given by Jack Novey, a side-gunner on a B-17 over Europe, in his classic autobiographical book *The Cold Blue Sky*. He described a living thing, always there, probing, seeking . . . 'the cold was like a serpent, crawling over my body, enveloping and numbing my mind, roaring into my ears, Let me in. Let me in and I'll kill you.' And kill them it did, exhausted Germans, Americans and Britons, during days and weeks of continuous fighting in unimaginable conditions; the coldest winter in over a quarter century of recorded European history, with little food, no sleep, no feeling in their frozen extremities. Some lay down for a brief rest, and slept an eternal sleep, never to awaken; literally frozen to death by the serpent cold of the Ardennes.

Then meets now in the village of Arbrefontaine, Belgium. The author's BMW 524tds pulls up alongside a perfectly restored US Army Jeep next to a classic Ardennes farmhouse.

Intelligence gathering inside a bar in Wiltz, Luxembourg. Francois holds court while the author captures the scene. Local citizens were always eager to help out.

Today the Ardennes is a vast, living, open-air museum. Its scenic beauty and peaceful farming communities all constitute a massive battlefield, replete with relics, saturated in history, and populated by towns and villages whose names to the learned read as a roll-call of military honour. Walking amongst them, down their streets, through their fields, was physically and emotionally exhausting, yet always rewarding. Handing a wartime photograph to an old farmer could generate a quiet gaze, as he nodded knowingly, a faint smile crossing his lips. He would look up and sort of mentally drift away for a moment. Perhaps he once played on the tank with his friends . . . or tried to move the great gun from its position . . . or watched as the post-war scrap merchants began their slow and methodical task of cutting the tank apart. Whatever it was, he remembered, and yes, he could take me there now, just follow him . . . and so it would go. Four years filled with anecdotes as well as film, scanners and CDs. The craziest moment: being chased by a bull through a muddy field in Wallerode, Belgium, while Francois laughed hysterically, all the while translating in German to the farmer what I was trying to accomplish. And the most somber: standing alongside a hedgerow outside La Maison Legaye on the outskirts of Stavelot, Belgium. I listened in horror as an elderly member of the Legaye family patiently told me how her friends and relatives, mostly women and children, were lined up along the hedge next to the house and executed in cold blood by the 1. SS-Panzer-Division on the evening of December 19, 1944. She happened to be gone that night, and today lives in the same house.

Investigating the minute-by-minute tactical aspects of a battle drew me deeper and deeper into the historical human emotion each conflict contained. Without actual site visits, such historical information by itself would have been limiting. It is possible to understand that, on such-and-such a date, tank X, after proceeding down street Y, encountered a US soldier standing in full frontal view, calmly aiming a bazooka at it. His shot disabled the tank, which in turn blocked the road, which in turn held up the panzer-grenadier regiment for two vital hours, which nonetheless resulted in the US soldier be torn apart by the tank's bow machine gun, while his unit successfully regrouped in the storm of the invasion.

'Someone has to stop this tank. . .'

Today, walking the streets of the twin villages of Krinkelt-Rocherath with my friend and 'northern shoulder' expert/author William Cavanagh, this encounter takes on a new, real and emotive meaning. Citing the soldier by name; the Panther tank turning the corner here and sighting its gun down this road. The soldier had already told his unit to withdraw through this field while he held them off. A single soldier, calmly taking on the surging sea of the 12. SS-Panzer-Division in its furious and vengeful entirety, in the fog and mist of a December morning in 1944. Surviving occupants of the Panther, interviewed over four decades later, would speak of the awe-inspiring courage of the US soldier. Perhaps this courage is what Thomas Brokaw spoke of so eloquently in his superb book, *The Greatest Generation*: a calm, profound, utterly selfless sacrifice for the greater good. Having visited Krinkelt-Rocherath many times, one cannot help but wonder what went through the mind of a soldier of that unit when, in the confusion, thunder and panic of the moment, he heard his friend with the bazooka say to him: 'Go. I'll hold them off. Someone has to stop this tank.' Time must have frozen for a split second, as the soldier realised what the statement meant; death for his defender, and through it, freedom for the rest.

What's an American or Briton to make of all of this today? Having lived in Belgium for nine years, I have a few suggestions for your next vacation. You should escape your everyday life for a few days or weeks and visit the Ardennes. You and a friend could bring your wives or friends to Europe. The flights across the Atlantic are relatively inexpensive. Fly into Brussels, and operate out of an inexpensive but nice hotel. Give your wives the tourist maps for Brussels and Brugges and tell them to have a great time together. You and your friend hop in a rental car with this book in the front seat, plus a purchased Michelin map No. 214, and have a great time. Drink superb beer in each village, eat terrific food in the smallest of cafés. Meet your wives every evening back in Brussels for din-

ner and swap stories. They'll love it, *and you'll never forget it*. Or if you can get a group together, contact Will Cavanagh by e-mail via the web site (www.tours-international.com) to arrange an Ardennes tour that will have you ducking for cover. And if you're a veteran of the battle of the Ardennes, you need none of my trite explanations to understand the meaning a return visit would hold.

Which leads me to the sobering thought that there are indeed fewer and fewer battle veterans of this terrible campaign alive today. Having survived their unlucky friends and companions and perhaps laden with a tinge of guilt, they have long since assimilated themselves back into civil society. Throughout the 'nifty fifties', when their former supreme commander led the nation as the chief US executive into the beginnings of the Cold War, they strove to catch up with their lives. College attendance, a childhood sweetheart as a bride and a new house in the suburbs served to complete the circle for so many Battle of the Bulge veterans. Now, as they approach the end of their lives and their numbers grow fewer with each passing year, one wonders when, not if, their thoughts return one last time to the snows of Belgium. Whether or not, in the banality and ease of present-day life, a particular time, incident, or terror surfaces once again from their memories . . .

Like so many men in his division, he had vowed that he would never, ever be that cold again. In doing so, he had unwittingly joined a post-war demographic exodus towards California and the west coast, to relish the endless summers, and prosper in the postcard skies. It had made living so much easier then, and now, as he approached his eightieth birthday, it was one less thing that would not fail or leave him.

He could no longer remember exactly when he had finally decided to leave the bay area of San Francisco for good. He had only known that the relentless pace of technology, progress and congestion had made the decision a surprisingly easy one. One fine, summer day in the backyard of his Cupertino home, relaxing in his favourite chair, he had found himself simply and casually suggesting to his wife that they should sell their house and move away, somewhere, anywhere. He didn't quite know what surprised him more at the time; the ease with which the thought came to him, or the enthusiastic and immediate confirmation of the same feelings from his wife.

It didn't really matter now. They had done it, a decade or so ago. Sitting content in a redwood chair, on the porch of his retirement home high in the central forested hills of Grass Valley, California, he now watched the snow falling gently through the pine trees, a soft gift from the grey leaden skies of winter. In the heart of California's gold country, winter came swiftly and quietly, and on this fresh morning, the air was sharp with the sting of a temperature that had plunged during the night. As a soft light began to wake up the mountain top, he gazed out at the valley below him, the thick carpet of dense conifer trees already wearing a thin coat of freshly fallen snow.

He took a sip of strong coffee from the mug he held in a gloved hand, a wry smile crinkling his face. Strong coffee, freezing temperatures, falling snow, and conifer trees. Things had come full circle indeed.

Down in the slope of the valley, off to the left by a dense copse of trees, the carpenter's cabin was waking up. A wisp of smoke from the short, stubby chimney signaled its owner stirring. From his chair he watched the scene as eventually the carpenter emerged, girded against the cold, to once again attack several choice California Douglas fir trees to provide new wood for his project. Sharp slap-crack noises echoed loud and clear through the valley as the carpenter began to work methodically, in a cadence. His breath formed puffs of frost.

He sat up in his lounge chair and listened, as the noise rose up the valley and met his ears. He slowly closed his eyes. The cold, the noise.

He opened them again, this time looking upwards toward the light grey clouds. The conifer trees, piercing skyward all around him, formed a cathedral of sharp, green spires, standing silently in defiance of the snow, now falling stronger, stinging his face. He blinked the flakes from his lashes, and listened once again with his eyes wide open.

Now his mind began to listen as well. The cold, the noise, the snow. Cold. So cold. More slap-cracks . . . got to get away . . .

He had returned.

His mind's eye opened completely now, opened from a deep, mental sleep. The scene was frighteningly familiar. On his back, looking upwards. The trees, the snow, the cold. Another enormous slap-crack, followed instantaneously by an almost imperceptible hiss. 88! The number itself stirred his legs at once. He frantically rolled over onto a prone position, instinctively grasping his helmet and clutching his rifle. The mortar concussion had thrown him from his position, stunned yet intact. He dug into the snow, sweeping his frantic gaze around, his mind working furiously as he assessed the situation in a moment. Crumpled, misshapened bodies confirmed the toll. Only a low moan from one of them prevented the tally from climbing higher. Tommy! It can't be . . . He crawled frantically through the thick, white snow towards the sound of pain. He brushed up against red and green fabric as he met his friend lying on his back.

Another slap-crack rent the air around him, pounding his ears. He instantly buried his face in Tommy's chest. The ground shook and heaved, then stopped. He looked into Tommy's face. His eyes were wide with surprise, terror and fear. His lips trembled, as large bubbles of bright red blood popped and gurgled from his mouth. He began to shake and shiver.

His mind raced as he frantically began to tear open Tommy's wool coat, hidden under the pathetic white sheet they all wore in a meagre attempt to hide themselves from their adversaries. A sea of blood flowed over his hands, which began to slip and slither as he vainly tried to search for his friend's wound. He finally flung aside a portion of Tommy's coat, only to be met with an horrific geyser of blood, jetting out to stain the perfectly white snow around him. (*My god, I can't stop it . . .*)

Tommy slowly turned his shaking head to face him, uttering slowly and carefully: 'It's OK . . . Go.' His head sank back in his hands. Tommy gazed at him with fading eyes and a trembling smile, and spoke his last words to his closest friend: '*It's coming!*'

Another slap-crack. Another earthquake. He left his dying friend in a clumsy snow-crawl towards a thick hedge, finally finding refuge in its dense base roots. His mind began to skid back into training gear. Localise. Field of fire. Flank. He raised his head cautiously to assess the situation. It was then that he felt it, sensed it, saw it through the mist.

It sat at the edge of the field, an enormous beast of battle. His eyes screamed silently as he took in its girth, its titanic size. Tank. A whole fieldful of tank. He held his breath, desperately trying to stay calm while he scanned the threat. Panther! . . . No. Having prided himself on his recognition skills, he cursed and squinted hard. A gust of wind parted the mist, and he sucked in his breath as saw it clearly for the first time. Special Motor Vehicle 182, Panzerkampfwagen VI, Type II, Designation B. Tiger II. Königstiger. *King Tiger.* He was lying no more than a hundred yards from the ultimate killing machine.

As if to affirm his identification and presence, another enormous slap-crack rent the air, only this time he got the full show. A long, fat flame spat wickedly out the obscene length of the 88mm gun, quite visible in the low dawn light. The ground shook again, as the enormous beast rocked gently back on its massive tracks, the snow shaking from its armoured bulk. A small puff of smoke trailed briefly upwards from the end of its long barrel, capping a hellish performance.

He had just begun to determine an escape route along the hedge to the river below when it began. (*It's coming!*)

At first it took the form of a series of far-off crumping noises on the horizon, increasing in frequency, timing and ferocity. The tree line in the distance seemed to sparkle with tiny, flickering lights. He glanced back at the King Tiger, which came alive now with crawling, jumping forms. He instantly recognised them as panzergrenadiers, off loading and running towards an undetermined location. They frantically gestured and yelled in German, as if warning everyone of their upcoming attack.

The attack indeed came, yet it was not of their doing. At once, the air became filled with the sound of a hundred subway trains, roaring in unison overhead, hell-bent on arriving on time, on destination. The eruptions began seconds later.

Burying his face deep in the cold snow, he began frantically and instinctively to dig, deeper, away, as the ground heaved, bucked and rolled. The force of the explosions was cataclysmic as the air was torn, literally shrieking from the concussions which rocked his position. Pressure waves pounded his head and ears relentlessly, as the earth was ripped asunder by an almighty sequence of blasts, the field around him tilled by the fury. He screamed involuntarily and curled up into a ball, crying and rocking as the ground shook and quaked. He was thrown into the air by one of a series of proximal explosions, smashing back to earth in a painful heap. With a low moan, he raised his throbbing head in the midst of the bombardment, now deaf and numb to the catastrophe unfolding around him. He glanced in the direction of the King Tiger, just in time to witness a direct hit on its enormous turret. With a thunderous detonation, the proud beast's seven-ton head separated cleanly from its massive body and flew lazily skyward, spinning slowly in a sickening arc. His eyes saw, yet did not believe. *What kind of force?*! He slumped forward unconscious in the snow, the sounds of battle receding around him into blackness.

The din and destruction tapered off, leaving only the sounds of burning brush, moaning men, and the cold frozen earth, now hissing and hot, its snowy blanket horribly mutilated.

A single, intelligent, clear human voice crackled quietly and placidly across the scene of destruction. It emanated from the field radio clutched in Tommy's cold, dead right hand. It persistently and professionally inquired of anyone present to render and update the situation . . .

'*Able One to Harper Five. I say again . . . Able One to Harper Five. One-Five-Fives have sung, repeat, Long Toms have sung, low and sweet, request coordinate update.*'

His closest friend, Thomas A. Colligan, 'Time-on-Target Tommy', would never reply.

'*More coffee, dear?*'

He sat transfixed, gazing glassy-eyed out towards the valley. His wife saw to her amazement that he was covered with a quarter-inch of snow, yet sat perfectly still.

Dear?

She tapped his hearing aid gently.

He woke with a start, sending the snow falling from his head. He looked down at himself, embarrassed, and began to brush the snow from his coat and pants.

Are you OK dear?

"It sat at the edge of the field, an enormous beast of battle. . ."

And let us never forget the enormous sacrifices that all young men made in the snow and cold of the Ardennes; young Germans, misled and deluded by a monstrous ideology; young Americans and Britons, led by a heartfelt desire to extinguish the same. And all united in conflict, suffering and death.

Turn back the pages of time now, and remember.

Philip Michael Vorwald
Waterloo, Belgium
April 29, 1999

'One-Five-Fives have sung, low and sweet.'

After reassuring her that he was fine, he stood, stamped the snow from his feet, and took another refill of coffee. She left him again, as he walked to the railing of the porch, placed the coffee down, and put his hands in his pockets. He looked long and hard down into the valley. The carpenter had called it quits for the morning as the snow continued to fall. He sighed heavily.

So long ago. Another time, another country, Belgium. So many friends, gone. Who will remember?, he thought. His lined face tightened, lips trembling. A bitter anger rose in his aged body.

'Who will remember ?!', he shouted hoarsely into the valley.

We will remember.

The 'then and now' photo technique is the final, permanent link to the past, a gateway to a glimpse of our human mortality, a record of what transpired where. To return to and accurately portray the scenes and locations of past struggles, conflicts and horrors in their modern-day setting is to do more than record history and document military occurrences. In a sense, it is to capture time itself on film, for the technique brings together history, poignancy and a terrifying banality in a way that can be profoundly moving. And the final realisation of what man overcame is an encouraging testament to the human spirit.

The landscapes of a former war are rapidly changing on the old continent. Soon they will forever lose their visual links with the past, rendered unrecognisable by progress, save only for the earthly features themselves, to be worn away under the pitiless assault of time.

While we still can, let us pause and reflect on the events that once took place in the countries of Belgium and Luxembourg. Let us mark their locations for posterity: *it happened here, they came this way.* Let us visit these sites with our friends, and stand in the freezing cold and fog of a forest in the Ardennes, or in the back roads of a small farming village. Let us stare at the scars of battle that still exist in the brickwork of ancient buildings in a town square, and reflect on the struggles which caused them. Let us realise that while memorials remember the fallen, they do not show where they fought, where they fell, where they died. Let us find these locations, see them, stand on them, experience them. Let us trace the name carved in stone of a young boy who came from a farm in Pennsylvania and died on a farm in Belgium.

A small cross in the clearing of a forest, south of the village of Melines, Belgium. On an early Sunday morning, far from the nearest farm or house, the flowers are fresh.

"All the News That's Fit to Print"

The New York Times

Copyright, 1945, by The New York Times Company.

NEW YORK, THURSDAY, JANUARY 4, 1945.

THREE CENTS NEW YORK

XCIV...No. 31,757.

Entered as Second-Class Matter, Postoffice, New York, N. Y.

T ARMY OPENS DRIVE AT TOP OF BELGIAN BULGE,
D GAINS BEYOND BASTOGNE, 7TH FORCED BACK
U. S. FLIERS BOMB LUZON, FORMOSA AND JAPA

ENEMY HIT HARD THROUGHOUT FAR EAST THEATRE

U.S. MOVE IS W

Y ASKS STATE
PEND BILLION

**Mayor Forecasts Increase
In Realty Valuations Here**

One-Cent Toll-Tax Rate for Next

DIES GROUP IS PUT
ON PERMANENT BASIS
BY HOUSE, 207 TO 186

Point of Drive
Salient Not Disc
Patton Widens

OUTER MONGOLIA   MANCHURIA   Sea of Japan
SINKIANG   Peiping   KOREA   TOKYO
Dairen   Yokohama

Then: A sunny, early afternoon in January, 1945 finds a Panzer IV sitting deserted in front of a farmhouse [1] in Aisomont, Belgium. Part of 7. Kompanie of SS-Panzer Regiment 1, 1. SS-Panzer-Division, it was part of a split column with 6. Kompanie and 3. Kompanie of the SS-Panzer-Pionier-Bataillon 1 sent as a probing effort towards Wanne on the afternoon of December 18, 1944 by Obersturmbannführer Jochen Peiper. Kampfgruppe Peiper as a whole was then making desperate attempts to find alternative routes westward as bridge after bridge was blown in their faces by retreating American engineers.

Now: The exact location 50 years later finds a renovated farmhouse with a second storey and a lower stone fence yet the characteristic shed on the left still exists in perfect order, providing a final link with the past. The house is No. 39, situated immediately before a turn as the eastbound road forks into westward and eastward directions, north-west of Wanne. The eastbound road eventually becomes Champ des Pierres as it heads towards the Amblève river. Today, only a scrap heap remains where the Panzer IV once sat . . . perhaps symbolic of a fate surely suffered by the great tank itself.

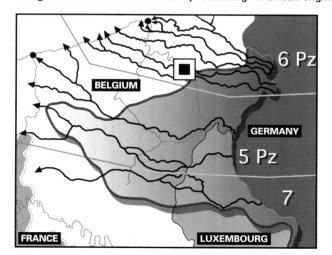

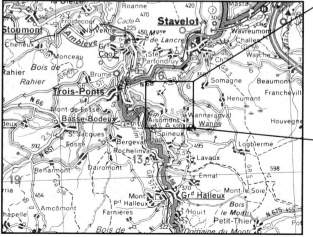

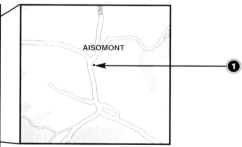

Aisomont: Michelin 214, Col. 8. 5° 53' East, 50° 22' North. Along the N633 southbound from La Gleize, exit at Rue de la Gare immediately before Salm river. Head east, direction Wanne, along Rue de la Gare, then Noupre, then Manonfat, which enters Aisomont from the west. If following the N68 west from Stavelot, turn left onto N633 (Route de Coo) and proceed as above.

Then: Late December 1944, and the way is made clear for the American advance once again. On December 22, Task Force Orr of the US 3rd Armored Division encountered the 116. Panzer-Division of the LVIII. Panzerkorps, 5. Panzer-Armee, immediately outside of the village of Amonines, Belgium. The German SdKfz 251/7 half-track vehicles, unceremoniously cleared to the roadside [1] were part of the 116. Panzer-Division's futile efforts to advance towards the Meuse river.

Now: They came this way, challenging the village over 50 years ago, along the present-day N841. The house on the right is No. 30 on Rue de Dochamps (the N841), as it enters the village from the east. The structure retains its original window and door arrangements, despite having played host to a variety of activities through the years, including those of a restaurant and a youth hostel. The telephone pole likewise retains its exact pride of place and helps to align the comparison perfectly. Today, Amonines is a picturesque village sleeping peacefully along the Aisne river.

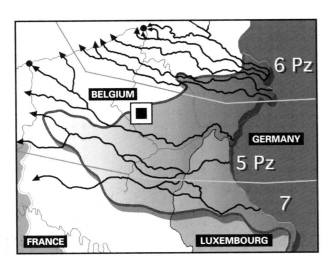

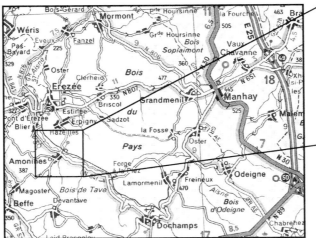

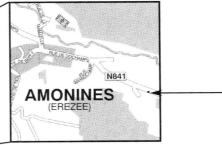

Amonines: Michelin 214, Col. 7. 5° 33' East, 50° 16' North. Lying directly south of Erezée, which itself is due west of Manhay, Amonines is best reached by exiting the E25 southbound at Exit 49, then heading west on the N651 to Manhay. From Manhay, take the N807 west to Erezée. Continue through Erezée west; upon crossing the Aisne river, go left on southbound N841 which enters Amonines from the east.

Then: **Military police attached to the 84th Infantry Division halt and interrogate traffic at a vital crossroads directly north of Marche at Baillonville, Belgium. Removed from the Ninth Army by General Bradley on December 19, by December 22 the 84th Division was joined to the VII Corps of the US First Army and pressed into service near Marche. The 84th was under constant pressure from the 116. Panzer-Division in the Marche-Hotton area during a series of great battles around Christmas 1944.**

Now: **The wartime photograph was taken at the junction [1] of the N929 (Route de France) and the N63 (Rue de Marche) in Baillonville, which lies 7 km due north of Marche. Looking out of a third-storey window of No. 1 Rue Marche, the photograph can be perfectly matched westwards across the intersection. The author was escorted by the owner through his house on an early Sunday morning, who then patiently sipped coffee while the picture was taken from the window ledge. The owner's wife, resplendent in dressing gown and slippers, was startled to see a photographer stomping up the stairs at 8.10 a.m.!**

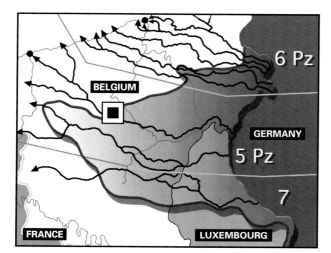

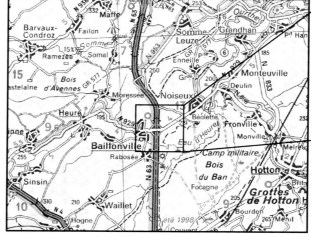

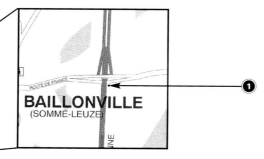

Baillonville: Michelin 214, Col. 6. 5° 21' East, 50° 17' North. The Baillonville crossroads lies directly north of Marche along the N63, where it intersects the N929 running west-east. Exit the N4 (E40) at Marche and head due north through the city following signs to the N63; continue 7 km north to the intersection.

Then: **On December 24, Christmas Eve, 1944, vengeful members of the dreaded Sicherheitsdienst (SD) police, attached to the 2. Panzer-Division, rounded up 33 young men in a reprisal raid against the Armée Secrète, a Belgian resistance organisation. The SD then summarily executed all but one in front of a burned-out house [1] alongside the Café de la Poste at the entrance of the village. A single man, Léon Praille, refused to be shot down with his friends and, when his turn came, punched an SD guard in the face and ran. In the confusion, he survived to tell the tale of atrocity.**

Now: **Fifty years later, on a quiet, peaceful Sunday morning, a solitary parked car sits on the site. Today, the Café de la Poste is no more, and the actual site where it stood remains empty, a visible gap between the characteristic house and telephone pole on the left (No. 10, Grand Rue) and No. 6 on the right. The memorial to those that lost their lives in the massacre lies further up the hill, on the same side of the street, across from the village church, where many of the victims lie buried.**

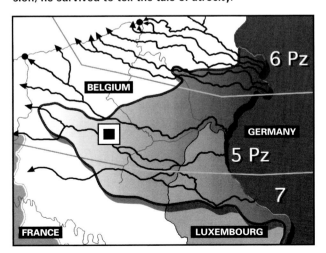

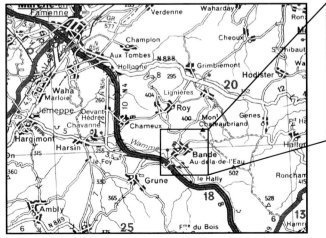

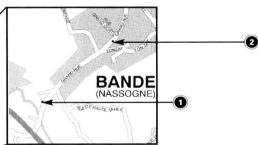

Bande: **Michelin 214, Col. 7. 5° 25' East, 50° 10' North. Just off the N4 between Marche-en-Famenne and Barrière de Champlon. Drive 10 km south-east of Marche, exit either direction on the N4 at village name and cross the flyover to the village which lies at the top of a hill.**

Then: A haunting, moving photograph outside of the church [2] in Bande, Belgium, as the villagers gather to remember their friends and family members massacred in the village weeks before.

Now: The church where the bereaved gathered still stands quietly alongside the Grand Rue in the village centre. Only the mourners have passed into the history books carrying with them the horrors of war as it once swept through their peaceful village. Directly behind the photographer lies a memorial to those young men massacred on that fateful Christmas Eve. A special information sign along the present-day N4 calls the attention of passing motorists to the memorial and the notoriety of the village.

Baronville

Then: A British Sherman 'Firefly' negotiates a tight corner along a side street. Part of the British 29th Armoured Brigade defending the Meuse (Maas) river from Namur to Dinant, this specimen was one of a substantial number of British-modified Sherman Fireflies assigned to each British armoured regiment in 1944. The British mounted a 17-pdr gun in the turret and put it to use against German armour, even though this gun proved wanting against the heavily-armoured panzers. This photograph was taken on January 6, 1945, as the 29th Armoured Brigade moved forward east of the Meuse.

Now: The exact location of the photograph pictured 50 years later in the small village of Baronville [1], south of Dinant and north of Beauraing. The southbound tank was in fact just turning off of the present-day N95 onto the Rue de Wiesmes, next to No. 1 to the right of the author. The same old-style electrical pole visible in the wartime photo background can still be seen today, and helps to align the comparison though the intersection has been widened somewhat since the war.

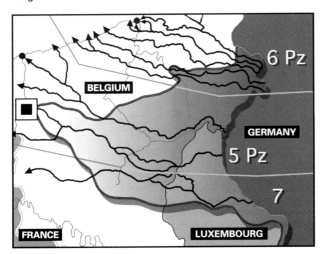

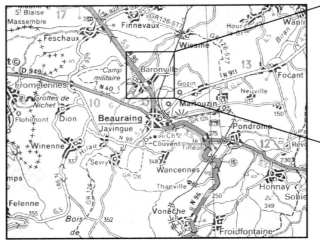

Baronville: Michelin 214, Col. 5. 4° 57' East 50° 7' North. 2 km north of Beauraing along N95; 18 km south-south-west of Dinant. From southbound E411 (A4), exit 22 to N94 southbound. At Vignée turn right onto N911, proceed to Beauraing, then head north along the N95 to Baronville.

19

Then: **The business-end of the British 17-pdr gun points directly at the camera as a Sherman Firefly tank proceeds down a snowy road [2] in the Belgian village of Baronville. The tank is in fact moving away from the photographer, as the turret has been reversed. This is the same tank shown in the previous photo in the same village, as denoted by the open hatches and the angle of the gun barrel, as well as the positions of the men in the tank. It was attached to the British 29th Armoured Brigade in the Dinant-Namur area.**

Now: **Over 50 years later, the same stretch of road in sunlit contrast. This is the present-day N95 (Rue de Dinant), looking south towards the town of Beauraing. The comparison photograph was taken standing out in front of No. 184 on the author's left, along the Rue de Dinant. The electric power lines still run on the same side of the road (albeit with new poles), and the characteristic house on the left in the wartime photo still exists today though it is hidden by trees in the photograph.**

Then: Christmas Day 1944, and Bastogne is under siege; an island of embattled Americans inside the sea of the German offensive. The main town square [1] on the morning after two Luftwaffe Christmas Eve bombing runs reveals wanton destruction of buildings, vehicles, even cattle. With the 5. Panzer-Armee now to the north and east, and the 7. Armee immediately due south, the town was poised to be overrun . . . yet it was not to be.

Now: The present-day town square (Place MacAuliffe) gives no hint to the degree of destruction that once rained upon the town. This is the view alongside the Rue du Vivier looking west. Many of the buildings along the western end of the square have been rebuilt in the same style. Vehicular parking likewise resumes en masse, this time without fear of bombs, though the possibility of impoundment always remains!

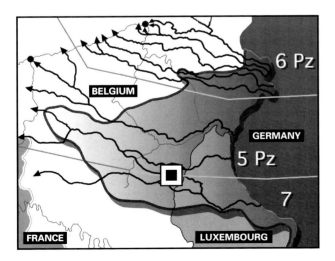

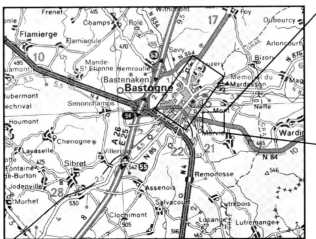

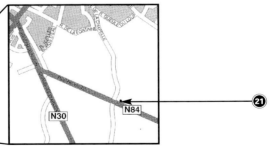

Bastogne: Michelin 214, Col. 8. 5° 42' East, 50° 0' North. A vital crossroads of the Ardennes, Bastogne lies at the intersection of the N4 and the E25(A26), which runs north-south. Exit 54 from either the N4 or E25 to town centre. N84 also enters Bastogne from the east while the N30 approaches the town from the north.

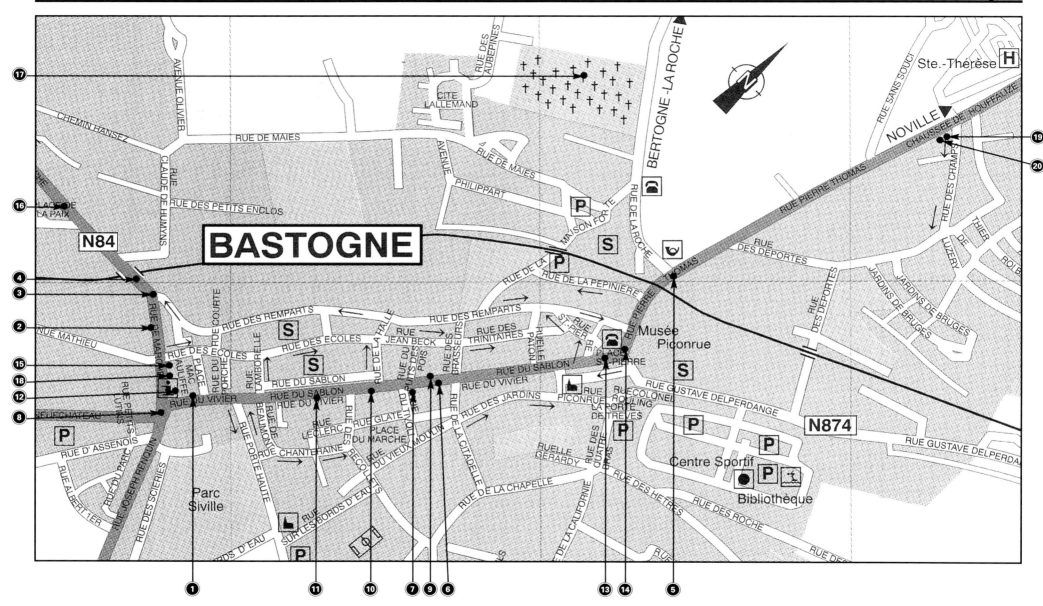

BASTOGNE

N84

N874

Parc Siville

Centre Sportif

Bibliothèque

Musée Piconrue

Ste.-Thérèse

NOVILLE

CITE LALLEMAND

Then: December 19, 1944, and elements of the 110th Regiment, 28th Infantry Division, having reached Bastogne at the beginning of the siege, regroup outside a garage [2] across the street from the Hotel Lebrun. Organisation was initially confused and sporadic, though eventually American logistics gained the upper hand and the siege was broken.

Now: Along the present-day N84 (Rue de Marche), as it enters the town centre directly from the west, the exact location of the wartime photograph is identified as No. 15, Rue de Marche. Once a garage — now a hair salon! The façades of the buildings in the centre and right retain the same arrangement of windows and doors.

Then: December 31, 1944, and Bastogne has been relieved from the south. US Signal Corps photographer Mallinder captures the snowy view down the main street [3] leading from the town square. To the left is the Hotel Lebrun, which served as the headquarters of the 10th Armored Division. The solitary cow wandering the street seems to reflect the abandonment of the town itself as townspeople began to leave the town after the siege had been broken.

Now: Standing in the left-turn-only lane looking west up the Rue de Marche, the author captures the identical photo location. The Hotel Lebrun is on the right with accommodation slightly less taxing than those of half a century ago. The building on the left in the wartime photo with the balcony is the present-day Nos. 9-11. Today, Bastogne is a strong, vibrant town, growing and developing at a rapid pace.

Then: Bastogne, December 1944, looking across the bridge [4] over the railway lines running north-south through the western edge of the town. With the city worn and exhausted from the siege, American soldiers mill about a scene of empty desolation. The combination of shelling, bombing, deprivation and isolation had left Bastogne a virtual shell.

Now: Looking in a westward direction along the present-day N84 (Rue de Marche), across the same rail bridge. Virtually every building has survived except for the massive water tower razed after the war. The characteristic house on the right sits on the corner of Rue de Marche and Rue Claude de Humyns.

Then: Mid-day December 19, 1944, and elements of the 1st Battalion of the 506th Parachute Infantry Regiment march northwards from the town limits [5] of Bastogne towards Noville. They are to shore up the defences of Task Force Desobry against the onslaught of the 2. Panzer-Division.

Now: The same intersection at the corner of Route de la Roche and the Rue Pierre Thomas, as the latter street heads north towards Noville and Houffalize. The building on the corner, No. 1 Route de la Roche, has been completely rebuilt and expanded though the house on the far left retains its tell-tale façade. They came this way, long ago, in the defence of the town.

Then: The initial stages of the defence of Bastogne take shape, as elements of the 10th Armored Division gather along the Grand Rue [6] in the centre of Bastogne. Men huddle about in small groups, eventually being assigned to one of three defence task forces:, Team O'Hara, Team Cherry, and Team Desobry. Many in these task forces were to receive a rude awakening at the hands of the Wehrmacht just outside the town limits. Team Cherry in particular was to be virtually annihilated by the 2. Panzer-Division east of Bastogne on December 19, 1944.

Now: The exact location of the 10th Armored Division's meeting point, looking north-east down the present-day Rue du Sablon, where it intersects Rue de la Citadelle and Rue des Brasseurs. The cobblestone streets have long since been tarmaced over, and today the area is a bustling shopping area in the heart of the town. Several of the original buildings on the right have survived virtually intact but the remainder lining the main street have not been so lucky.

Then: Early morning, late December 1944. The sunrise greets the haunting stillness and desolation of a town under siege. A few remaining civilians mill about the deserted Grand Rue [7] in Bastogne, reflecting on what has occurred overnight, and what may yet befall their town at the hands of the Wehrmacht. But the fall of Bastogne is not meant to be. All around the town, American infantry fortify defence perimeters. And from the south, a great armoured fist pushes northward, racing against time, to rescue their compatriots and lift the siege.

Now: Looking up the present-day Rue du Vivier 50 years later finds the scene changed in terms of fortune, yet many of the buildings remain. The characteristic curved façade overhang on the white building to the right (No. 99, on the corner of Rue de la Halle and Rue du Sablon) establishes the alignment point, while the building at the top of the street completes the scene.

Then: December 1944, Bastogne, Belgium. Remaining residents who sat out the siege in their shattered homes now leave the town after it was relieved at 4.50 p.m. on December 26, 1944 by forward elements of the 4th Armored Division pushing up from the south. History records the Belgians huddled in the oxcart as the Legrand family.

Now: Over a half a century later, traffic of a different sort moves eastward down the N84 as it passes the town square and intersects the N85 [8]. Military police have long since been replaced by the remorseless traffic light. Many of the characteristic buildings lining the square and the street survived more or less intact, despite intense shelling and bombing.

Then: The morning of December 30, 1944, and American soldiers examine the results of an overnight Luftwaffe raid on Bastogne. This particular strike took out the command post of Combat Command B of the 10th Armored Division [9] along the Grand Rue in the heart of the city. While a mournful group looks on, soldiers dig for survivors. The Christmas period saw heightened bombing by the Germans, first strategically then, later, out of frustration as the siege was lifted.

Now: Fifty years later, two motorcycles rest on top of the exact spot where the bomb fell and US soldiers perished. The two buildings in the centre right of the photo with their twin windows help recreate a moment in history. From left to right, the shops are Nos. 134, 130, and 128 along the present-day Rue du Vivier in the heart of Bastogne. The photograph was taken directly in front of No. 143 along the Rue du Sablon behind the author.

Then: A truly momentous photograph amidst the destruction and debris of Bastogne. Lieutenant General Omar N. Bradley, commander of the US 12th Army Group, General Dwight D. Eisenhower, Supreme Allied Commander; and Lieutenant General George S. Patton, Jr., commanding US Third Army, stand in the middle of the rubble-strewn Grand Rue in the heart of Bastogne. On January 16, 1945, the two armies commanded by General Bradley, Lieutenant General Courtney H. Hodges' First and Patton's Third, would link up from the north and south in the town of Houffalize. Sealing off the 'Bulge', this action signalled the beginning of the end of the Third Reich.

Now: **Crosswalk of history. The exact location [10] where some of the most powerful men on earth once stood; the crossing in the middle of the Rue du Sablon in the centre of Bastogne. Despite the previous wartime destruction, the building in the background on the right, with its unique window shapes, confirms and aligns the photo location today. The building is No. 1, Rue de la Halle, as this street enters the Rue du Sablon from behind the building in the foreground, which is No. 97, Rue du Sablon. On this precise spot, the progress (and end?) of the war was no doubt discussed.**

Then: **On an early December morning, an American tank thunders up the Grand Rue in the centre of Bastogne during the siege when it was cut off from the outside world. The area around the Grand Rue suffered substantially during numerous Luftwaffe bombing runs over the Christmas period. Though significant material damage was sustained, the spirit of the town and its defence was never broken.**

Now: **On a Saturday morning, over 50 years later, traffic of a different sort thunders up the same street. This is the precise section [11] of the Rue du Sablon today in the centre of Bastogne. After the war, many of the buildings and shops were rebuilt along different lines, though several of those on the right have survived as they once were, and serve to align the present-day photo with the visions of the past. From left, the main shops are Nos. 85, 87, 93 and 97.**

Then: **The dreary heart of the town in the grey light of winter, looking south-east. This main intersection [12] formed the confluence of four key roads, intersecting at the town square. During the Christmas siege of 1944, all roads in Bastogne eventually led straight out to the 5. Panzer-Armee and 7. Armee as the town was encircled. Note the white-shrouded Sherman tank beside the house to the right in the photo.**

Now: **Incredibly, this is the exact same junction and same photo angle as that of 50 years ago. In addition to the resurfacing and widening of the roads, virtually all of the former buildings have been razed, including the house on the immediate left. Only the sloping roofline of the building in the left-centre of the photo remains to fix the location. Today, new apartments and office space rise up where the Sherman tank once huddled. This is the major intersection of Bastogne, where the N84 and N85 meet across from the Place MacAuliffe.**

Then: **The remembrance of one calamity in the midst of another. Two US soldiers pause along the Grand Rue [13] in the centre of Bastogne to reflect upon a memorial to the fallen soldiers of World War I. It is more than likely that the soldiers are reflecting on the sad irony of it all: the Great War — the 'war to end all wars' — was but a prelude to a larger, more destructive worldwide conflict, one swirling about them now in the snows of Belgium. Didn't we do all this before?**

Now: **The pace of progress has swept the memorial away but this is the precise spot where it and the soldiers once stood. Today, cars park where soldiers once paid homage. The house in the centre left of the present-day photo, with its unique horizontal oval window at its top, still matches the old photo perfectly, despite all other changes. This is the 'Maison Mathelin', situated on a small church access road called Rue Gustave Delperdange, immediately north of the main church in Bastogne.**

Then: **A view looking south-west down the Grand Rue as the pummelled town rests under a fine layer of Christmas snow. Bastogne slowly suffered under the incessant bombing and shelling, yet the town remained in American hands, never wavering or losing hope of eventual relief. Such relief came on the day after Christmas, when the Third Army technically broke the siege entering the town from the south, though resupply and reinforcements would stretch ahead for days.**

Now: **The exact location [14] and view today, 50 years later. On a decidedly more cheerful day, traffic of a different kind moves along the timeless Rue du Sablon, next to the church on the left. Widened and paved long ago, at this turn the road now becomes Rue Pierre Thomas and eventually the Chausée de Houffalize and the N30 itself as it heads north towards Foy and Noville.**

Then: **January 18, 1945. An historic photograph captures Major General Troy H. Middleton, commander of VIII Corps, shaking hands with Major General Maxwell D. Taylor, commander of the 101st Airborne Division. Major General Taylor used this impromptu occasion to 'officially' hand over Bastogne to Middleton's care, after his 'Battered Bastards of the 101st' had survived the siege and defended the town against overwhelming odds. This handshake ceremony took place on the south-west corner [15] of the town square in Bastogne (known then as the Place du Carré), before a formal review of troops.**

Now: **With the town square now renamed Place Général A. C. MacAuliffe, in honour of the then acting divisional commander who directed the defence, the exact location of the historic photograph is identified: in front of a pizzeria! Yes, Giorgio's Pizzeria, standing on the corner of Rue des Ecoles, is the site of history. Yet through the waiters, tables, and tourist trappings, the characteristic stonework on either side of the awning and the corner façade can still be seen. Where once the fate of nations was decided, the only decisions being made here today are about the size and type of the pizzas — and whether to order with extra cheese!**

Then: Three American GIs walk past the massive water tower which once rose alongside the main road leading into the town directly from the west. Rows of houses in the background stand idle, where a few remaining inhabitants rode out the siege of December, 1944. The water tower itself bears the scars of shelling and bombing.

Now: The exact location [16] of the soldiers' sojourn 50 years later along the present-day N84. The water tower itself was razed after the war, yet the architecture of the houses and the building on the extreme left help to frame the location. These houses (Nos. 1, 5, 9 and 11) sit along Avenue Tasiaux, where it meets the N84 (Rue de Marche). The small park where the water tower once stood is now known as Place de la Paix.

Then: During the siege of Bastogne, US soldiers bury their comrades in the municipal cemetery on a cold, snowy day in December 1944. One of the few, somber advantages to the freezing weather was the preservation of corpses yet their burial in the frozen earth was a difficult, lonely and sad affair.

Now: The exact location of the burial plot over 50 years later, in the crowded town cemetery [17] just off of the Route de la Roche in the north-west area of Bastogne. Despite the crowded tombstones, this exact photo angle and location was pinpointed thanks to the headstone cross in the upper left-hand corner of the wartime photo. Today this grave, with its characteristic slanted shoulders, can still be seen in its original location peeking through the others.

Then: Enormous devastation in the town square of Bastogne after a Luftwaffe bombing run. In futile attempts to soften the town up for subsequent armoured attacks, the Germans routinely shelled and bombed Bastogne in the early stages of the offensive. Most likely taken on Christmas Day, 1944, this photo taken looking north-east [18] shows the town square where a disabled US half-track lies abandoned amidst the carnage.

Now: Bastogne's town square today, looking out across it in the same direction from the Rue de Marche. Despite significant structural damage to the majority of the buildings in this area, the tall white building in the background, with its characteristic portico and window (left-centre in the present-day photo), confirms the photo angle. Fifty years later, modern French and German vehicles reside where the half-track once sat.

Then: Heavily-armed members of the 101st Airborne Division march northwards out of Bastogne on December 19, 1944, as they attempt to bolster the defensive positions operating against the 2. Panzer-Division in the Foy-Noville sector. Many of the soldiers are carrying bazookas, which they hope to use with telling effect against German armour. Unfortunately, they will have to get fairly close for an effective kill shot against the heavily armoured panzers!

Now: Fifty years later, the same stretch of road, the present-day Chaussée de Houffalize, leaves the town for points north. Though new buildings adorn the street today, the set of houses along the far-upper left background of the photo identically match those in the old wartime photo, fixing the location [19]. Immediately behind the author is the Rue de Champs at the point where it intersects the Chaussée de Houffalize from the east.

Then: December 19, 1944, and US Signal Corps photographer Tech/5 Wesley Carolan pauses on the steps of a house [20] on the outskirts of Bastogne to picture elements of the 101st Airborne Division moving north towards Foy and Noville in an attempt to repel the advances of the 2. Panzer-Division outside the town limits of Bastogne.

Now: The stillness of a Sunday morning on the N30 50 years later. Then this was on the outskirts of the town but today substantial development has taken place including the building of a new hospital for Bastogne on the right. The author stood outside the front door of No. 20 Chaussée de Houffalize.

Then: December 29, 1944. The siege having been lifted on the 26th, on a cold, snowy morning elements of the 101st Airborne march eastwards out of Bastogne. This famous photo has been reproduced many times in books on the battle. The battered sign on the right represents the beating the town endured in the battle.

Now: The author resisted the temptation to include a current day sign for 'Bastogne' on the Rue de Wiltz [21] which stood immediately behind; while it would have made a compelling match to that of 50 years ago, its new replacement now lies too far east of this photo location (by six metres!) to afford a proper match. The price of perfection!

Then: With Bastogne under siege by Christmas Day, six Belgian civilians attempt to escape the brutal conditions by heading towards the town of Longchamps, which lies 8 km north-west of Bastogne. They were subsequently turned back by a road-block manned by the 502nd Parachute Infantry Regiment. This particular soldier is dug in directly at the base of a small bridge, establishing an outer perimeter of the Bastogne pocket against the German tide swirling all about the city.

Now: The identical stretch of road [1], now the present-day N834, that runs between Bastogne and Longchamps, with only a modern guard rail to indicate the presence of the bridge. The view is looking east directly towards the E25 motorway running along the top of the photo; beyond the motorway along the N834 lies Savy, with exit 53 just off the photo to the right. No trace remains of the foxhole, and the forest in the background has only recently been felled.

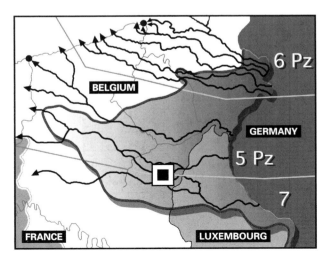

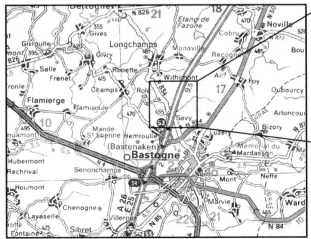

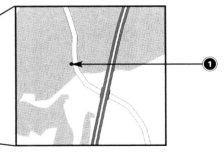

Bastogne-Longchamps: **Michelin 214, Col. 8. 5° 41' East 50° 2' North. Along the E25 in either direction, exit 53 onto the N854. Turn northbound onto the N834 direction Longchamps. Just west beyond the underpass of the E25 and N834 lies a curve in the road, the location today.**

Then: **A snowy day in late December 1944, directly east of Bastogne, finds the business end of a German Jagdpanzer IV/70 guarding the approach towards the town, near the border between Belgium and Luxembourg. Most likely taken after the siege of the town had been lifted, this photo shows off the 75mm gun and sloping front glacis to good effect. This specimen could have been part of SS-Panzer-Jäger-Abteilung 1, which was operating in the area at the time.**

Now: **A virtually identical weather match 50 years later along the present-day N15, just inside the border between Belgium and Luxembourg where the Belgian N84 becomes the N15. The barbed-wire fence, house corner and snowy conditions complete the scene. This photo location [1] lies precisely 350 metres east of the Belgium-Luxembourg border; the sole house along this particular stretch of N15 being No. 10 seen on the right.**

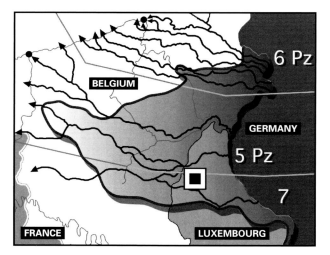

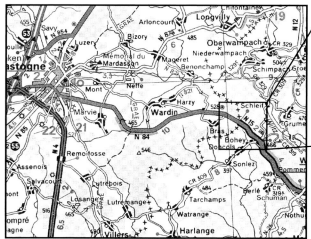

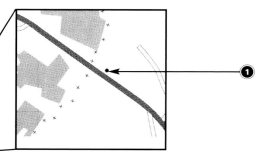

Bastogne-Wiltz: **Michelin 214, Col. 8. 5° 51' East 49° 58' North. From Bastogne, head directly east along the N84; at the Belgian-Luxembourg border the N84 becomes the N15 in Luxembourg. 350 metres east of the border is the location.**

Then: Early January 1945, looking across a snowy field [1] of atrocity at the crossroads at Baugnez, Belgium, three kilometres south-east of Malmédy. At 8 a.m. on January 13, 1945, elements belonging to the 120th Infantry Regiment, 30th Infantry Division, attacked from Géromont towards Baugnez where they had heard of 'large numbers of American bodies' lying in a field at the crossroads. Heavy snow had just fallen the evening before. In early afternoon, they reached this field and secured the area. The next morning, January 14, 71 bodies were uncovered (three unrelated to the actual massacre).

Now: The field today, the view being north-east towards the crossroads of the present-day N62 and N622. The junction itself is just off the photo to the left. The road is the N62 (Route de Luxembourg) heading south (left to right) towards Ligneuville. The field shown is actually now the front of No. 4 Route de Luxembourg. Across the road in the background is the erroneously (or conveniently) placed Mémorial Americain, commemorating the fallen. The memorial indicates that that is the massacre location; in point of fact, it is this field instead.

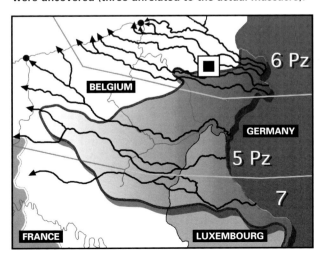

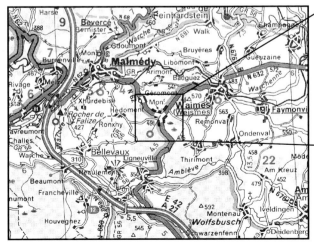

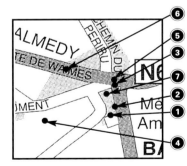

Baugnez: Michelin 214, Col. 9. 6° 4' East 50° 24' North. From either direction on the E42, take exit 11 and head east on the N62 through Malmédy and Géromont to Baugnez and the crossroads of the N62 and N622.

Then: **Just after noon on Sunday, December 17, 1944, Battery B of the 285th Field Artillery Observation Battalion came under fire from Kampfgruppe Peiper at the Baugnez crossroads. They subsequently surrendered and between 2.15-2.20 p.m., as the entire group stood prisoner in a field, machine-gun fire cut them down where they stood.**

Now: **Looking directly north [2] now across the massacre field, with the rebuilt Café Bodarwé in the background. The same tree line along the perimeter in the background remains today to frame the comparison, though certainly more fully grown. This is the view parallel to the present-day N62, lying off to the right heading south towards Ligneuville.**

Then: **Having retaken the area around Baugnez by January 14, 1945, the investigation into the Malmédy massacre took place amidst a scene covered in snow. This is the view looking westward from the crossroads, down the farm lane running next to the Café Bodarwé. Destroyed vehicles belonging to the 285th Field Artillery Observation Battalion line the road to Géromont and Malmédy on the right.**

Now: **The matching photo [3] 50 years later on a similar snowy day in Baugnez. The power lines have since been moved across the road. The same farm lane is now known as the Route du Monument, after the memorial site which lies across the road. The house in the distance, No. 4, is unchanged since the war.**

Then: **Several bodies of the now-infamous 'Malmédy Massacre' — those of victims having run away wounded and falling — lay further away from the actual massacre field itself, alongside a hedgerow marking a small farm lane leading away from the crossroads. All told, 82 men were killed at or near this crossroads area.**

Now: **The exact spot [4], approximately 110 metres from the massacre field. The lane which runs from the crossroads is now the Route du Monument; the house in the background, is No. 4. Some months later, the author returned to find this field the site of further housing developments.**

Then: **Vehicles and detritus lay strewn down the road towards Malmédy at the Baugnez crossroads. Having encountered Kampfgruppe Peiper coming from Thirimont to the south-east, it is likely that the 285th Field Artillery Observation Battalion came under initial fire before even reaching the junction. The truck with the US Army star insignia on the left is actually at the turn and is pointing towards Ligneuville.**

Now: **Fifty years later, looking directly west down the present-day N62 (Route de Waimes) towards Malmédy [5]. The house in the left background is No. 4 Route du Monument. Despite the modern electrical and signal trappings, the crossroads retains its original layout. The rebuilt Café Bodarwé is off the photo to the immediate left.**

Then: **With the tail-end remains of vehicles belonging to the 285th Field Artillery Observation Battalion lining the road to Baugnez, a US Signal Corps photographer recorded the view looking east [6] along the route out of Géromont and Malmédy.**

Now: **The same view today along the widened and paved N62 (Route de Waimes) heading uphill to the Baugnez crossroads.**

Then: **The grim task of body documentation lasted three days, as the snowy execution site was uncovered and photographed in great detail. This view was taken looking south-east [7] across the field of death.**

Now: **The same field and direction 50 years later finds the opposite side of the road now fully developed with houses and commerce. The trees have long since been felled, as have so many of those which once lined roads in the Ardennes.**

Then: **Dawn of the New Year in 1945 sees the US counter-attack moving forward in the Hotton — La Roche area. Soldiers of the 290th Regiment of the 75th Infantry Division move through the village of Beffe, Belgium, on January 5 amidst the snow, cold and destruction. Behind them lay Devantave. The 75th passed into VII Corps reserve when the First Army's counter-offensive started on January 3.**

Now: **Fifty years later, the scene of their march [1] is in fact the intersection of the Rue de l'Eglise (foreground to background), the Sous le Tonan (on the right), and the Route d'Amonines (to the left) in the very centre of the village of Beffe. From the left, the two houses are Nos. 12 and 10 respectively. Up the hill in the distance lies Devantave while directly behind the author is the village church.**

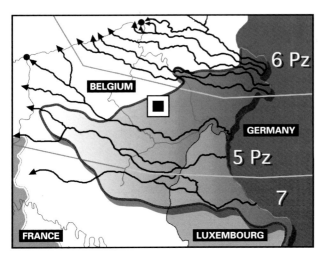

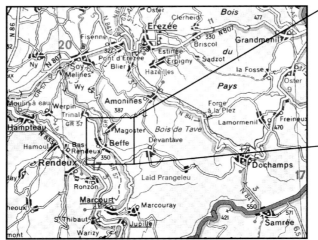

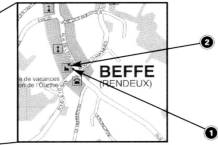

Beffe: **Michelin 214, Col. 7. 5° 32' East 50° 15' North. From Hotton (north-east of Marche), take the N833 (Route de Hotton) south-east to Rendeux; at the intersection of the N833 and the Route de Marche in Rendeux, turn left, direction Beffe, to enter the village from the south. From La Roche, take the same N833 north-west, turning right towards Beffe in Rendeux.**

Then: With the 290th Regiment still marching to the rear, the US Army Signal Corps photographer moves approximately ten metres to his left, faces north-west, and takes another picture as the GIs continue their trek through Beffe past the local cemetery on the right. The village church is now to his immediate left. Note the position of the electrical pole on the left.

Now: Fifty years later, the author performs the same manoeuvre, capturing the present-day view [2] down the Rue de l'Eglise next to the village cemetery. The power lines are now supported on a modern concrete post. The road, though widened a bit, still runs past the same stone cemetery wall which has changed little since the war.

Then: **The centre of war-torn Berdorf, Luxembourg, looking directly north [1] down the main street in the village. The large building on the right, the Parc Hotel, was the scene of an heroic last stand by approximately 60 soldiers of Company F, 12th Infantry Regiment, 4th Infantry Division. Holding out against the 212. Volks-Grenadier-Division for three days at the beginning of the offensive, their situation gradually became untenable and the village had to be given up.**

Now: **Fifty years later, looking north down the present-day Rue de Consdorf, finds an identical scene on the left and a completely changed scene on the right. The Parc Hotel site is now occupied by the Scharff Hotel, the large white building in the far right. The building on the left, identical through half a century, is No. 12 Rue de Consdorf, now home to the Tourism Board. Today, Berdorf is a clean, quiet, picturesque Luxembourg town, giving no hint of the carnage which once came its way.**

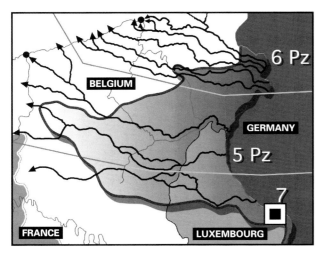

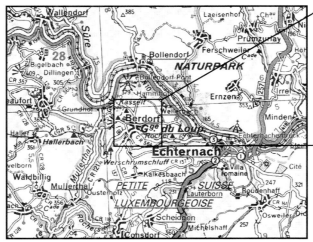

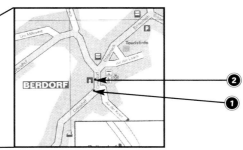

Berdorf: **Michelin 214, Col. 10. 6° 21' East 49° 49' North. Situated high on a hill overlooking the valley of the Sûre river, Berdorf lies north-west of Echternach, Luxembourg. From Echternach (or points west), exit the N10 along the Sûre river at road CR364, direction Berdorf. Berdorf is approximately 3-4 km up the road into the hills.**

Then: With the priest's Jeep parked outside, GIs enter the shell-scarred church [2] in the centre of Berdorf in late December 1944. The town, which was held by the Americans at the beginning of the Ardennes offensive, felt the fury of the 212. Volks-Grenadier-Division of the LXXX. Armeekorps as it swept on and around Berdorf on December 17. After a specific attack by I. Bataillon of Grenadier-Regiment 423 of the 212. Volks-Grenadier-Division, Berdorf was evacuated on December 20. Five days later, on Christmas Day, two companies of the 2nd Regiment, 5th Infantry Division, counter-attacking with the full weight from mechanised units of the 9th and 10th Armored Divisions, had encircled the town. One day later — on December 26 — Berdorf was retaken.

Now: The restored church nestles quietly amongst the trees along the Rue de Consdorf. Its façade has been completely restored, though the wrought iron fence is gone.

Then: December 17, 1944, and men of the 26th Regiment, 1st Infantry Division, move forward into the town of Dom Bütgenbach in Belgium, passing under a dropped railway bridge [1] near the village of Berg. The 26th Regiment was engaged two days later by the first of a series of attacks on Dom Bütgenbach led by SS-Panzer-Grenadier-Regiment 26 of the 12. SS-Panzer-Division. For two days, American artillery pounded the Germans, keeping them scattered and ineffective.

Now: Identical weather and time of year though the passage of 50 years finds the same span perfectly restored. Close examination of the arch on the right, particularly as one stands directly underneath the huge bridge, finds the tell-tale difference in the age of the stonework. Though beautifully done, the repaired section is much less weathered and appears a little lighter in colour. This photo was taken directly north of Bütgenbach along the N647 (Monschauer Strasse) where it intersects with Klosterstrasse, just before the N647 dives beneath the bridge itself.

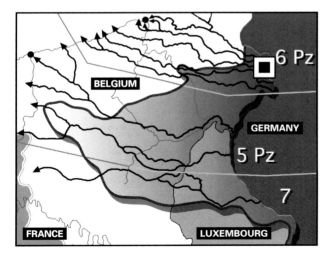

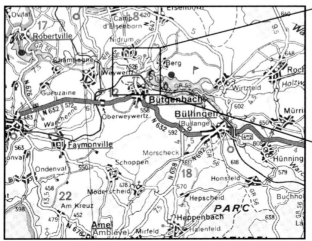

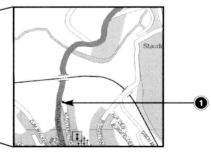

Berg: Michelin 214, Col. 9. 6° 12' East 50° 26' North. From points west, exit E42 southbound at exit 11; head east along the N632 through Malmédy, Baugnez and Waimes until you enter Dom Bütgenbach from the west. Turn left onto N647, direction Elsenborn. 1 km north of Bütgenbach is the railway span. From the east, enter Dom Bütgenbach from Büllingen on the N632 from the south. Continue through Bütgenbach towards Elsenborn as above.

Then: With the failure of the I. SS-Panzerkorps to launch Panzerbrigade 150 into action in secrecy on December 16 (the actual documents detailing its operations had already been captured by the Americans on the same day in Heckhuscheid, Germany), Operation 'Greif' was essentially doomed from the start. News of German soldiers in American uniforms spread quickly in the Malmédy area and the road-blocks were set up. This one, supported by an anti-tank gun in a sandbagged emplacement, was erected in the small village of Bernister, north of Malmédy.

Now: The same corner in Bernister, Belgium, 50 years later. The author was surprised to find the location rather remote from the Malmédy area, high on a hill and quite difficult to reach from that city. This corner also lies at the furthest western end of Bernister, itself a rather small and dispersed village. Today, many more homes dot the area and more are being built. The exact location [1] is next to a farm on a road called Vieille Voie de Liège, literally in the shadow of the massive E42 motorway heading north to Liège.

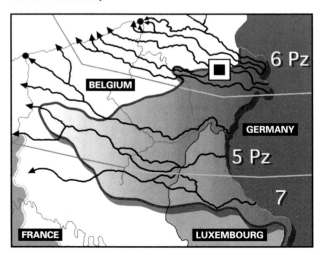

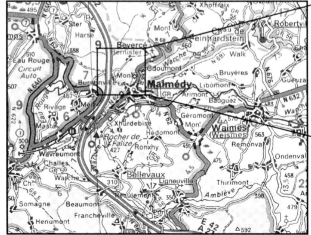

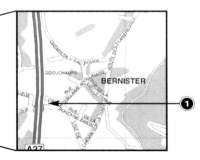

Bernister: Michelin 214, Col. 9. 6° 2' East 50° 26' North. From north or south, exit E42 at exit 11, direction Stavelot/Francorchamps at the circle. Turn right onto the N62, northbound to Francorchamps. At Burnenville, turn right onto a street called Chemin du Bois du Loup; pass underneath the E42 itself and the road-block site will be immediately in front of you.

Then: **Lying four kilometres directly east of Diekirch along the Sûre river, Bettendorf was hit by artillery of the 352. Volks-Grenadier-Division of the LXXXV. Armeekorps the very minute the Ardennes offensive began on December 16, 1944. Under constant pressure, the 3rd Battalion of the 109th Regiment (28th Infantry Division) withdrew from the town on December 18 back to Diekirch. The Americans returned in force on January 18 from Gilsdorf to the west, with the 3rd Battalion, 8th Infantry Regiment of the 4th Infantry Division moving into the town from the south bank of the Sûre.**

Now: **Approaching Bettendorf from the south 50 years later along the Route d'Eppeldorf, the author suddenly came on the spot where the GMC with the flat tyre once stood. The fencing which once held the village sign still remains in situ though the sign board itself has gone. In the background, the same house can be identified with its four-window arrangement, barely visible in the upper right of the wartime photo. Today, on a cold afternoon, it stands clear and distinct. The present-day photograph was taken just outside the front door of No. 10.**

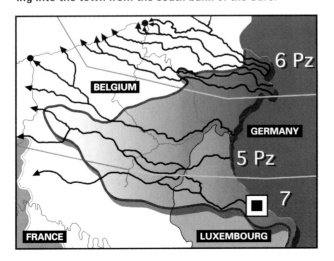

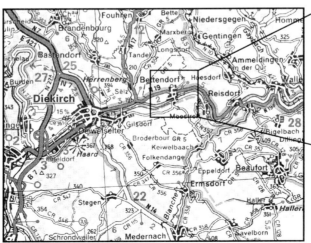

Bettendorf: **Michelin 214, Col. 9. 6° 13' East 49° 53' North. From Ettelbruck/Diekirch, head east along the N19, direction Echternach. Bettendorf is directly on the N19, approximately 4 km east of Diekirch. The photo location is in the south part of Bettendorf, across the Sûre (Sauer) river.**

Bihain

Then: Against a classic Ardennes winter backdrop of fog and snow, elements of the 83rd Infantry Division move forward through the small village of Bihain, Belgium, south of Lierneux. Two Sherman tanks move slowly along with the infantry column, perhaps giving them the reassurance to chat, joke and smile at the Signal Corps photographer.

Now: Fifty years later, almost to the day, one of the author's favourite comparisons comes to life. This is the farm village of Bihain on a similar cold, foggy, snowy day. The view is looking directly north down an unnamed road [1] east of the village church. The two farmhouses on the right are No. 18 and No. 19.

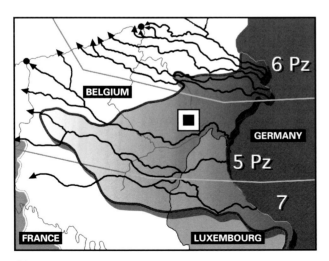

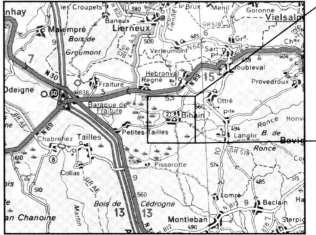

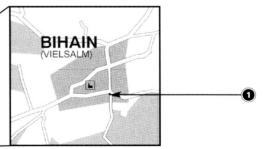

Bihain: **Michelin 214, Col. 8. 5° 48' East 50° 14' North. From north or south, exit E25(A26) at exit 50 onto the N89, heading east towards Vielsalm/Salmchâteau. Approximately 5 km east of the E25 lies Hebronval. Turn right at Hebronval, direction Ottré/Bihain. Follow signs to Bihain, where you will enter the village from the north-east. Streets in Bihain are without names.**

Then: Late December 1944, and a stream of wounded leaves the small village of Blier, north of Amonines, as US Army corpsmen care for their comrades. These men were most likely wounded in the battle between the 3rd Armored Division and the LVIII. Panzerkorps, engaged immediately south in Amonines. In general, the US Army medical efforts during the Ardennes offensive were rapid, caring and efficient, including forward-based operating areas. These, in turn, were aided by the relatively close proximity of large cities such as Liège and Namur, and further points west under Allied control for advanced evacuation.

Now: An exact comparison 50 years on in the little Belgian village, looking south [1] along the present-day N841 (Route de l'État). The two châteaux provide the historical backdrop where American wounded were once carried from the scene. The road forking to the right in the background is Rue Croix Henquin, leading to both the Gite de la Ferme, No. 1 (the building on the right), and the Château de Blier on the left. Amidst the stillness and quiet of today, one can only ponder the fate of wounded as they were carried down this road: back to their friends in foxholes for more battle or, perhaps, whisked back to the States in peace?

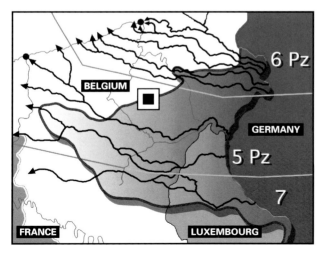

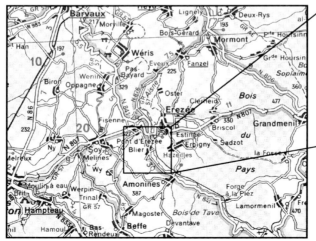

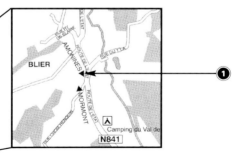

Blier: Michelin 214, Col. 7. 5° 33' East 50° 17' North. From north or south, exit E25 at exit 49, then head west on the N651 to Manhay. Pass through Manhay to Grandmenil and beyond, still heading west, now on the N807 to Erezée. Move through Erezée, crossing the Aisne river at the Pont d'Erezée. Immediately after crossing the river, turn left on the N841, direction Amonines/Dochamps. Blier is on the N841 1½ km south of the Pont d'Erezée.

Then: **North of La Gleize, American engineers clean up the detritus of battle. Kampfgruppe Peiper, having been shelled into oblivion and driven out of the village, left behind all manner of armour, including this massive King Tiger II. In the small village of Borgoumont north of La Gleize, this tank, along with two Panzer IVs, was sent to engage and stop Task Force McGeorge, one of three sent into the area on December 20, 1944 by the 3rd Armored Division. The Sherman lying next to the King Tiger was most likely one of its victims.**

Now: **The exact resting place [1] of the mighty King Tiger, looking south-west down an unnamed road north of La Gleize. The concrete posts carrying electric power which line this stretch of road on the left-hand side, though hidden with foliage, remain to help with the identification. When combined with other photographs taken in this immediate area (including the one reproduced overleaf), the location is determined with accuracy. Fifty years ago, this road was indeed impassable!**

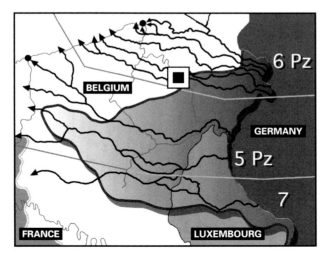

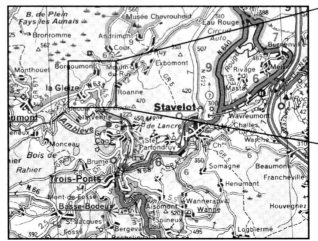

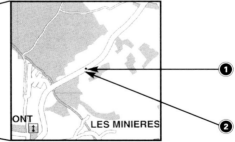

Borgoumont: **Michelin 214, Col. 8. 5° 52' East 50° 26' North. From Stavelot to the east, take the N68 west to Trois-Ponts. Turn right onto the N633 and head to La Gleize. At the north end of the village of La Gleize, signs indicate a road to Borgoumont north. Approximately 1 km along this road lies a small creek; just over this creek and halfway up the hill is the photo location. Coming from Stoumont, head east along the N633 until you enter La Gleize, and follow as above.**

Then: To clear the roads, the same Tiger II No. 334, its number now visible on the side of the turret, was unceremoniously pushed off the side of the road. It rests (now minus its tracks) in front of the same electric post seen in the previous photo. It belonged to the same unit of 1. SS-Panzer-Division which blocked Task Force McGeorge from entering La Gleize from the north through Borgoumont.

Now: Beside the same concrete pylon, the precise location [2] is fixed by determining the distance from the house in the wartime photo. Though new trees block its view today, one of its chimneys can just be seen peeking out over the tree-tops, and subsequent examination close up showed the house to be identical.

Then: With the Ardennes offensive essentially at an end, an awards ceremony was held in late January in the courtyard of a building in the centre of Born, Belgium. Members of the 393rd Infantry Regiment, along with medics of the regiment's medical detachment, (both part of the 99th Infantry Division) stand at attention while the citations are read out. The small vertical white stripes on several of the helmets denote officers and the crosses medical corpsmen. It is rather unusual to see photos from this period which show large gatherings of medics in a single formation.

Now: Fifty years on, the courtyard was found to be the playground of the main school in Born located on the corner of Schulstrasse and St Vither Strasse [1]. The school building on the left is identical, but, whereas the wartime photo had a clear line of sight to the bridge in the background, the view today is blocked by foliage and classroom buildings. However, it is interesting to note that the three trees in the wartime picture still stand.

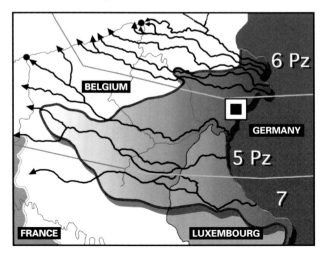

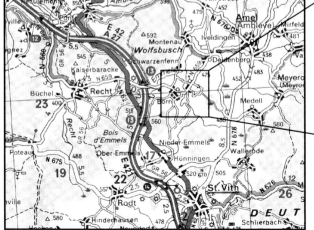

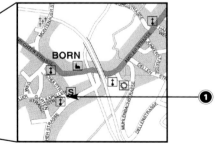

Born: Michelin 214, Col. 9. 6° 7' East 50° 20' North. Southbound on the E42(A27), exit 13 eastbound onto N659, direction Born, 2 km. Note: The bridge is inexplicably missing on the Michelin map whereas the Belgian counterpart enlargement clearly captures it. The author can attest to its existence!

Then: A month after the battle, a German Wirbelwind Flakpanzer lies half-buried in the snow at Buchholz, Belgium. This rather unusual vehicle was attached to SS-Panzer-Regiment 1, Kampfgruppe Peiper of the 1. SS-Panzer-Division, which moved through the hamlet early on the morning of December 17, 1944. It was destroyed by American aircraft operating in the area in support of the 99th Infantry Division near Losheimergraben on the same morning. Buchholz was situated along Rollbahn D — the pre-designated attack route assigned to the Kampfgruppe.

Now: Fifty years ago, the Wirbelwind once sat on this exact spot [1] on a small track just off the main forest road connecting Buchholz with the village of Honsfeld. Buchholz station, which lay in the distant background along the railway line which runs left to right along the ridge, has now disappeared after having existed as an abandoned structure until the early 1980s. Although it has now been demolished, its former location helps to align the comparison. The house on the left is No. 1 along the unnamed road.

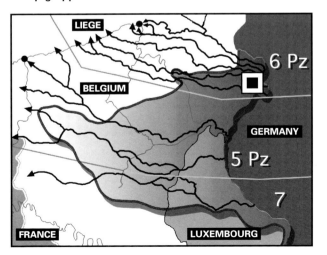

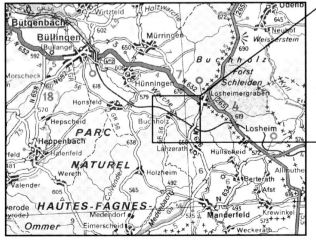

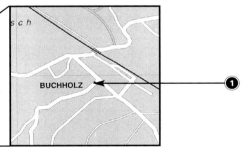

Bucholz: Michelin 214, Col. 9. 6° 19' East 50° 23' North. From Büllingen, head east along the N632. Immediately before the German border, turn right onto the N626, direction Lanzerath. Just before the village of Lanzerath, signs on the right point down a road towards Buchholz. This is the road Kampfgruppe Peiper took coming from Lanzerath to Buchholz. The photo location is on the left just next to house No. 1.

Then: On January 30, 1945, with the Ardennes offensive all but over, American soldiers walk down the snowy main street of Büllingen, Belgium, a key town that once lay along Rollbahn C of the attacking panzer spearheads. It was captured at 8 a.m. on the morning of December 17, 1944, by Kampfgruppe Peiper moving north from Honsfeld. Technically assigned to Rollbahn D, Kampfgruppe Peiper detoured north to Büllingen in a bid for fuel, a gamble which proved successful. Having captured 50,000 gallons of US military gasoline, the 1. SS-Panzer-Division used the village for a brief refuelling stop.

Now: The town was subsequently shelled by American guns sited along the Elsenborn ridge, the results of which can be seen in the wartime photo. Büllingen was eventually retaken by the 1st Infantry Division on January 29, 1945. Over 50 years later, this is the same view from position [1] looking north-east down Hauptstrasse. Though many buildings have since been rebuilt, the small portico of the building on the centre-left (No. 334 Hauptstrasse) matches that in the wartime photo enabling the comparison to be aligned.

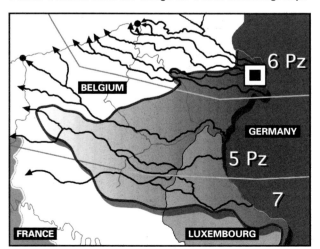

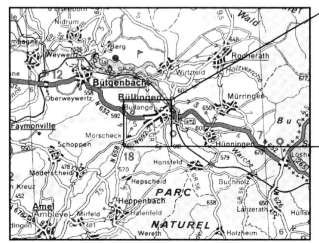

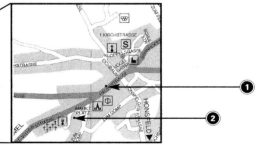

Büllingen: Michelin 214, Col. 9. 6° 15' East 50° 25' North. From Malmédy and Waimes, head east along the N632 into Bütgenbach. In Bütgenbach centre, turn right continuing on N632, direction Büllingen. You will enter the town along from the west. To follow in Peiper's footsteps, head directly north from Honsfeld, approaching the town from the south along Honsfelder Strasse.

Then: January 29, 1945 and US Signal Corps photographer Bill Augustine pictures German prisoners marching south-westerly along a road on the outskirts of the town of Büllingen, Belgium. These panzergrenadiers were taken prisoner by elements of the 26th Regiment, 1st Infantry Division, which reoccupied the town.

Now: The road the prisoners were marching down was in fact the present-day N692 (St Vither Strasse) in Büllingen, and this is the exact vantage point [2] from which the Signal Corps photographer took his picture 50 years ago. This small tree-lined road from the N692 leads up to the building of the Forstamt (forestry office) Büllingen which lies directly behind the author. A small area known as the Marktplatz lies just off to the right.

Then: **November 1944 and Bütgenbach supply logistics continue in front of the large village church. These men could belong to either the 9th or the 99th Infantry Divisions, which during November held this 'quiet sector' of the front. Such supplies would be sorely required one month later as the 12. SS-Panzer-Division launched its first assault on the village at 2.25 a.m. on the morning of December 19, 1944. After two days of intense pressure, the German assaults were eventually repelled, aided in large part by massive US artillery support from the Elsenborn ridge area.**

Now: **Today, the landscaping in front of the village church [1] belies the former area of military activities. Instead of the wartime supply trucks, only worshippers park their cars, perhaps to offer thanks for 50 years of peace in the village.**

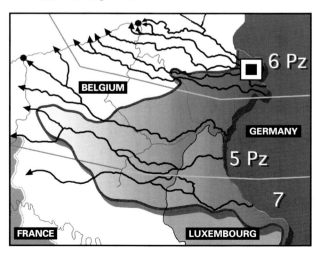

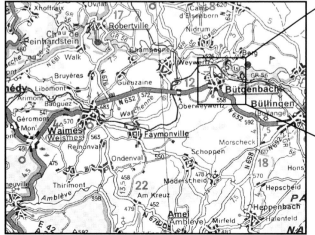

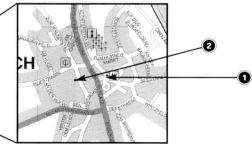

Bütgenbach: **Michelin 214, Col. 9. 6° 12' East 50° 26' North. From Malmédy and Waimes, head east along the N632 directly into Bütgenbach from the west. Bütgenbach lies 3½ km west-north-west of Büllingen.**

Then: **Early in November 1944, General Eisenhower, the Supreme Allied Commander, toured the area near the German border, conferring with his senior staff whose forward divisions were comfortably positioned in the Ardennes. This photograph shows General Eisenhower and Lieutenant General Omar N. Bradley, the 12th Army Group commander, discussing matters with Major General Louis A. Craig (centre), commander of 9th Infantry Division, in the front garden of a house in Bütgenbach, Belgium. The 9th Division was covering the Monschau-Hohen area adjacent to the German border, north of Elsenborn and Bütgenbach. During the early desperate days of the Ardennes offensive, Craig's forces would be called upon to assist the 99th and 2nd Infantry Divisions facing the full onslaught of the 6. Panzer-Armee.**

Now: **The photograph was taken in what is today a car park in front of the same house [2]. This is No. 11 Zum Walkerstal, in the centre of the town, looking west away from the market square. The ornate stonework around the door and the window on the right match up though the stone fence post and iron gate are long gone. Here the architects of battle once pondered their strategy; today, perhaps the three gentlemen would turn around, hop into the nearest Renault and be off to the front!**

Then: In a triumphant pose of conquest, six Belgian soldiers proudly stand on top of a Panther tank which has turned turtle at Celles, Belgium. Members of the 5th Fusiliers Battalion, these Belgians were operating with the British 29th Armoured Brigade, helping to stem the westward advance of the 2. Panzer-Division. The Panther belonged to Kampfgruppe von Cochenhausen which moved up in support of the Kampfgruppe von Böhm reconnaissance unit in the Foy-Notre-Dame area.

Now: The precise location of the belly-up Panther lies at position [1] just off the side of the N94 (Route de Neufchâteau) 50 metres south of its intersection with the present-day N910 (Route d'Achene) in Celles. The chateau on the hill in the background provides the perfect historical and structural comparison point of alignment. This picture is representative of one of the furthest points west into Allied territory achieved during the entire von Rundstedt offensive, reaching almost to Dinant which lay on the Meuse river itself.

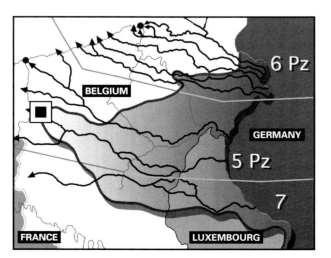

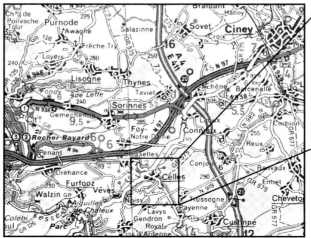

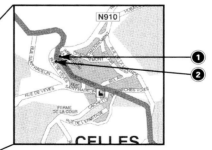

Celles: Michelin 214, Col. 5. 5° 1' East 50° 13' North. From north or southbound E411, exit 20, heading west on N97. Just past Foy-Notre-Dame and Boisselles, leave the N97 for the N94, heading south through Boisselles to Celles.

Then: As the lead tank forming the tip of Kampfgruppe von Cochenhausen, this Type A Panther struck a mine while advancing near Celles on December 24, 1944. By then, Kampfgruppen von Böhm and von Cochenhausen had pushed past Buissonville and entered the area around Celles, where this tank was disabled. This photograph reveals the Panther already substantially stripped of it accoutrements. Comparing this photo with the one on the previous page reveals that the château itself has since been enlarged with an entire wing, complete with turret! This clearly dates this photo as being post-war and offers an ironic 'then and now' situation on the château itself!

Now: The field [2] between the N910 and N94 at the apex of their intersection lies directly behind a café and house No. 3A. The château remains as it once was; at its foot runs Rue de Vêves. A German vehicle of a different sort — the author's own BMW 525tds — stands in the foreground. Ironically, it proved to be the precise spot where the Panther once sat, though at the time the author was simply looking for a parking space! Fate? The Panther still remains in situ close by, though now sitting on a stone plinth in front of the café.

Then: On December 22, Combat Command B of the 4th Armored Division set out from Habay-la-Neuve at 2.30 a.m. for the big push from the south to relieve the encircled town of Bastogne. At dawn they encountered elements of the 5. Fallschirm-Jäger-Division, engaging them in a fierce battle until 1.30 p.m. when US fighter-bombers forced a German withdrawal and American forces took the village of Chaumont, Belgium. Here a Jeep attached to the 25th Cavalry Squadron has struck a powerful mine while advancing on Chaumont from the south, sending it and its occupants blasting through trees.

Now: Fifty years later, this is the exact location of the tragedy [1] which occurred immediately south of Chaumont along an unnamed and unnumbered farm road. The track itself leads up north into Chaumont from the village of Burnon, some five kilometres directly due south. The Jeep met its fate right beside this oak tree, still easily identified by the tell-tale arrangement of its branches. Today, a small plaque at its base commemorates the American effort in liberating the town.

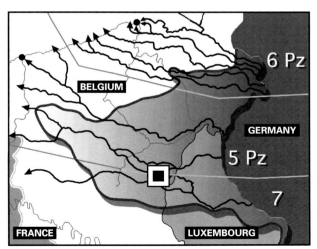

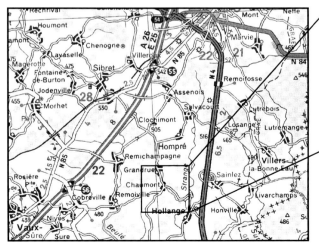

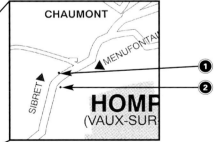

Chaumont: Michelin 214, Col. 7. 5° 40' East 49° 55' North. From the E25 south of Bastogne (north or southbound), take exit 56 onto the N848, direction Cobreville (south-east). Just through Cobreville, take direction Remoiville east. Upon entering Remoiville, continue east towards Chaumont entering just south of the village from the west. The photo location will be up the hill 100 metres to the right.

Then: The same scene of devastation as in the previous photo, viewed from a different angle. Bodies lie all around the splintered Jeep on both sides of the road, the face of the nearest GI being masked out by the censor to avoid identification. However, the 4th Armored could not be delayed or deterred; they pressed on into the village of Chaumont, which can be seen in the upper distance. Liberation of Bastogne from the south was now only days away.

Now: Taken from position [2], this picture shows an almost identical scene 50 years later, with the village in the distance. Apart from the odd farm vehicle, traffic is now much quieter and less frequent than the frenetic days of that December long ago.

Then: **By the morning of December 18, 1944, Kampfgruppe Peiper, denied vital bridges in Trois-Ponts, sought an alternative route south along Rollbahn E. After passing through the village of La Gleize advance elements of his column located a bridge still intact just east of Cheneux. As the spearhead crossed over at 2 p.m., it came under immediate, sustained air attack from the 365th, 366th and 404th Fighter Groups of IX Tactical Air Command. Panther 131 was one of the tanks hit. This frontal view confirms it as the Ausf. A version.**

Now: **The Panther once rested here by the roadside [1]. Today, 50 years later, cows peacefully graze in the field to the right and, once again, all is quiet in Cheneux.**

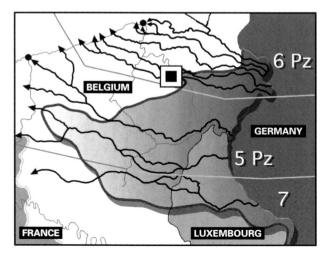

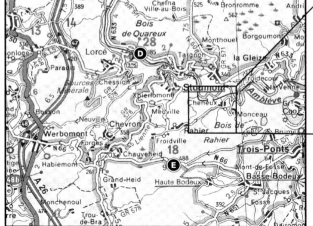

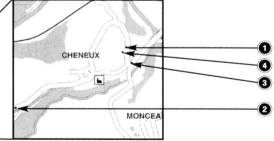

Cheneux: **Michelin 214, Col. 8. 5° 49' East 50° 23' North. North or southbound on the E25(A26), exit 48; head east on the N66, direction Basse-Bodeux, passing first through Werbomont and beyond Chauveheid (do not take the N645). Two km east of Chauveheid on the N66, turn north, direction Froidville/Rahier. Pass through Rahier to enter Cheneux from the west.**

Then: Aftermath of US air attacks in the valley of the Amblève river. This Maultier half-track lies smashed just west of Cheneux. The German spearhead pushed on westward to the Lienne river where it encountered increasing opposition, forcing a pull back to La Gleize.

Now: The precise location [2] today where US fighter-bombers came calling. The German vehicle lay on this curve between Cheneux and Rahier. Though the road is unnamed and unnumbered, the house on the right is No. 73 (La Maison Boutet) and lies just west of the village of Cheneux.

Then: Despite difficult flying conditions, US fighter-bombers made their presence felt as they strove to stop or delay the advancing German spearheads in the early days of the offensive. Attacking Kampfgruppe Peiper on December 18 as it passed through Cheneux was a key objective. This house (La Maison Dumont), situated directly on a hairpin turn just up the hill from the bridge across the Amblève, received a direct hit.

Now: Missing the tank, the blast killed a number of Belgian civilians hiding in the cellar. Now, the ill-fated house [3] has been completely rebuilt beside the same hairpin turn on the road leading from La Gleize through Cheneux and onto Rahier. This particular house (No. 2) is located directly east of Cheneux.

Then: **After the battle, just east of Cheneux. During initial US air attacks on Kampfgruppe Peiper on December 18, 1944, this Panther (No. 131) of the 1. SS-Panzer-Division was put out of action. In the background can be seen the Cheneux bridge across the Amblève river, one of the few the German spearhead found intact on its drive westward.**

Now: **The identical view of the valley [4] looking east 50 years later. With metal fence posts standing in for the wooden ones of yesterday, the comparison is complete. The characteristic curves in the road and sloping hills match the scene; only the trees surrounding the bridge, being now much larger and denser, display the tell-tale passage of time.**

Then: By December 20, the pressure in the St Vith sector from the LXVI. Armeekorps of the 5. Panzer-Armee was increasing rapidly, exploiting initial American confusion. In an attempt to solidify the defences around St Vith, Brigadier General Robert W. Hasbrouck, commanding the 7th Armored Division, hastily put together various line units to form Task Force Jones. Including elements of the 14th Cavalry Group, this force was given the objective of protecting the crossroads at Cherain and other villages along the east-west lines of American defence.

Now: When the American forces arrived, Cherain was already under attack by Grenadier-Regiment 1130 of the 560 Volks-Grenadier-Division, but Task Force Jones successfully defended Cherain. The post-battle photograph captured a lone Jagdpanzer IV abandoned by the roadside. Today, 50 years later, the identical scene complete with a blanket of snow recreates one of the author's favourite comparisons. The Jagdpanzer IV has vanished, leaving only the more prolific hedgerow on the left to indicate that time has indeed passed. The view is looking south-south-east.

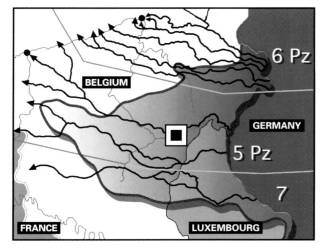

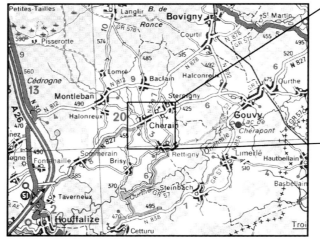

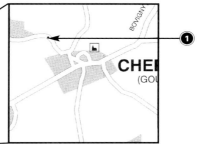

Cherain: Michelin 214, Col. 8. 5° 52' East 50° 11' North. From the E25 (A26) north or southbound, exit 51, Houffalize. Head north on the N30 to the intersection of the N827, direction St Vith. Cherain lies approximately 7-8 km north-east of Houffalize on the N827. You will enter the village from the west. The photo location lies just behind Cherain, along a small unnamed road that heads north-west to the village of Montleban.

Then: The commander of the 2. Panzer-Division, Oberst Meinrad von Lauchert, after initial successes in Marnach to the east, chose dawn of December 17, 1944 to attack Clervaux, Luxembourg, in strength. Opposing him was the 110th Regiment of the 28th Infantry Division, commanded by Colonel Hurley F. Fuller. The battle for Clervaux was joined at 9.30 a.m. when the leading Panzer IVs of II. Abteilung of Panzer-Regiment 3 were met head-on by Sherman tanks of the 707th Tank Battalion. In a battle lasting all day, more armour was thrown into the town by both sides; with tanks in the narrow streets, house-to-house fighting ensued.

Now: Clervaux basks in serenity of a lazy Sunday afternoon. This is the precise location [1] where the Sherman of the 707th Tank Battalion once lay disabled and dismembered. Clervaux is now a bustling tourist venue nestling in the valley of the Clerve river, and no casual tourist could possibly imagine the titanic struggle which once raged for control of the town which finally fell after the onslaught by 2. Panzer-Division. The characteristic spire of No. 61 Grand Rue confirms and aligns the comparison. The view is looking east-south-east.

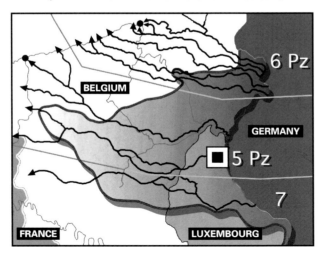

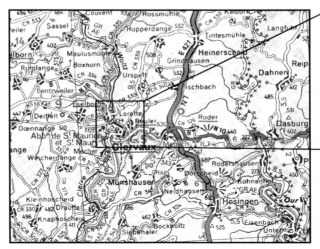

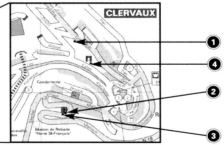

Clervaux: Michelin 214, Col. 9. 6° 2' East 50° 3' North. From the E42 (north or southbound) exit 15 (St Vith) onto the N62 (E421) south, direction Ettelbruck/Diekirch/Clervaux. Then N62 becomes the N7 heading south to Clervaux. Exit the N7 at the N18, direction west into Clervaux. You will enter the city from the east on the N18 (Rue de Marnach). As you wind down the valley into the city, you will pass the cemetery seen in the photo comparisons.

Then: Although taken in February 1945 after the 26th Infantry Division recaptured Clervaux, this photograph typifies the encounters which characterised the fighting earlier in December 1944. A Sherman M4 from the 707th Tank Battalion lies next to its nemesis, a Sturmgeschütz III assault gun. Once, armour from opposing forces met head on at this hairpin [2].

Now: The same bend today in Luxembourg. This tight corner lies along the N18 (Rue de Marnach) as it leaves Clervaux, ascending the valley of the Clerve towards Marnach to the east. The difference in the stone colour and type used to repair the damage to the cemetery wall is clearly visible, more noticeable on the far side.

Then: The same location as in the previous photo, though nature is already acting to reclaim its own. Taken on January 31, 1945, soon after Clervaux was recaptured on January 26, two American GIs reflect on the snowy scene of destruction [3]. Overall, a rather surreal photo, with a peaceful cemetery violated by two armoured hulks, and everything covered with a gentle mantle of snow.

Now: With several of the headstones in the cemetery now aiding the comparison, the exact photo angle is captured along the Rue de Marnach 50 years later. The deceased rest eternal, while the tanks have vanished, gone to the scrap merchants long ago.

Then: **Clervaux having been retaken, US forces guard the city in all directions, including the sky. This M16 belonging to the 777th Anti-Aircraft Artillery Battalion is seen standing guard in front of the prominent town church [4] on February 13, 1945.**

Now: **The timeless church, which survived the war intact, now calls worshippers without the aid of anti-aircraft guns. This is the view along the Rue Eglise, looking up and west, in the centre of the town.**

Then: On the morning of December 20, 1944, three US task forces organised by Combat Command B of the 3rd Armored Division set out to repulse the I. SS-Panzerkorps' ambitious Kampfgruppe Peiper. Task Force Jordan moved on Stoumont, Task Force McGeorge against the area directly north of La Gleize (Borgoumont) and Task Force Lovelady against the vital Trois-Ponts/La Gleize road near the village of Coo. Task Force Lovelady succeeded in reaching its position at 1 p.m. when it surprised SS-Panzer-Artillerie-Regiment 1 trying to reinforce Kampfgruppe Peiper from the south.

Now: Numerous pieces were destroyed including an SdKfz 165 self-propelled artillery gun which was pictured along the main road. This is the exact spot today [1] on the present-day N633 (Avenue Pierre Clerdent), just east of Coo. The view is looking directly west over the railway tracks, approximately 100 metres north of the overpass of the N633 and railway, next to the Rue Biester.

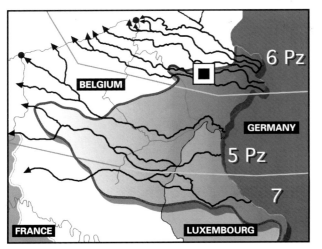

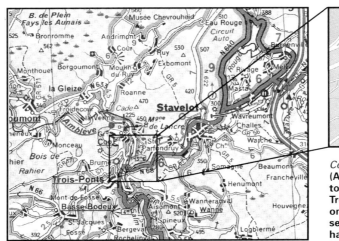

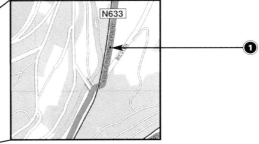

Coo: Michelin 214, Col. 8. 5° 53' East 50° 24' North. From the E42 (A27) north or southbound exit 11 onto the N62, direction Stavelot to the west. Pass through Stavelot heading west on the N68 to Trois-Ponts. At the intersection of the N68 and the N633, head north on the N633, direction Coo. Approximately 1 km north of this intersection, the N633 ducks under the railway, emerging on the right-hand side of the track. The photo location lies just beyond.

Then: Pictured in the spring of 1945, an M36 tank destroyer still lies where it was disabled during the battle to retake Dahl in Luxembourg. The village was the scene of activity involving the 319th Infantry, 80th Infantry Division, on January 8 when Sergeant Day G. Turner, attached to Company B, fought a successful 'battle of the Alamo' when, with his nine-man squad, he held off wave after wave of German assaults in hand-to-hand combat. For his heroic, tenacious defence, Sergeant Turner was awarded his nation's highest decoration, the Medal of Honor.

Now: Situated high on a hill between Wiltz and Ettelbruck, 50 years later Dahl sleeps under a blanket of snow in an Ardennes winter. Today the village is spreading out with former farmland having been handed over for housing developments. The village church still stands though, as do other farm structures of half a century ago, enabling the photo comparison [1] to be made. This is the view looking directly east along the side of d'Weltzerstroos. The house is No. 4.

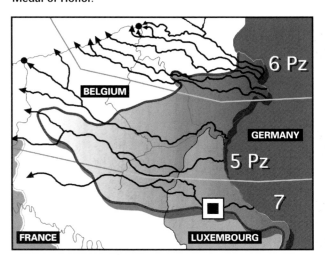

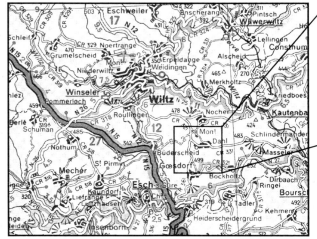

Dahl: Michelin 214, Col. 8. 5° 58' East 49° 56' North. Dahl lies high in the hills south-south-east of Wiltz, Luxembourg. From the N15 (from direction Bastogne or Ettelbruck) take the N27 at Esch-sur-Sûre east, direction Goesdorf/Dahl. CR361 off the N27 heads north to both villages, with Dahl laying beyond Goesdorf. You will enter the village from the south and drive straight on to d'Weltzerstroos, the site of the comparison.

Then: The crossing of the Our river at Dasburg, Germany, was a vital objective on the first day of the German offensive for the 2. Panzer-Division. Yet a month later, on January 21, remnants of the once-proud 5. Panzer-Armee would be retreating across this same site. American aircraft bombed the bridge on January 22 attempting to block their withdrawal. This photo, taken after the battle shows a wooden trestle bridge built by the American forces after they had successfully destroyed the previous structure. A German Panther lies at the foot of the eastern bank on the German side, perhaps a victim of the bombing.

Now: The Our river forms the border between Luxembourg and Germany and the photograph of the famous bridge today, looking towards Germany, reveals the same sloping eastern bank, reached now by a much-stronger bridge across the present-day N10. On the German side, the road becomes the Bundestrasse B410. The photo was taken next to the Café du Pont, situated right on the crossing, next to a Q8 petrol station. This is a popular refreshment point for both nationalities.

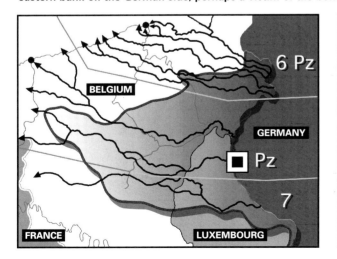

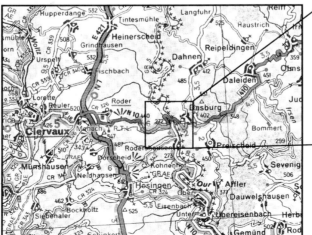

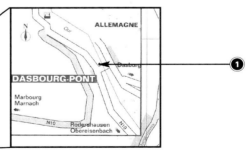

Dasburg: Michelin 214, Col. 9. 6° 8' East 50° 3' North. Along the E421(N7) running north-south through Luxembourg, exit at the N10 (east of Clervaux), direction Dasburg. The bridge lies 6 km to the east on the N10, spanning the Our river which forms the frontier between Luxembourg and Germany.

Deidenberg

Then: Taken late on the morning of December 18, 1944, this German cine still records the panzer might moving west through Deidenberg. Bringing up the rear, as always, a massive Tiger II thunders through the intersection, carrying elements of Fallschirm-Jäger-Regiment 9 on its broad shoulders. Fifteen of these kings of battle were active in support of the 1. SS-Panzer-Division — the 'Leibstandarte-SS Adolf Hitler' — commanded by SS-Oberführer Wilhelm Mohnke. This particular King Tiger (No. 222) was part of schwere SS-Panzer-Abteilung 501.

Now: The precise comparison view today. Taken eastwards looking down the present-day N659 at position [1], just one metre away from the location of the following photo, the house on the right is No. 88. Note the patches of moss on its roof, still there after 50 years! What a sight — and sound — it must have been to stand on this spot and watch the enormous 67-ton beast thundering past!

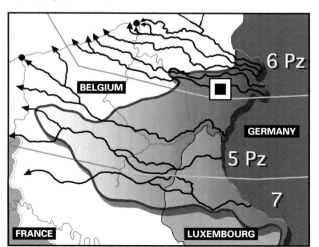

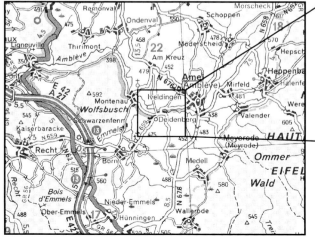

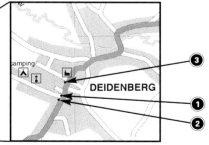

Deidenberg: Michelin 214, Col. 9. 6° 8' East 50° 22' North. Southbound along the E42 (A27), exit 13 onto the N659, direction Born. Pass through Born east to Deidenberg, which lies just west of the Amblève river. You will enter the village from the west.

Then: The children of Deidenberg, Belgium, turned out along designated Rollbahn E to wave on the 1. SS-Panzer-Division. This attack route, assigned to Kampfgruppen Hansen and Knittel, ran straight through the main street of their village.

Now: The exact spot [2] 50 years later almost to the very day, where innocence once cheered on mechanised evil. A similar gloomy, rainy day colours the view looking north-east down the present-day N659 which runs through the centre of Deidenberg. The characteristic farmhouse structure in the background provides the perfect alignment for the comparison.

Then: It is January 1945 and the Americans have finally retaken the village. Vehicles belonging to the 23rd Armored Infantry Battalion of the 7th Armored Division line the snowy main street [3]. Picture taken by Signal Corps photographer Tech/5 Robert Runyan.

Now: The photo comparison 50 years later finds vehicles of a different sort parked outside the Café Erkes, No. 86, along the present-day N659. The building on the extreme right in the wartime photo has since been demolished, exposing the café in its entirety. Today, the centre of Deidenberg is undergoing significant renewal with a new main square being laid out to the right.

Then: On the evening of December 20, 1944, the 116. Panzer-Division, LVIII. Panzerkorps, 5. Panzer-Armee, succeeded in taking the Belgian village of Dochamps, just east of the La Roche–Hotton road. Exploiting the gap between Task Force Hogan and Task Force Tucker of 3rd Armored Division, Kampfgruppe Bayer of the 116. Panzer-Division moved west into Devantave. It was only later — on January 9, 1945 — three days after elements of the 84th Infantry Division had been able to recapture the village, that this photo was taken. It shows vehicles belonging to the 84th amidst the snow and devastation.

Now: Devantave sleeps on a Sunday afternoon. This is the identical view matching the picture taken 50 years ago looking directly south down the Rue Saint-Donat [1] in the heart of the village. The house on the left is No. 5; the large one on the right No. 10. Substantial damage makes the comparison a difficult one though this is the same location. The village church is immediately off to the left and behind.

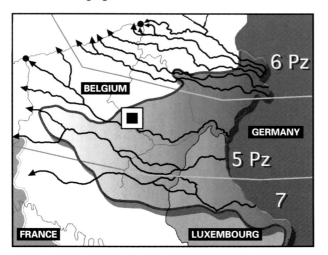

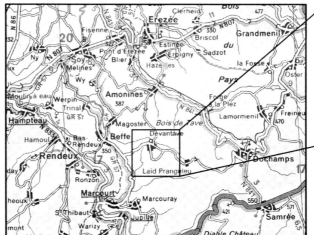

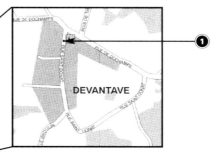

Devantave: Michelin 214, Col. 7. 5° 33' East 50° 14' North. From La Roche, take the N833 northbound direction Hotton (or from Hotton, the N833 southbound direction La Roche). Exit the N833 direction east to Marcourt/Marcouray. Pass through Marcourt, but before Marcouray head north in the direction of Beffe. Before Beffe, turn right to Devantave, entering the village from the west.

Then: **Men of the 109th Infantry Regiment, 28th Infantry Division, parade in the town square [1] of Diekirch, Luxembourg, on December 15. The next morning, artillery of the LXXXV. Armeekorps began to pound the town, while the 5. Fallschirm-Jäger-Division and the 352. Volks-Grenadier-Division moved forward to the attack. One by one the villages east of Diekirch fell: Fouhren, Longsdorf, Bastendorf. On December 19, Grenadier-Regiment 914, attached to the 352. Volks-Grenadier-Division and fighting alongside Grenadier-Regiment 915, attacked Diekirch itself and in the dead of night the town fell into German hands.**

Now: **The town square today. The view is looking west across the Grand Place, bounded by Rue du Palais to the south and Rue de Stavelot to the east. The great expanse is now a large parking area though the two buildings on the left in the distance help align the comparison with the fuzzy wartime photo of long ago. Here on December 10, 1944, Marlene Dietrich entertained the troops and on this very spot American bands played on as the Germans put the finishing touches to their plans.**

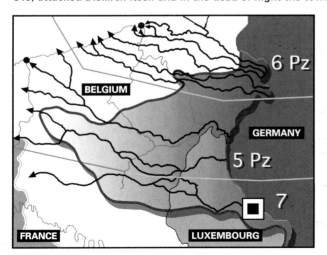

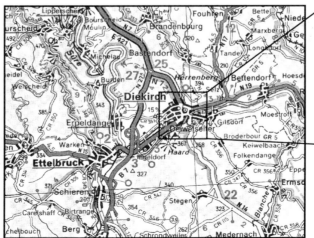

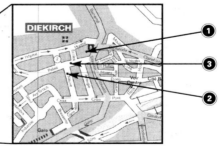

Diekirch: **Michelin 214, Col. 9. 6° 10' East 49° 52' North. Diekirch, north of the great city of Luxembourg, can be reached directly from the four corners of the compass. From Bastogne in the west take the N84/N15; from St Vith in the north take the E421; from Echternach in the east, take the N19; and from Luxembourg City, the N7/B7 north.**

Then: **Just over a month later, Diekirch was retaken by the Americans in a tactically bold action. At 3 a.m. on January 18, silently and without artillery preparation, two regiments of the 5th Infantry Division crossed the Sûre river in flat-bottom boats. The German defences were totally surprised and on January 19 the town was liberated.**

Now: **This is the view 50 years later looking down the Rue Neuve [2] towards houses lining the Rue du Palais. The house with the four windows is No. 12. Though the house to its left has been completely rebuilt, the other buildings lining both sides of Rue Neuve, together with the width of those on Rue du Palais, enable the comparison to be confirmed.**

Then: **Post-battle damage assessment along the Rue du Palais [3] in the centre of Diekirch in the spring of 1945. American shelling, ever present and effective, caused a great deal of damage in the town itself. This is the view looking west.**

Now: **A modern day view in the same direction reveals the restoration and tidiness of Diekirch today. Some of the structures have changed, though the house on the far right, with its characteristic shutters and step railing, remains.**

Then: On the afternoon of December 20, the Belgian village of Dochamps came under attack by the 116. Panzer-Division, supported by elements of the 560. Volks-Grenadier-Division. Opposing the effort was Task Force Tucker of the 3rd Armored Division though by nightfall Kampfgruppe Bayer (Panzer-Regiment 16, a battalion of Panzer-Grenadier-Regiment 60 with artillery and engineers) of the 116. Panzer-Division had taken the village. It would be several weeks before the 2nd Armored Division would retake Dochamps. This photo shows men of the division next to the church [1] which suffered from American shelling as did the whole village.

Now: Fifty years later, the US troops have long since departed and the church in Dochamps looks none the worse for wear. This is the view looking south along the present-day Rue du Lavoir, where it intersects the Rue du Vieux Frêne. On the far right runs the Rue des Fontaines, where the American sentry once stood guard as his friends rolled by.

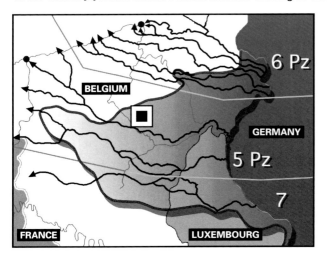

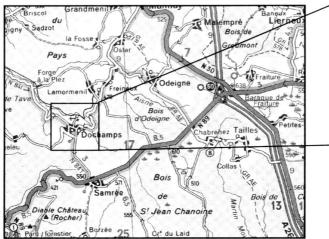

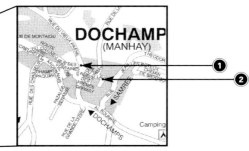

Dochamps: Michelin 214, Col. 7. 5° 37' East 50° 14' North. From the E25 (A26) north or southbound, exit 50 onto N89 west. At Samrée on the N89, turn right onto the N841, direction Dochamps, which lies 3 km to the north of Samrée. You will enter the village from the south.

Then: **Having retaken Dochamps from the 2. SS-Panzer-Division (of the follow-up II. SS-Panzerkorps) on January 7, elements of the 2nd Armored Division consolidate their gains in the centre of the village. An M4 Sherman tank stands guard east of the church while a half-track moves up in the distance.**

Now: **The view along the Rue du Lavoir [2] on a similar snowy day 50 years later. With the fog beginning to settle on the peaceful scene, the same area in Dochamps shows little change, save for the new house on the left (No. 7, Rue du Lavoir). The house on the right is No. 20. The village church, seen in the previous photo, lies up the hill to the left, its spire just visible through the mist.**

Then: **Early January 1945, and a column belonging to the 2nd Armored Division, led by an M36 tank destroyer, slowly makes its way along a snowy road northwards back towards Dochamps, Belgium.**

Now: **The precise location [1] of the wartime photograph on the same road 50 years later. This is the present-day N841 running between the villages of Samrée to the south and Dochamps to the north. The photograph was taken just south of the edge of the latter village, about a hundred metres from the Chemin du Bois, looking south. The characteristic curve of the road, along with the drop-off on the left shoulder, confirm the location, though several of the trees on the left have long since disappeared. With snow on the ground and continuing to fall, the comparison is eerily reminiscent.**

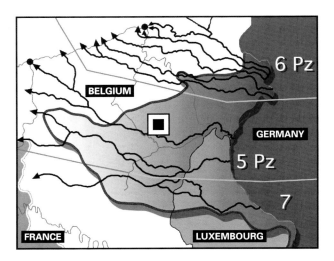

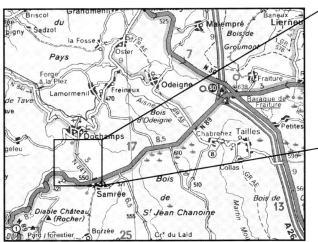

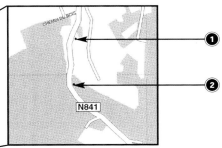

Dochamps-Samrée: **Michelin 214, Col. 7. 5° 38' East 50° 12' North. From the E25 (A26) north or southbound, exit 50 onto N89 west. At Samrée on the N89, turn right onto the N841, direction Dochamps. The N841 runs between Dochamps to the north and Samrée. This is the road used by the 2nd Armored Division as it moved men and material back and forth between the two villages.**

Then: The 2nd Armored Division now on the move southwards from Dochamps to Samrée, gingerly inching their M4 Shermans down a twisting, snowy road. After having retaken Dochamps from the 2. SS-Panzer-Division, they continued to move southward in conjunction with the 84th Infantry Division, further reducing the German bulge.

Now: The same curve [2] in the present-day N841 finds conditions a little more conducive to driving. This photo was taken just south of the location in the previous photo, now looking north towards Dochamps.

Then: On the morning of December 16, 1944, the Luxembourg village of Drauffelt lay directly in the path of XXXXVII. Panzerkorps commanded by General der Panzertruppen Heinrich von Lüttwitz. Grenadier-Regiment 77 of the 26. Volks-Grenadier-Division had already begun to move on the village which lay astride a vital railway. Late the next morning Kampfgruppe 902 of the Panzer-Lehr-Division crossed the river here. By the middle of January, the Third Army was pushing the 7. Armee back along a broad front, and the 26th Infantry Division recaptured the village from the 5. Fallschirm-Jäger-Division of LVIII. Armeekorps on the 25th.

Now: Seen over 50 years later, the same spot along the railway reveals no sign of the M4 Shermans of the 69th Tank Battalion (6th Armored Division) assembled at the marshalling yards [1] at Drauffelt in late January 1945. This is the view looking directly north up the area known as the Eiseboonswee, the photo being taken at the southernmost end. The wartime photo was taken from the second-storey window of the stationmaster's quarters but, unable to gain access to achieve the necessary height, the author had to make do by standing on the roof of his car!

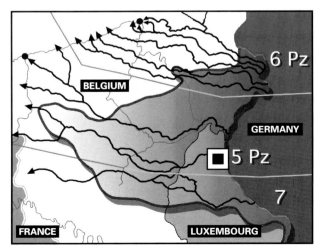

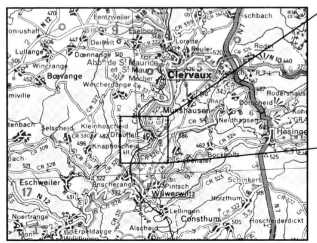

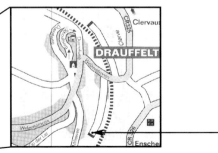

Drauffelt: **Michelin 214, Col. 9. 6° 1' East 50° 1' North. From the E421 (N7), exit on the N18 west to Clervaux. In Clervaux, head south, direction Wiltz on the CR325 following the Clerve river. Drauffelt lies approximately 6 km south of Clervaux.**

Then: Echternach in Luxembourg, like other key cities situated along the Sûre river, was a major objective of the German 7. Armee. From the outset, it was under sustained attack by forces of the 212. Volks-Grenadier-Division of the LXXX. Armeekorps, which faced the 12th Regiment of the 4th Infantry Division, and on December 20 the beleaguered Company E had to surrender the city. The attack to recapture Echternach began in early February 1945, and by the 10th the city was back in American hands. Here, with a Bofors gun at the ready, the skies over Echternach are guarded by Battery C of the 457th Anti-Aircraft Artillery Battalion.

Now: Over 50 years later, the author identified the exact location [1] of the anti-aircraft gun emplacement. This is the view looking due west from high on a hill in the south-eastern outskirts of the city, just beyond the termination of Rue Ste Croix, next to an old chapel. The chapel remains today looking much as it did during the war, its spire, along with the mountains in the background, serving as an alignment point. The author was amazed to find the gun pit almost as if it had just been filled in, still distinguishing the site from the rest of the open field.

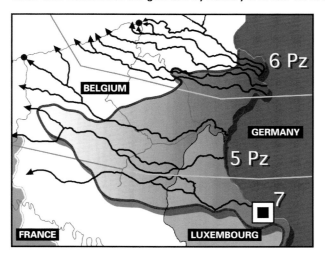

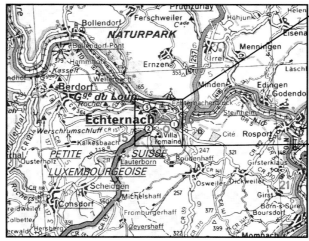

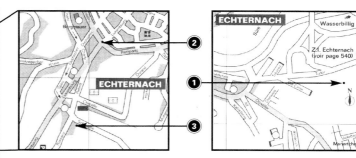

Echternach: Michelin 214, Col. 10. 6° 25' East, 49° 48' North. From Luxembourg City, take the E29 (N11) north-west in the direction of Echternach and enter the city from the south. From the west, take the N10 along the Sûre river from Ettelbruck straight into Echternach.

Then: Giving the term 'commanding at the front' a whole new meaning, Major General Manton S. Eddy, commander of the US XII Corps, heads for cover in the centre of Echternach as his boys lay down artillery fire. Taken on February 9, 1945, the fight to recapture Echternach from the 212. Volks-Grenadier-Division was underway. Echternach was liberated soon after.

Now: Looking down the same street 50 years later, things are a bit tidier and certainly much quieter. The view is north-east down the Rue de Luxembourg [2], with the Rue Maximilien to the left and Rue des Remparts to the right. Like many towns and cities in Luxembourg, Echternach suffered a great deal from artillery of both sides in the conflict.

Then: With the city retaken in February 1945, the artillery of the US XII Corps is redeployed in its defence. Here a massive 155mm self-propelled gun peeks around the corner of a house near the centre of Echternach as the crew ready it for firing.

Now: With the same iron fencing still in place, and the brick corner still standing, the author captures the precise photo angle and location as that taken over 50 years ago. He is standing directly in front of No. 4 Rue Gregoire Schouppe [3] in the south-west section of Echternach. Substantial housing development has taken place in the field across the street, though this corner location remained recognisable.

Then: Unbeknown to its inhabitants, the small Belgian town of Elsenborn was to be cleared by forward elements of the 277. Volks-Grenadier-Division during the start of hostilities. Yet due to tenacious American defence to the east, instead the town became a tactical 'pull back' location for both the 99th and 2nd Infantry Divisions. After the initial six days of fighting in the northern sector, a formidable defensive line had been consolidated on the Elsenborn Ridge, geologically favourable terrain for further action. Shown under a blanket of snow in late December 1944, this is the Hotel Leinen [1] in the centre of Elsenborn.

Now: A virtually identical comparison 50 years later, minus snow. Today the hotel is still standing on the Lagerstrasse running through the centre of the town although renamed Gaststätte Leinen. History records the successful defence of the Elsenborn Ridge area in the early days of the Ardennes offensive as one of the key elements leading to eventual Allied victory.

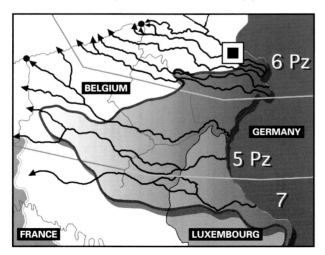

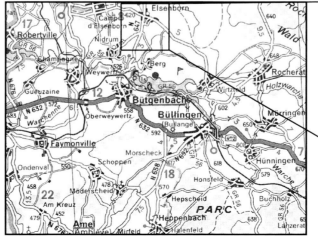

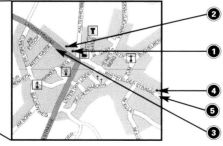

Elsenborn: **Michelin 214, Col. 9. 6° 13' East 50° 28' North. From Malmédy to the west, take the N632 east direction Bütgenbach. In Bütgenbach, turn left (north) on the N647, direction Berg/Elsenborn. You will enter the town from the south.**

Elsenborn

Then: Along the same street, members of the 99th Infantry Division wait with their Jeeps outside the forward regimental command post of the 393rd Infantry Regiment.

Now: This same building [2] on Lagerstrasse is now the Café Thonnes.

Then: Looking east down the snowy main street [3] towards the centre of Elsenborn.

Now: Extensive housing development along the right-hand side reveals the passage of time in this comparison taken 50 years later. The garden wall on the left has been replaced with a more modern version.

Then: **Having waited for two M4 Shermans to pass, a Weasel pulls out from the Dakota Aid Station of the 393rd Infantry Regiment onto the main road from the east heading into the centre of Elsenborn. Medical corpsmen often used these types of vehicles for transporting supplies and wounded.**

Now: **Today, the former aid station [4] on the immediate right is No. 41 Wirtzfelder Strasse. The Weasel would have emerged from the garage space of this same house; quite a different vehicle from that residing there today! The oak tree on the left of the photo still stands, helping to align the comparison.**

Then: **A Weasel attached to the medical group of the 393rd Infantry Regiment moves slowly down the road to the village of Wirtzfeld, east-south-east of Elsenborn.**

Now: **Looking down the same road today, Wirtzfelder Strasse, towards Wirtzfeld itself. The characteristic house, No. 49 [5] on map, in the centre of the forked road remains, as do most of the trees on the left of the photo.**

Then: After initial success in Manhay to the east, the II. SS-Panzerkorps launched its main attack on Erezée, Belgium, on December 27, 1944. Initiated by SS-Panzer-Grenadier-Regiment 25 of the 12. SS-Panzer-Division (the 2. SS-Panzer-Division being now thoroughly pinned down by the US effort to retake Manhay), it moved south-east on Erezée through Sadzot, where it was met and stopped by the 509th Parachute Infantry Battalion. The attack on Erezée was the last forward, offensive action by the 6. Panzer-Armee during the Ardennes offensive.

Now: An identical comparison in the centre of Erezée where 50 years ago stood the massive implements of destruction which carried the day in the Erezée-Grandmenil-Manhay sector; two American 155mm (8-inch) M1 howitzers parked in the town square next to the church. This is the view today looking directly south across the Place du Capitaine Garnir [1] at the junction of three streets: Rue des Combattants, Rue Général Borlon and Rue des Hachets. The house on the right is No. 1 Avenue du Centenaire.

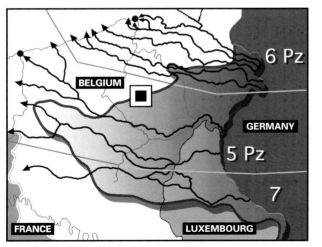

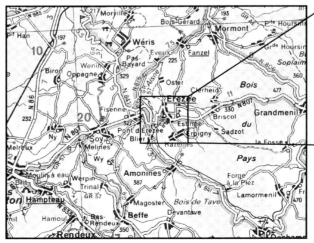

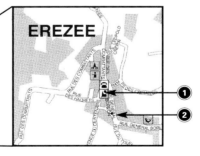

Erezée: Michelin 214, Col. 7. 5° 33' East 50° 17' North. From the E25 (A26) north or southbound exit 49, then head west on the N651 to Manhay. From Manhay, take the N807 west into Erezée. Erezée lies 11 km west of Grandmenil.

Then: Far from home, GIs maintain the holiday spirit before the battle for Erezée begins. A local horse is pressed into service to field-test a 'US M1 Christmas sled'. Although it was able to move through snow at a fairly rapid clip despite its one-horsepower rating, nonetheless it lacked firepower, though its very low silhouette made it difficult to hit at a distance!

Now: Fifty years on, the exact location of frivolity [2] finds the same side street in Erezée alone and deserted. The house, modified since the war, is No. 8 Rue Général Borlon. The view is looking north towards the town square with the church in the distance.

Then: **Having overrun Diekirch and Ettelbruck, by December 24 the 352. Volks-Grenadier-Division (LXXXV. Armeekorps, 7. Armee) had moved as far as Bettborn before the US III Corps began to decisively push them back. The Luxembourg village of Eschdorf was a key objective for the 104th Regiment of the 26th Infantry Division and on Christmas Eve they began an attack which battled on throughout Christmas Day. The following day Eschdorf was back in American hands. After the battle, three members of the 104th Infantry stand at attention before their unit commander.**

Now: **The same courtyard [1] in Eschdorf where 50 years ago three soldiers — Sergeant Farsfield, Tech/5 Trueblood and Tech/4 Breda — once stood to attention. Today a refurbished façade frames the scene across the street from the village church. This photo was taken in front of No. 4 Haaptstrooss-Dricht.**

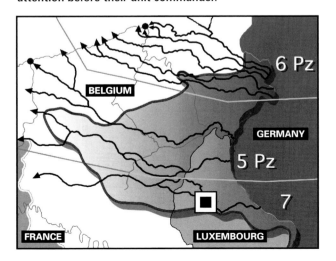

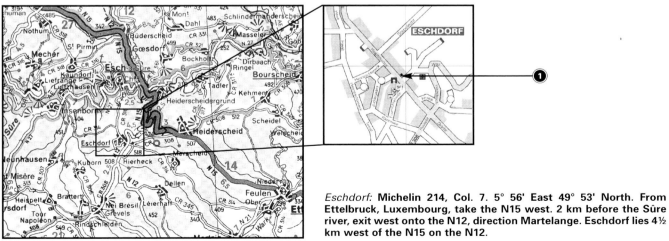

Eschdorf: **Michelin 214, Col. 7. 5° 56' East 49° 53' North. From Ettelbruck, Luxembourg, take the N15 west. 2 km before the Sûre river, exit west onto the N12, direction Martelange. Eschdorf lies 4½ km west of the N15 on the N12.**

Then: **By December 21, 1944, Fallschirm-Jäger-Regiment 15 (5. Fallschirm-Jäger-Division, LXXXV. Armeekorps), had moved westward as far as Martelange in Luxembourg, an impressive achievement. They had moved through Wiltz and overrun the town on December 19 and captured six Sherman tanks which they quickly put into the service of the Reich. After the recapture of Esch-sur-Sûre on January 19, 1945, by American forces, one of these Shermans was found in the village. This photo taken five days later shows the turncoat tank parked in front of the Hotel des Ardennes [1] in the centre of the town.**

Now: **On a similar snowy day 50 years later, this is the precise spot where the imposter was brought to book. No. 1 Rue du Moulin lies on the corner intersection of this street with the Rue de l'Eglise. When the author tried to book a room there for a Luxembourg holiday, his local travel agent in Waterloo said that the hotel did not exist. Upon being presented with the 'now' photo shown here, the travel agent was perplexed, spending the better part of a day finding out it had since been converted into private residences while retaining the hotel facade!**

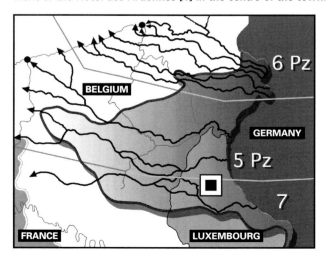

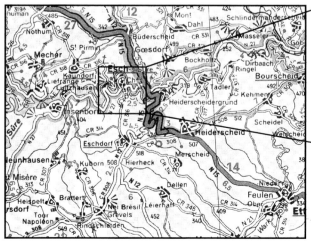

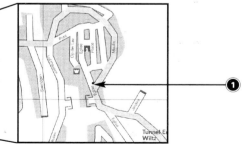

Esch-sur-Sûre: **Michelin 214, Col. 8. 5° 56' East 49° 55' North. From Ettelbruck to the east, take the N15 west direction Wiltz. Just after crossing the Sûre river at Heiderscheidergrund, turn left onto the N27, direction Esch-sur-Sûre. You will enter the picturesque village from the east. Coming from Bastogne to the west, take the N84/N15 direction Wiltz. Continue beyond Wiltz on the N15, direction Ettelbruck. Before the river, turn right onto the N27 as above.**

Then: Having liberated Ettelbruck in September 1944, late on December 20 the men of the 109th Regiment of the 28th Infantry Division were pushed out of the city by Grenadier-Regiment 915 of the 352. Volks-Grenadier-Division (LXXXV. Armeekorps, 7. Armee). The 80th Infantry Division struck back and, on the evening of December 23, its 318th Regiment was thrown back with heavy losses. However, continued pressure saw Ettelbruck fall into American hands on Christmas Eve.

Now: In the same view today, the city church steeple provides a reference point while the identical house on the left completes the comparison. We are looking directly east down the Rue Michel Weber [1] with the junction of Rue des Vergers behind the author. The house on the left is No. 86 Rue Michel Weber with No. 35 on the far right, Today, Ettelbruck is a prosperous, attractive city with a rich military past.

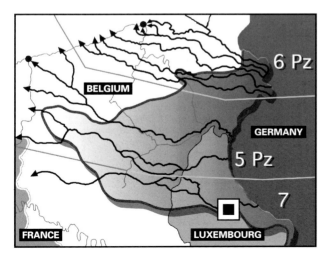

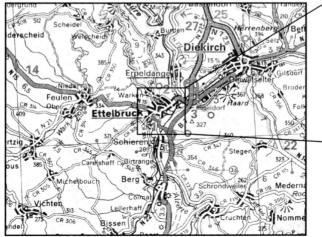

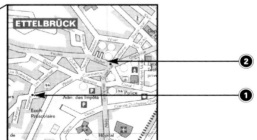

Ettelbruck: Michelin 214, Col. 9. 6° 6' East 49° 51' North. From Bastogne to the west, take the N84/N15 west direction Wiltz/Ettelbruck. Ettelbruck lies 41 km to the south-east of Bastogne along the N15. From Echternach, take the N10/N19 west to Ettelbruck along the Sûre river. Ettelbruck lies 28 km west of Echternach off the N19.

Then: By December 24, 1944, elements of the newly-arrived 5th Infantry Division were arriving to support the exhausted effort being led by the 80th Infantry Division. This wartime photo, taken most likely on December 26, shows members of the 11th Regiment of the 5th Infantry marching through the town. Note the white bedsheets many soldiers had taken to wearing as de facto snow camouflage.

Now: The centre of Ettelbruck, Luxembourg, 50 years later. The view is looking south up the Grand Rue [2] with Rue Guilliaume to the author's back. The large store on the left is No. 46 and five decades later it is still a shoe shop! However, since this photo was taken the street has been pedestrianised and closed to motor traffic.

Then: **Faymonville, Belgium, where the 1st Infantry Division (the 'Big Red One') is now firmly in control having retaken the village from the 3. Fallschirm-Jäger-Division on January 16, 1945. Sergeant Augustine attached to the unit pictured transport making its way through the deep snow next to the battered Hermann family home. The house was most likely damaged by American artillery fire in the move to recapture the village. Faymonville was situated along Rollbahn D of Kampfgruppe Peiper though the battlegroup passed by just south of the village on December 17, moving west from Schoppen to Ondenval.**

Now: **The same venue [1] in Faymonville today. The passage of 50 years finds the Hermann's house completely repaired with a new addition. The view is looking north-west along the Rue de la Laiterie. The house, No. 19 Rue de la Warchenne, sits on the corner of this street as it intersects Rue de la Laiterie and Rue Mon Antone just north of the railway bridge. With the road widened and Faymonville sleeping peacefully, there is little reminder today of the violence which once struck this corner of Belgium.**

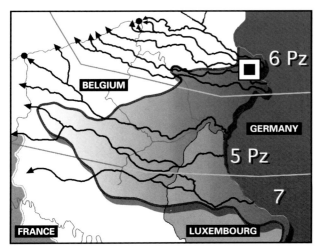

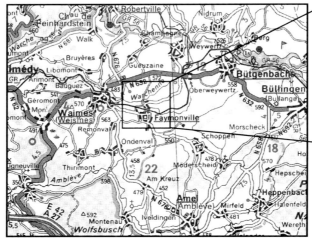

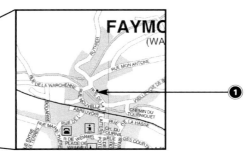

Faymonville: **Michelin 214, Col. 9. 6° 8' East 50° 25' North. North or southbound on the E42 (A27), exit 11, direction Malmédy. Pass through Malmédy direction Waimes on the N62. In Waimes, head south on the N67 to Faymonville; the approach to Faymonville will be a road leaving the N67 just south of Waimes, heading east into the village.**

Then: **Having taken Clervaux by the evening of December 17, 1944, the 2. Panzer-Division kept up the attack and, through the dead of night and into the morning of the 18th, moved westward in strength. In response, the 9th Armored Division sent three task forces to try to halt its advance: Task Forces Rose, Harper and Booth. Task Force Rose was quickly overrun by von Lauchert's forces at Antoniushaff, and Task Force Booth met its fate at Hardigny. Task Force Harper was virtually annihilated with Colonel Harper himself killed in the battle. This well-known photo reveals the destruction of Task Force Harper at the Fetsch road junction.**

Now: **Today Fetsch is still little more than a few houses and cafes at the intersection of the present-day N12 and N874 [1]. It was in this field that Task Force Harper met its fate at the hands of the 2. Panzer-Division for this is the view looking north-east towards the same houses, virtually unchanged since that fateful day. The large house on the left is No. 4 — the Café op der Fetsch — standing beside the N12.**

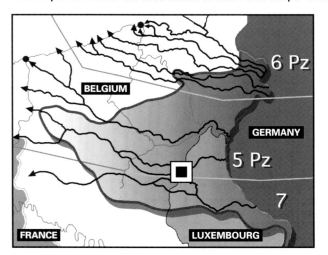

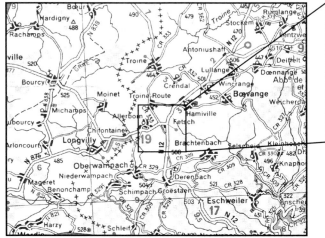

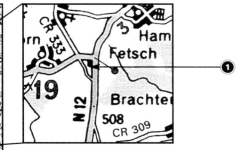

Fetsch: **Michelin 214, Col. 8. 5° 53' East 50° 2' North. From Bastogne, take the N874 east, direction Longvilly/Clervaux. N874 runs into the N12 in Luxembourg, running north/south. The field is on the south-west side of the road junction, behind the large café.**

Then: In 1945, after the battle of the Ardennes was over, a young Belgian named Jean Collignon rode the battlefield on his bicycle, making drawings of the vehicles of war which still littered the area. In this particular sketch Collignon depicted a Sturmgeschütz which had been put out of action yet still appeared to be hiding behind two farm houses. He drew the picture in a small village north of the town of Houffalize called Fontenaille.

Now: The accuracy of Jean Collignon's rendering can be confirmed today, as illustrated in this present-day photo comparison taken by the author showing that the 50-year-old drawing matches perfectly with its location. Though several other structures have been added on around them, the two farm houses still stand in the little Belgian village just as they once did. They lie right beside the N30; this is the view looking south back towards Houffalize. The small road immediately behind the farmhouse heads directly into the small village to the left of the photo. Off the right, the village of Mont.

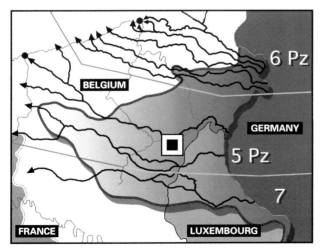

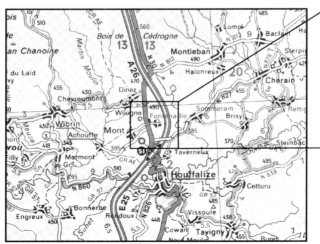

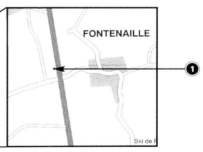

Fontenaille: **Michelin 214, Col. 8. 5° 47' East 50° 9' North. North or southbound along the E25 (A26), exit 51 onto the N30, direction Baraque de Fraiture northbound. Fontenaille lies 2 km north of Houffalize along the N30.**

Then: A blanket of snow covers German war dead buried on a hillside at the foot of a small chapel in Forge à l'Aplé, Belgium. Wooden crosses, many topped with the helmets of the fallen, still mark their names and location. Though unconfirmed, these men could well have belonged to SS-Panzer-Grenadier-Regiment 25 of the 12. SS-Panzer-Division as this unit commenced an attack on Sadzot — and hence Erezée — on the night of December 27 by slipping through a gap in the lines of the 1st and 2nd Battalions of the 75th Infantry Division's 289th Regiment at Forge à l'Aplé. The attack was eventually stopped just outside Sadzot.

Now: Fifty years later, the same small chapel [1] still stands just inside the woods. The hillside where the German dead were buried runs down from it towards the camera position. The view is looking south, just off the Route de Lamormenil across the street from house No. 5. Though the site is quite overgrown today, the hillside retains a sense of poignancy and tragedy, marking the place where Germans who once fell in the final offensive effort of the 6. Panzer-Armee were given a field grave.

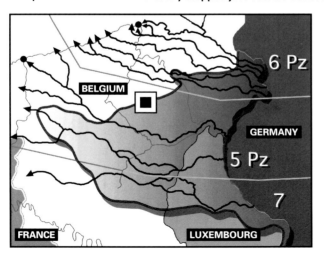

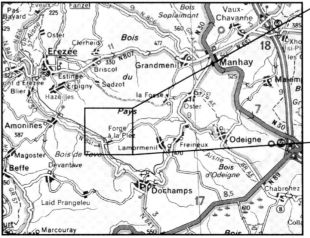

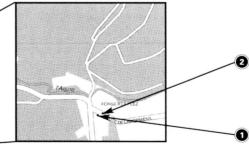

Forge à l'Aplé: **Michelin 214, Col. 7. 5° 36' East 50° 15' North. From the E25 (A26) north or southbound exit 49, then head west on the N651 to Manhay. From Manhay, take the N807 west through Erezée to the bridge across the Aisne river; immediately across the river, proceed south on the N841 approximately 3½ km until signs point left to Forge à l'Aplé, just across the Aisne river.**

Then: A snowy afternoon in January 1945. With the 6. Panzer-Armee long since on the defensive, elements of the 84th Infantry Division pass through the small hamlet of Forge à l'Aplé, Belgium.

Now: Fifty years later, almost to the day, the same route used by the US troops is pictured by the author. This is the view looking west along the present-day Route de Lamormenil [2]. The house with the characteristic archway is No. 5; the one beyond it on the right with the pointed roof No. 7. Only the two trees, now much taller and broader along the road in the background, gives a hint that time indeed has passed on by.

Then: **With Kampfgruppen von Böhm and von Cochenhausen of the 2. Panzer-Division stopped at Celles by the combined efforts of the British 29th Armoured Brigade and the American 2nd Armored Division, men of the 75th Infantry Division (VII Corps) follow in the footsteps of the 2nd Armored. They are pictured here on the afternoon of December 26 marching through the small village of Forzée, east of Celles. The comforting attention of an M4 tank lends support, its gun trained down the road.**

Now: **Forzée, Belgium, 50 years later, and the matching shot is captured exactly on a similar long-shadowed afternoon in December. In one of the author's favourite comparisons, little has changed. Though a few windows have been added to the house in the foreground, everything including the overhead power cables line up. This is the view looking north along the Rue des Coures [1] which is the street just off of the N949 as one enters the village from the north-east. In the fields of Forzée today, the only mechanised sounds come from farm machinery.**

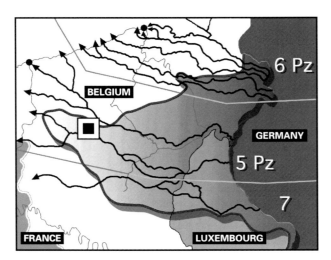

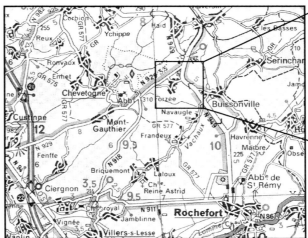

Forzée: **Michelin 214, Col. 6. 5° 11' East 50° 13' North. Along the N4 south of Namur direction Marche, exit onto the N929 before Sinsin, 10 km north-west of Marche. Head west on the N929 through Haversin. 5 km north of Buissonville, the N929 splits into the N949 as well. Take the N949 direction Rochefort. Immediately on the right is a sign for Forzée, entering the village from the east.**

Then: Early on the morning of December 20, the Belgian village of Noville was cut off from the south by the 2. Panzer-Division, and the 506th Infantry Regiment was brought up from Bastogne to shore up the northern defence at Foy. By Christmas Day, this perimeter had shrunk further south and the town was completely encircled. Following the relief of Bastogne on December 26 by the Third Army, Foy was eventually retaken by the 101st Airborne. This photograph, taken on January 16 by Pfc E. L. Martin, shows the clean-up following its recapture, as the medical corps go to work amidst the destruction.

Now: The same view 50 years later, almost to the very day, reveals a decidedly more civil and peaceful scene. A small village, Foy lies directly on the N30 running due north from Bastogne. This is the view looking south-east from point [1] on the map down the road into the village. The house on the right, still retaining its tell-tale diamond emblem design above the door, is No. 15 on an unnamed street. The building on the extreme left of the wartime photo has been razed. And, today, the ambulance would have to wait for a green light at the junction.

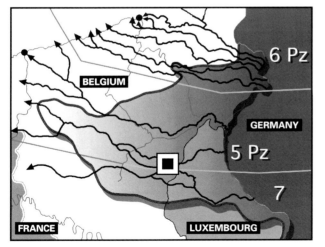

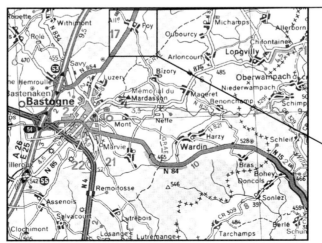

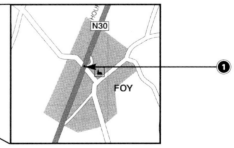

Foy: Michelin 214, Col. 6. 5° 45' East 50° 2' North. North or southbound on the E25 (A26), exit 53 at Bastogne onto the N854 eastwards. The N854 becomes the N30 heading north to Foy. The village lies approximately 6 km north of Bastogne on the N30.

Then: After the battle, a Sturmgeschütz, looking decidedly the worse for wear, sits basking in the noonday sun in a field in Géromont, Belgium. Though already stripped by souvenir hunters, and targeted for destruction by the scrap merchant's code on its front glacis, the Allied white star recognition symbol remains displayed in an effort to masquerade as an American tank. Carrying the markings of Company C, 81st Tank Battalion, 5th Armored Division, this imposter was in fact part of Kampfgruppe Y of Panzerbrigade 150, taking part in Operation 'Greif'.

Now: The same field 50 years later, where the stealth armour of the SS once met its fate. Operation 'Greif' was commanded by Obersturmbannführer Otto Skorzeny and the Stug was one of a number of those lost by the brigade just east of Malmédy. This location can be viewed today from approximately 30 metres from the edge of the present-day N62 looking eastwards, just to the west of No. 85 Route de Waimes, where the characteristic forest patterns and treelines in the background help to align the comparison.

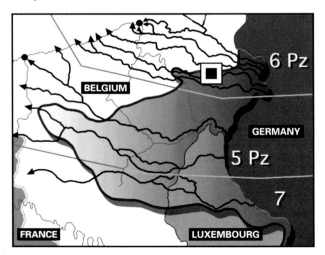

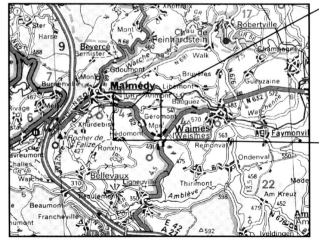

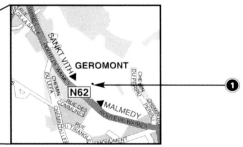

Géromont: **Michelin 214, Col. 9. 6° 3' East 50° 25' North. North or southbound on the E42 (A27), exit 11 at Malmédy onto the N62 eastwards. Pass through Malmédy on the N62, direction Waimes. Géromont lies 2 km east-south-east of Malmédy directly on the N62.**

Then: **Two views of a 'friendly fire' Christmas Day tragedy. This ambulance, operating with the 5th Medical Battalion, was headed into the village of Gonderange, Luxembourg, no doubt carrying casualties from the fighting up north near Echternach. Spoiling for a kill, an American P-47 Thunderbolt pilot mistook the ambulance for German and shot it up causing it to crash into this tree and catch fire. In turn, the infantry fired back and brought down the aircraft. The pilot survived but the driver and wounded in the ambulance did not.**

Now: **The scene of the tragedy 50 years later. This is the view [1] looking directly north down the Rue du Village, which eventually joins the E29/N11 heading for Echternach. Though the original tree is long gone, newer versions have been planted along the road, and further foliage blocks the confirming aspect of this comparison. In the far right of the wartime photo, one can just make out two buildings with rather distinctive architecture. Although now hidden by the trees on the right, these identical buildings still stand further down this road.**

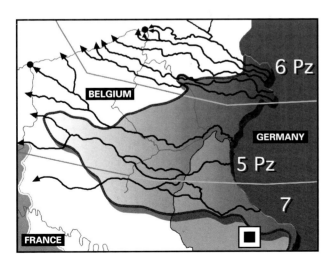

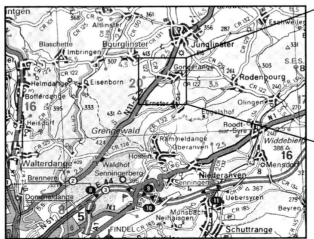

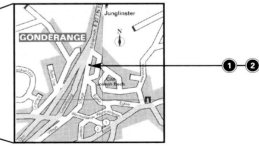

Gonderange: **Michelin 214, Col. 9. 6° 15' East 49° 42' North. Gonderange, Luxembourg lies between the city of Luxembourg to its south and Echternach to its north. From Luxembourg city, take the E29/N11 north-east, direction Echternach and Gonderange is approximately 10 km out of the city. From Echternach, take the same E29/N11 south-west, towards Luxembourg city. Gonderange is approximately 2½ km south of Junglinster.**

Then: **The US Army photographer then walked five yards further north, around the burned-out ambulance, to record the scene from the opposite direction [2]. A senseless accident midst the fog of war.**

Now: **The author performed a similar manoeuvre in picturing the site today. Now looking directly south straight back into Gonderange, the shadow cast by the tree in the previous photo falls on the road leading into the village. Ironically, a human stick figure painted on the bicycle lane as a warning to present-day motorists is in fact positioned directly on the spot where the accident occurred, an ironic double for a crime scene outline!**

Then: **By the evening of December 23, 1944, the 7th Armored Division had completed a hasty, confused withdrawal through Vielsalm as German units swept into the area. West of the town, the 9. SS-Panzer-Division moved into the village of Goronne in the face of the withdrawing 82nd Airborne Division. Yet the Americans would return and by January 16, 1945, the XVIII Airborne Corps of the US First Army would be back in control of Vielsalm. In this photo, American soldiers investigate King Tiger No. 312 while Belgian girls throw a smile their way.**

Now: **This particular King Tiger operated with schwere SS-Panzer-Abteilung 501 in support of the 9. SS-Panzer-Division and it was disabled by men of the 628th Tank Destroyer Battalion, a unit attached to the 82nd Airborne, immediately west of the village. In another of the author's favourite comparisons, the final resting place of the oft-described 'king of battle' is identified and pictured 50 years later — almost to the day. Exactly 300 metres due west of the Goronne village limit sign, on a gentle curve in the present-day N822, with the chimney of a small house No. 47 in the left distance.**

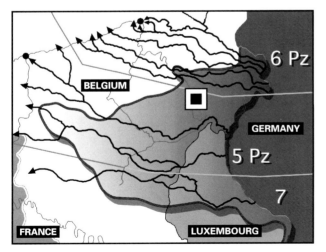

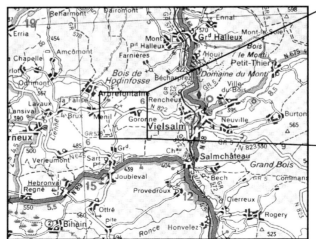

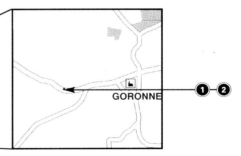

Goronne: **Michelin 214, Col. 8. 5° 52' East 50° 17' North. North or southbound on the E25 (A26), exit 50 at Baraque de Fraiture and head east on the N89, direction Vielsalm. At Salmchâteau head north on the N68 into Vielsalm from the south. In Vielsalm, turn westwards on the N822, direction Lierneux. Goronne lies 4 km west of Vielsalm on the N822.**

Then: **The locals must have had second thoughts of trying to move a 67-ton vehicle stuck in gear and out of petrol, for the summer sun finds Tiger II No. 312 still lying by the roadside outside Goronne. With the snow having long since melted and the souvenir hunters having had their pick, a magnificent specimen comes into full view. What a prize it would make today!**

Now: **The season having similarly changed, the author returns to the same location to capture the photo scene of the summer of '45. The view is looking east off the side of the N822 which enters Goronne on the right and Vielsalm further east. Though out of the picture, the stretch of road today is marked by a large oak tree just off to the right.**

Then: On December 24 the infamous 2. SS-Panzer-Division 'Das Reich' swept through the village of Manhay to the east of Grandmenil in a spectacular night tank battle. After taking Manhay on Christmas Day, it then swung west and attacked Grandmenil. Despite an effort to contain the German thrust by Task Force Kane (3rd Armored Division), the village was captured the same day. However, on the afternoon of the 26th a co-ordinated series of US artillery and air strikes, and an attack by Task Force McGeorge (3rd Armored Division) drove 'Das Reich' back towards Manhay.

Now: A distinctly more tranquil view today outside No. 31 Route d'Erezée at the intersection of Rue Alphonse Poncelet [1] where once a soldier of the 289th Regiment (75th Infantry Division) examined a Type A Panther. Though having added a second storey, the house remains identifiable and traffic once again moves freely on the N807 between Grandmenil and Manhay. Immediately out of the picture to the author's left stands today a sole surviving Panther of the 2. SS-Panzer-Division — displayed on a plinth as a fitting memorial to the fighting of 50 years ago.

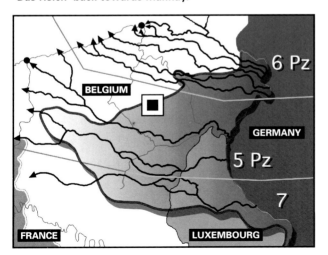

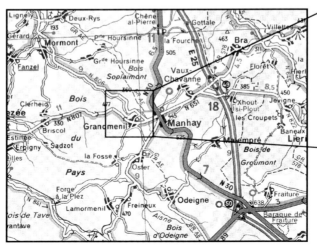

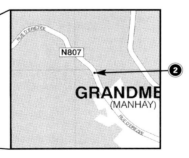

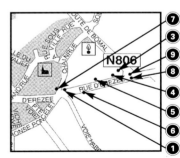

Grandmenil: Michelin 214, Col. 7. 5° 40' East 50° 17' North. North or southbound on the E25 (A26), exit 49 at Manhay. Head west on the N651 through Manhay itself and into Grandmenil from the east.

Then: After the battle in Grandmenil, Belgium, January 1945. American soldiers, having hitched a ride aboard an M4 Sherman of the 2nd Armored Division, pass another Panther which once belonged to the 2. SS-Panzer-Division 'Das Reich'. In the Manhay-Grandmenil sector, things were not always this sanguine.

Now: The former resting place [2] of another 'Das Reich' Panther exactly 900 metres west of Grandmenil along a curve in the present-day N807 (Rue d'Erezée). Once again the surrounding area has seen substantial reforestation, trees being planted and harvested for timber in the Ardennes on a regular basis. Ahead lies Erezée, 11 km to the west.

Then: January 1945 finds yet another Panther of the 2. SS-Panzer-Division lying abandoned and definitely out of action just off the road between Manhay and Grandmenil. A US Army bulldozer prowls the area, keeping things clear for the advance of American logistical support.

Now: The same intersection [3] on a sunny summer day 50 years later. This is the junction of the present-day Route de Bomal (N806) and the Route d'Erezée (N807), midway between Manhay and Grandmenil. The concrete of a modern drainage system leaves no clue as to what once came to rest here.

Then: A US Army M5 high-speed tractor, pulling a 155mm M1 howitzer, passes another knocked out Panther which belonged to the 2. SS-Panzer-Division during their brief but tenacious occupancy of the village. This particular Panther was disabled along the road running from Manhay to Grandmenil and on to Erezée [4].

Now: Looking west down the present-day N807 (Route d'Erezée) towards Grandmenil finds all of the vehicles long gone, though the house in the distance, No. 27, remains timeless. The intersection of the Route de Bomal (N806) is immediately behind the photographer. Today, Grandmenil is remarkably unchanged, save for the trees which once lined the road.

Then: A snowy January view [5] in 1945 of the same Panther as in the previous photo but this time looking east towards Manhay. American soldiers stand upon its carcass, no doubt relieved to be examining it in death and not alive on active duty! Most likely the tank was cleared from the road by bulldozers active in the area after the late December battle.

Now: The location 50 years later is incongruously marked by a small tree, as well as a small barbed-wire fence running the length of the Route d'Erezée which runs east into Manhay. The owner of No. 27 is well aware of the historic aspect of his property and, upon requesting permission to gain access to take these photographs, he immediately proceeded to point out to the author the various locations in the area where the knocked-out panzers once lay.

Then: Grandmenil was a tank graveyard for the 'Das Reich' division. No fewer than ten Panthers lay scattered all around part of a last-ditch defence from the counter-attacks by the 3rd and 7th and, later, the 2nd Armored Divisions. Under the ruthless leadership of SS-Brigadeführer Heinz Lammerding, the 2. SS-Panzer was once one of the elite panzer divisions.

Now: The same field [6] where the might and pride of 'Das Reich' ignominiously met its match. This is the view looking south-east directly across the N807 from No. 27 on the Route d'Erezée. The wooden fence posts still trace their same paths though the only heavy machinery in action today on these fields belongs to the local farmer!

Then: Yet another example of the defeated rolling stock of the 2. SS-Panzer-Division which lay about Grandmenil in January 1945. This picture shows Corporal James Gordon and Private L. C. Rainwater of the 2nd Armored Division posing rather nonchalantly on this superbly intact Panther. In the background to the right lies the village church.

Now: The identical field [7] where the Panther lay over 50 years ago. The village church in the background provides the perfect landmark to complete the comparison. The photo was taken from the junction of the small Rue Alphonse Poncelet with the Route d'Erezée, looking west just in front of No. 31 which lies behind the author.

Then: **The battle over, one leviathan confronts another, yet only one is mobile. On the left, a US M10 tank destroyer, most likely attached to the 2nd Armored Division, pushes on past a disabled Panther of the 2. SS-Panzer-Division. Having taken a hit on its right track, the Panther's subsequent reversal manoeuvre unwound the track from the drive sprocket and road wheels.**

Now: **Despite substantial change, this is the spot [8] on the road where the Panther ground to a halt. We are looking directly east into Manhay from Grandmenil, at the junction of the present-day N806 (Route de Bomal) and the N807 (Route d'Erezée). The houses on the right are Nos. 38 and 24.**

Then: **Grandmenil, December 30, 1944. In a photo which typifies both the type and ferocity of the action which took place in the village, yet another charter member of the 2. SS-Panzer-Division lies destroyed in front of an equally wrecked house. Artillery pounded both Grandmenil and Manhay in the US effort to retake both villages. The road sign directions are incorrect having been twisted, probably by the violent shelling.**

Now: **Photographed 50 years later virtually to the exact day, this is the spot where the Route de Bomal and the Route d'Erezée meet west of Manhay. The house [9] has been rebuilt pretty much along the same lines and certainly on the same foundation, the Panther long ago now consigned to the pages of history.**

Then: The low light of evening finds the US Army on the move through Habay-la-Neuve, Belgium; the push to relieve Bastogne was now underway. On December 22, 1944, the counter-attack towards the town by the 4th Armored Division was launched on a dual axis: Combat Command B, commanded by Brigadier General Holmes E. Dager, was to move from Habay towards Chaumont, with CCA on its right coming up from Arlon. On the 29th the 6th Armored passed through Habay as well. Perhaps the two nuns in the background have prayed for the tide of battle to turn . . . and for the souls of those who would be lost in it.

Now: The nun's prayers answered — the battle is over. Over 50 years ago, a US half-track drove past this spot on the present-day N40 (Rue du Luxembourg) passing the junction [1] with the N87 (Rue Emile Bandrux), adjacent to Place Pierre Nothumbi. The village church lies behind the house in the background.

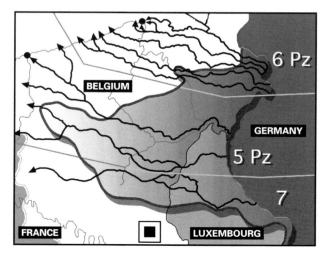

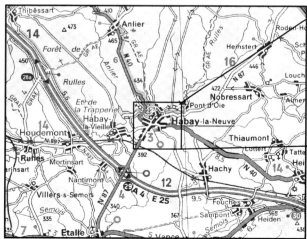

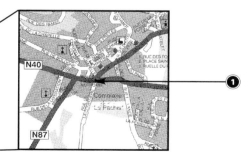

Habay-la-Neuve: Michelin 214, Col. 7. 5° 39' East 49° 43' North. North or southbound on the E411 (A4), exit 29 at Habay. Head north-north-east on the N87, direction Habay, and enter the village from the south.

Then: **Morning on December 16, 1944 — Day One of the battle for the Ardennes — and American prisoners are already streaming into Germany. Captured in the first hours of fighting in the Schnee Eifel sector, members of the 99th Infantry Division trudge past the local church on a street in Hallschlag, Germany. The village lay three kilometres east of the border and it was a small yet vital stepping stone between the staging areas near Blankenheim, further to the northeast inside Germany, and the Losheim Gap through which Kampfgruppe Peiper and other elements of the 1. SS-Panzer-Division advanced into Belgium.**

Now: **Fifty years later, this is the view [1] looking directly south, just off of the present-day Bundesstrasse 421 which becomes the N634 on the Belgian side of the border. Today, the church sports a smaller, more modern steeple and a new white façade.**

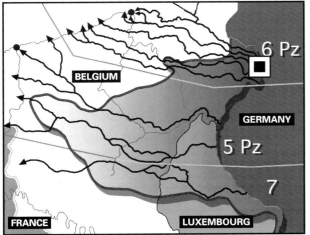

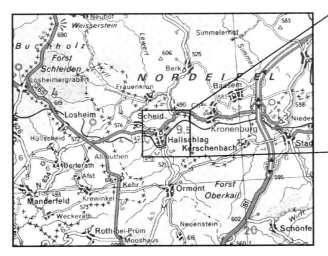

Hallschlag: **Michelin 214, Col. 2. 6° 26' East 50° 22' North. Southbound on the Belgian E42 (A27), exit 15 at St Vith. Head east on the N626, direction Schönberg/Manderfeld. At Manderfeld, take the N634 east into Germany, direction Stadtkyll. Hallschlag lies across the border along B421.**

Then: On December 19, 1944, the Panzer-Lehr-Division was drawing ever closer to Bastogne. Immediately east of Wardin, in the small hamlet of Harzy, its advance unit, which included the 8. Kompanie of Panzer-Lehr-Regiment 130, fought the just-arrived Company I of the 501st Parachute Infantry (101st Airborne Division) and in the ensuing battle they lost one Panzer IV to a bazooka. After the siege of Bastogne had been broken, elements of the 90th Infantry Division passed through the village heading east towards the Luxembourg border three kilometres away. The Panzer IV lost three weeks earlier lies off the side of the road.

Now: Fifty years later little has changed in this small Belgian village just four kilometres from Bastogne. Even an electricity pole still stands on the same spot. The view from [1] on the map is looking due west along the present-day N821, directly into Wardin. The characteristic house on the right is No. 8. Down this road, the soldiers came; first the Americans, then the Germans, then the Americans again.

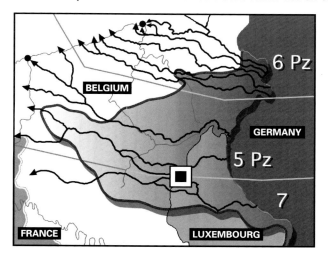

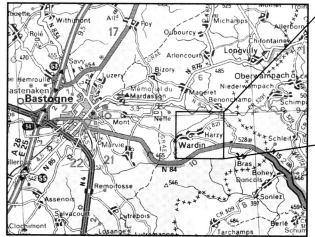

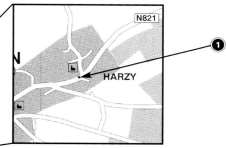

Harzy: Michelin 214, Col. 8. 5° 48' East 49° 59' North. North or southbound on the E25 (A26), exit 54 at Bastogne. Head east on the N84, direction Wiltz/Ettelbruck. Approximately 5 km east of Bastogne, take the N821 north into Wardin. Pass through the village heading east, where you will enter the hamlet of Harzy from the west, still on the N821.

Then: **By mid-day on December 23, 1944, the forward elements of the Panzer-Lehr-Division had reached the eastern outskirts of Rochefort, Belgium. After a brief defence of the town by units of the 84th Infantry Division, the town fell into German hands on Christmas Eve. In an effort to relieve the surrounded 2. Panzer-Division, on Christmas Day Kampfgruppe von Poschinger of Panzer-Lehr attacked and overran the village of Humain, four and a half kilometres north-east of Rochefort. With Humain secure, in turn Kampfgruppe von Fallois took the adjacent village of Havrenne but failed to take Buissonville to the north-west.**

Now: **The same stretch of road [1] between Havrenne and Humain, where 50 years ago the spearhead resupply efforts met their fiery fate at the hands of Allied airpower. Strong air attacks blunted von Fallois' advance and Havrenne was retaken by the 2nd Armored Division on the same day. This is the view looking west along the Rue de Humain, looking towards Havrenne in the distance, where the blasted and burned-out remains of the German effort once lay scattered along the road.**

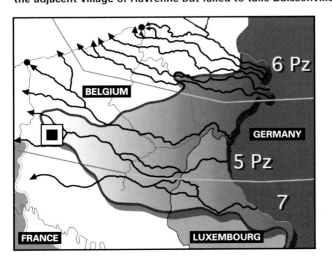

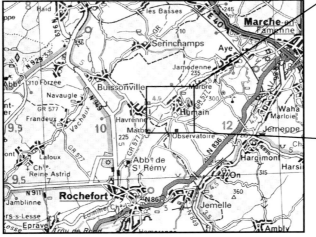

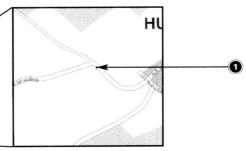

Havrenne: **Michelin 214, Col. 6. 5° 14' East 50° 12' North. North or southbound on the N4 (E40) (A4), exit at the N929 intersection, direction Haversin. Pass through Haversin heading south-west. South of Haversin, take the N949 south, direction Rochefort, and 2 km past the turn-off for Buissonville, turn left to Havrenne.**

Then: Moving east at midnight on December 22, 1944, the 2nd Battalion of the 319th Regiment of the 80th Infantry Division entered the outskirts of Heiderscheid in Luxembourg and, after heavy fighting against the 79. Volks-Grenadier-Division, who were supported by some armour from the Führer-Grenadier-Brigade, it had taken the town by noon on the 23rd. However, several furious counter-attacks ensued, provoking the 315th Field Artillery Battalion to open up on the village with its massive 155mm 'Long Tom' howitzers on the morning of the 24th. The Germans thereupon withdrew with heavy losses.

Now: Two days later, members of the 80th Infantry Division were pictured inspecting the abandoned German armour — this Panther Type A lies in a field in the northern part of the village. The precise spot [1] where it ended its days is exemplified in this perfect match. The farmhouse in the background is No. 13 An Der Grass but, to the author, the most striking aspect about this location was the fact that this plot had still not been built upon, a relative rarity as many villages expand! However, some time later the author passed this way again only to find the farm exterior transformed, marring a latter-day comparison.

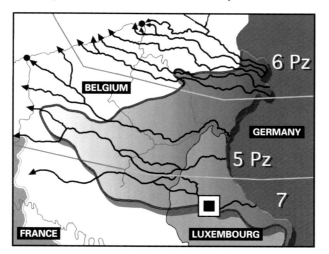

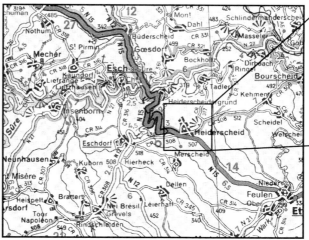

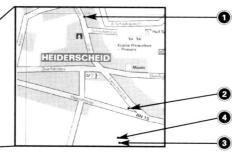

Heiderscheid: Michelin 214, Col. 8. 5° 58' East 49° 54' North. South-east from Bastogne, or north-west from Ettelbruck, take the Luxembourg N15 to CR308, exit Heiderscheid. Heiderscheid lies along the N15 itself, 5½ km south of the Sûre river crossing of Heiderscheidergrund.

Then: The spent armour of the Führer-Grenadier-Brigade lay all about the village of Heiderscheid. Several rounds of high explosive appear to have been fired into the house in the background. Curious soldiers of the 80th Infantry Division clamber over this beautiful example of a Sturmgeschütz III Ausf. G (SdKfz 142/1) assault gun. The 'trapezoidal head' of its gun mantlet identifies it as an earlier variant; this would later be replaced by the famous 'Saukopf' (pig's head).

Now: Over 50 years later, an exact comparison [2] at the intersection of a street called Eweschten Eck as it leaves the N15 (far left) to enter Heiderscheid itself. The large housing complex (No. 3, Eweschten Eck) remains virtually identical to the way it looked during the battle. The house in the distance on the far left completes the comparison. Then, a panzer made a valiant but vain attempt to hold the village against American counter-attacks; today, Heiderscheid sleeps on a rainy Sunday afternoon. Tempus fugit.

Heiderscheid

Then: The cost to the Führer-Grenadier-Brigade in the battle for Heiderscheid is inspected and tallied by US soldiers on December 26, 1944. Caught in an open field, a lone Sturmgeschütz III SdKfz 142 (left) is joined by two SdKfz 251 armoured personnel carriers (centre and right) in a scene of destruction immediately south of the village.

Now: The same field [3] in Heiderscheid today, under sunny, peacetime conditions. This is the view looking directly north, towards the village. In the distance, immediately in front of the houses, runs the N15. Despite substantial building in the village, including a new steeple, the church remains to marry up the location with that of yesterday.

Then: Having captured the general scene of destruction in the previous photo, the US Signal Corps photographer then approached one of the armoured personnel carriers to record a more gruesome scene: with German dead lying all about, a soldier peers into the open back-end of the vehicle. The arrangement of bodies suggests they were possibly shot down upon exiting or killed by a shell-burst.

Now: Retracing the footsteps of the wartime photographer, the author counts off the paces, turns slightly west, and pictures the precise patch of ground [4] where the destroyed vehicle once lay. The white house in the distance on the left is No. 8 Haaptstrooss, just along the present-day N15. Today, gazing on this sunny patch of green field, one can scarcely imagine the carnage of yesteryear.

Then: By nightfall on December 16, 1944, the 2. Panzer-Division had entered Marnach, one of the villages on the road to Clervaux. In a hasty response, Major General Norman D. Cota commanding the 28th Infantry Division sent elements of the 707th Tank Battalion forward to reinforce the 110th Regiment in the sector. The following morning, December 17, the Americans counter-attacked. A light tank company of 707th Tank Battalion, moving south from the village of Heinerscheid towards Marnach, was instantly engaged by forward elements of the 116. Panzer-Division and the American attack was smashed in a matter of minutes.

Now: Today the Luxembourg village of Heinerscheid basks in the quiet stillness of a Sunday morning. This is the view over 50 years later along the present-day E421 (N7), which runs north-south through Luxembourg, at the intersection [1] of an unnamed street near the village church. The house on the left in the distance is No. 28. Having suffered little damage during the battle, it retained its structural identity and serves to align the comparison. Its neighbour to the right (today No. 21) did not fare so well and has since been completely rebuilt. Now, only buses stop where tanks once clashed.

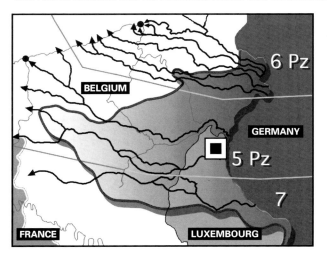

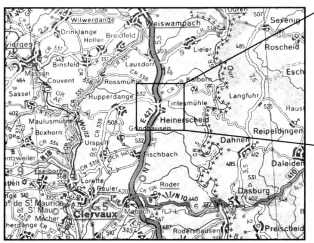

Heinerscheid: Michelin 214, Col. 9. 6° 5' East 50° 5' North. North or southbound on the E42 (A27), exit 15 just south of St Vith. Head due south along the E421 (N62). At the border of Luxembourg, the N62 becomes the N7 (though still the E421). Approximately 7-8 km south of the border with Belgium lies Heinerscheid, directly on the E421 itself.

Then: The tide of war having turned since the initial attack of the 5. Panzer-Armee, scarcely a month later the Americans were back. On January 23, 1945, the 90th Infantry Division once again crossed the Clerve river heading east. Two days later, Heinerscheid was once again in American hands and shattered remnants of the fighting lay about the village. Here the US Army Signal Corps photographer records two destroyed German SdKfz 251 armoured personnel carriers on a local farm. The vehicle on the left is a SdKfz 251/9, as indicated by the presence of a 75mm KwK 37 gun; that on the right, a more standard version of the same vehicle. Both belonged to the 1. SS-Panzer-Division.

Now: The precise location [2] of the wartime scene of destruction is captured over 50 years later along the CR339. This small road exits the E421 (the 'Skyline Drive') 400 metres north of Heinerscheid, and heads east towards the village of Kalborn. The house in the distance on the right remains though its façade now sports a layer of exterior insulation. The bend in the road as it heads into the distance serves to further line up the comparison.

Then: **On Christmas Day, Kampfgruppe Maucke (15. Panzer-Grenadier-Division) attacked Bastogne from the west just south of the village of Champs. A column of 18 panzers, loaded with infantry, broke through the lines of the 327th Glider Infantry and reached the road running between Champs and Hemroulle, where they were engaged by hastily assembled paratroopers of HQ and 1st Battalion of the 502nd Parachute Infantry. The panzergrenadiers were swept off the tanks by a hail of gun-fire, and 17 of the tanks knocked out by tank destroyers, tanks, and bazookas of the glidermen and paratroopers. One tank was captured intact.**

Now: **A classic 'weather match' comparison 50 years later, almost to the very day, where the battle once raged along this stretch of road between Hemroulle and Champs. The identical electrical poles and trees mark a timeless reflection of history; only the removal of trees on the right indicate the passage of time. This is now the N854, just over a kilometre west of Hemroulle. Returning to the same spot some time later, the author was disappointed to discover that the electricity posts had been removed. Let this comparison mark the site in history, as progress marches on.**

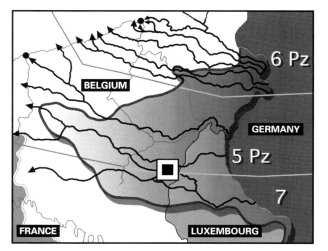

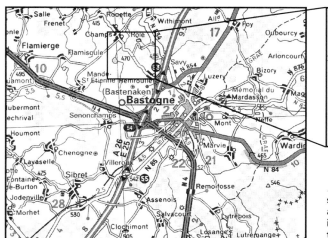

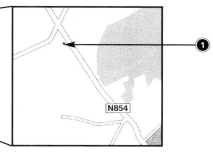

Hemroulle: **Michelin 214, Col. 8. 5° 41' East 50° 1' North. North or southbound on the E25 (A26), exit 53 at Bastogne. Head immediately west, direction Hemroulle/Champs. The village of Hemroulle is literally at the base of the exit, west of the E25 itself. The N854 terminates into a small road in the village.**

Then: In support of the I. SS-Panzerkorps, a special elite force was formed under SS-Obersturmbannführer Otto Skorzeny to aid in front-line deception in an operation code-named 'Greif'. Panzerbrigade 150 went into battle wearing American uniforms, using American-styled vehicles, and speaking various levels of American English. Eventually caught out, many of its personnel were executed as spies, among them three members captured on December 17 at Aywaille, Belgium: Gefreiter Wilhelm Schmidt, Oberfähnrich Günter Billing and Unteroffizier Manfred Pernass.

Now: At dawn on December 23, they were executed by a US firing squad at Henri-Chapelle. This is the site of their execution [1] over 50 years later. Despite substantial development, the impact marks of the firing squad's rifle rounds in the wall are still visible. The site itself is located at the intersection of the Chausée de Liège (N3) and a small dirt road known as Chemin du Moulin á Vent. The execution wall lies behind a sports centre, across from the Maison de la Repos Beloeil on the N3. Since taking these comparisons, the site has become a dumping ground and much of the wall has been covered up.

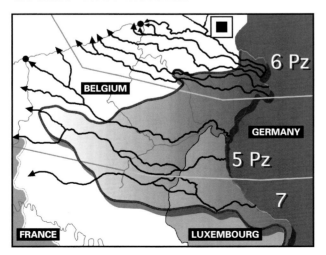

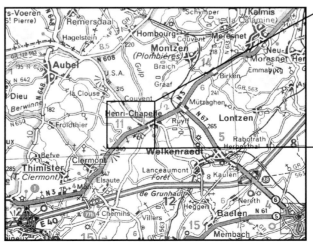

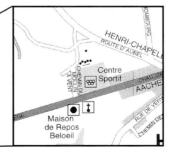

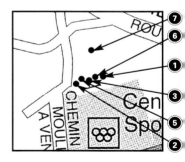

Henri-Chapelle: Michelin 213, Col. 8. 5° 56' East 50° 41' North. Eastbound from Liège on the E40 (A3), exit the major interchange with the E42 (A27) north towards Battice (N3). Head east on the N3 (Chausée de Liège) direction Thimister/Clermont, for approximately 10 km. The site of the execution lies just before Henri-Chapelle village limits on the N3, on the Chemin du Moulin á Vent.

Then: **Still dressed in their American uniforms (which justified their execution under the provisions of the Geneva Convention) and each guarded by their own MP, the three Germans await their fate. From L-R: Gefreiter Wilhelm Schmidt, Oberfähnrich Günter Billing and Unteroffizier Manfred Pernass. Colonel P. Schroder, a chaplain in the US First Army, gave a final blessing to each soldier though Billing in the centre refused the offer. Blindfolds were then tied on each man after which white 'heart' targets were pinned on each man's chest (see picture opposite).**

Now: **The same angle of the wartime photo on the present-day location [2] reveals how much the site has changed. A chain-link fence now surrounds the entire site and a cinder block wall on the left hides roughly half of the 'stop butt' from a frontal view. Vehicles of all types now sit upon the roof of the structure which is in fact a large concrete shed. Despite the obstacles surrounding the execution wall, it is still possible to stand directly in front of it, inside the fence. The author first did this the hard way; permission was granted to walk through the truck service centre to the back area where the wall stands but here the author encountered the classic scrapyard guard dog. A subsequent visit revealed much easier and less dangerous access via the small side road to the right.**

Then: Oberfähnrich Günter Billing, a true fanatical Nazi NCO to the end, is tied to the execution post. Unlike his two comrades, he remained defiant throughout the entire ceremony. At the precise moment of execution, he shouted out a tribute to Hitler. The shout was in vain, as the sharp crack of 12 rifles rang out and echoed down the valley.

Now: The impact marks of the bullets are easily discernable today [3]. A macabre yet rather interesting observation is the relation of the height of the marks to that of each executed German. Billing, in the centre was short and small compared to his much taller comrades, hence the marks are much lower than those on either side.

Then: Pernass glances nervously about as he waits to be tied to the post. Eyewitnesses to the execution reported that, unlike Billing to his right, Pernass seemed to be more anxious and agitated throughout the ceremony, understandable behaviour given what was soon to be his fate!

Now: Subsequent executions account for the additional pock marks [4]. The firing squad shot from a location on a sloping hill which led away from the wall, hence, the rounds would have passed through the men's chests at a slightly upward angle.

Then: With Unteroffizier Manfred Pernass now lashed to the post and blindfolded, Captain J. Eiser, a medical officer of the 633rd Medical Clearing Station, pins the four-inch white aiming mark over the German's heart. Pernass's 'personal valet', in the form of a US military MP on the right, watches over the tension-filled proceedings.

Now: The precise angle of the sombre ceremony over 50 years later along the wall of death [5]. The author was struck by the fact that the chain-link fence of the present-day site seemed to form an emotional barrier to the place of execution.

Then: Seconds later, Gefreiter Wilhelm Schmidt pays the ultimate price. The impact marks behind him complete the tragic scene. The firing squad's aim was true as indicated by the spreading blood stain on his back; death was instantaneous.

Now: The site of Schmidt's death is that most overrun by debris and rubble [6]; the smaller wall vent at the bottom of this photo would in fact be at Schmidt's waist today, as indicated in the wartime execution photo. Two impact marks from bullet strikes are clearly visible.

Then: The precise moment of execution on a cold, misty dawn on December 23, 1944, is captured forever in this historic Signal Corps photo. Often reproduced, it shows six of the twelve US soldiers having just fired up the slight hill towards the condemned. Puffs of impact dust from the wall behind each prisoner signal the task complete.

Now: A glimpse back in history from where the firing squad carried out its grim task [7]. This comparison reveals the state of the execution wall 50 years later, but now even this view is no longer possible as the block wall continues to be obscured by further debris.

Then: The execution ceremony complete, American soldiers approach the lifeless bodies to cut them down. No need to check for signs of life; four rounds per man was more than enough to do the job. The dead Germans were buried in a temporary field cemetery in Henri-Chapelle, only to be transferred later to the German War Cemetery at Lommel, Belgium. Today they lie side by side as they died: L-R: Schmidt, Billing, and Pernass.

Now: A final look at the execution site, slowly being overrun by the march of progress and the assault of time [8]. Since taking these comparisons, the site has become a dumping ground and much of the wall has been buried under piles of rubble and rubbish.

Then: On a small snowy farm in Hénumont, Belgium, paratroopers of the 517th Parachute Infantry Regiment lead captured German soldiers out of a bombed-out farmhouse on January 14, 1945. These Germans were most likely attached to the 62. Volks-Grenadier-Division which fought in Hénumont before retreating from the area. This wartime photo reveals an ironic sight. Having just witnessed the penalty dispensed at Henri-Chapelle towards captured enemy soldiers, this photo shows German prisoners of war carrying ammunition crates for the Americans in contravention of the provisions of the Geneva Convention.

Now: The same snowy farmhouse scene some four kilometres south of Stavelot. Despite additional rebuilding, the stylish arched door remains unchanged as does the building on the right which can be matched by the presence of several prominent stones in its walls. The farmhouse lies on an unnamed road running north-south through the village just past an intersection with a small road leading to Belle-Femme.

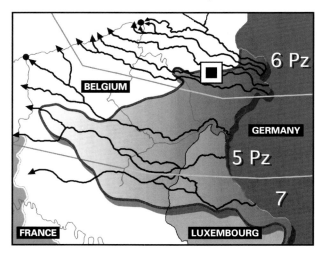

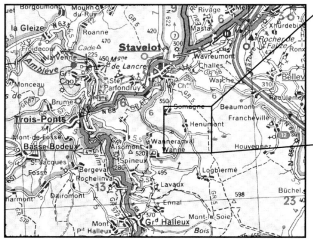

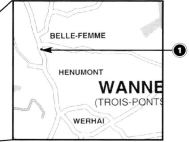

Hénumont: Michelin 214, Col. 8. 5° 57' East 50° 22' North. North or southbound on the E42 (A27), exit 11, direction Stavelot. Enter Stavelot off the N68, direction town centre. Pass through Stavelot heading south, across the bridge over the Amblève on the Rue G. Dewalque. Immediately head east along the Chemin du Château for approximately 1 km; turn south onto the Route de Somagne. Pass through Somagne. Hénumont is the next village.

Then: After passing through Merlscheid, Lanzerath and Buchholz on December 16, 1944, Kampfgruppe Peiper seized the Belgian village of Honsfeld the following morning. Having surprised American troops of the 99th Infantry Division and remnants of the 14th Cavalry Group, a brief yet bloody clash ensued as American forces scrambled to exit the village to the west. After the battle, these members of Kampfgruppe Peiper were pictured entering the village aboard a camouflage-bedecked SdKfz 251 Ausf. D armoured personnel carrier. Abandoned American vehicles lay all about the village.

Now: This is the view 50 years later looking east into the centre of Honsfeld [1] along the unnamed street which enters from Büllingen in the north. The comparison was taken standing next to No. 78 on the author's right; the large house on the left in the distance being No. 51, while that on the right is No. 60. Despite several houses being completely rebuilt, that on the left retains it characteristic shape. Without the original photograph in hand, it would be difficult to imagine the cacaphony of war when today all is stillness and silence.

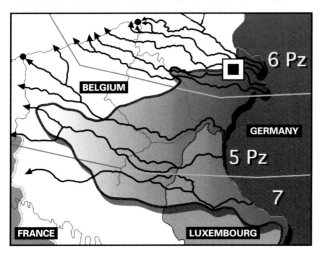

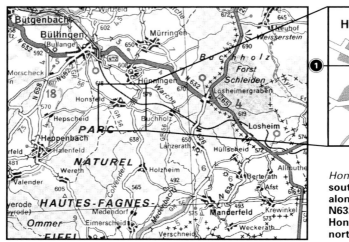

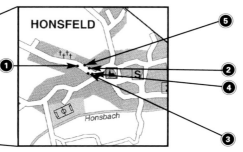

Honsfeld: Michelin 214, Col. 8. 6° 17' East 50° 23' North. North or southbound on the E42 (A27), exit 11, direction Malmédy. Head east along the N62 through Malmédy, Waimes (N62 then becomes N632), Bütgenbach and into Büllingen. In Büllingen, turn south onto Honsfelderstrasse, direction Honsfeld, entering the village from the north-west.

Then: **With American resistance crushed, men of the 3. Fallschirm-Jäger-Division, moving in advance of Kampfgruppe Peiper, examine the spoils of war in Honsfeld where a local farmyard yields all manner of hastily abandoned American matériel. Next to the Jeep a 76mm anti-tank gun still lies covered against the elements.**

Now: **With time having swept both vehicles and men into the pages of history, the same farmyard [2] is revealed in this comparison, complete with tree and sloping roofline. The farmhouse stands on the northern side of the road when entering Honsfeld from the direction of Büllingen.**

Then: **Having cleared the way for Kampfgruppe Peiper to enter Honsfeld, triumphant members of the 3. Fallschirm-Jäger-Division help themselves to items taken from the American dead lying in the streets and farmyards. US combat gear was highly prized and often favoured over German issue, particularly footwear and rations.**

Now: **The identical spot [3] today finds the water trough refurbished yet still intact. We are looking east, the photo being taken next to No. 77. The white house on the right across the street is No. 61. The signposts have been modernised, the small one on the right still indicating the direction of Büllingen, albeit under decidedly more peaceful conditions!**

Then: **With Honsfeld captured, a German Kriegsberichter walks about the village, graphically recording the price the Americans paid trying to defend it on that cold winter's day of December 17, 1944. Face down in the snow and mud, American dead lie about the crossroads in the centre of the village. As if pointing the way to fate, the signpost indicates the next village to the north: Büllingen.**

Now: **The precise spot [4] where the two dead American soldiers once lay. After taking this comparison with the trough and sign providing the alignment, it was only later that the author realised one macabre and chilling aspect that had previously gone unnoticed. The drainpipe running along the curb in the centre-right of the photo, when combined with the tuft of grass to its left in the centre, combine to form a visual 'head-shoulders-back' combination virtually identical to that of the posture of the dead soldier in the wartime picture. A truly chilling comparison.**

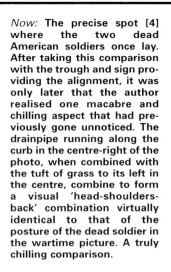

Then: After the war ended, several war crime trials took place in Dachau, Germany. This post-war photo shows Captain Raphael Schumacker, Lieutenant Colonel Burton Ellis and Corporal W. Wolfe investigating the location of a reported atrocity in a farmyard at Honsfeld on December 17, 1944. Though other massacres at Baugnez and Ligneuville were thoroughly documented, that purported to have taken place at Honsfeld remained unproven.

Now: Fifty years later, the scene of the alleged crime [5] is inspected by the author. The features of the house on the right confirm the location and help orient the comparison. This is in fact the rear view of the same farmhouse pictured on the opposite page with the abandoned vehicles in the farmyard. Today, a driveway enters the site where bodies once lay but the truth of what really happened here is now lost in the mists of time.

Then: On the morning of December 16, 1944, two regiments of the 5. Fallschirm-Jäger-Division, aided in the south by the 352. Volks-Grenadier-Division, crossed the Our river and fanned out in a series of sustained attacks. Fallschirm-Jäger-Regiment 14 moved on Stolzembourg, Putscheid and Hoscheid within Luxembourg itself while Fallschirm-Jäger-Regiment 15 attacked Vianden on the German-Luxembourg border. By late afternoon of December 17, the German paratroopers had ejected the defenders (an anti-tank company of the 28th Division plus a few Shermans) from the village.

Now: Following on the dramatic and successful crossings of the Sûre river on January 18, 1945 by the US 5th Division's 2nd and 10th Infantry Regiments, the 2nd Battalion, 11th Infantry, was ordered to recapture Hoscheid. At 7 a.m. on January 24 the attack commenced and by late afternoon Hoscheid was back in American hands. This Panther was knocked out on the Welbes-Marnach farm [1] right in the centre of Hoscheid where the passing of 50 years finds little that has changed. Today the village has a fair degree of modern homes along Haaptstrooss so the author was surprised to see the farm still nestling amongst them at No. 45.

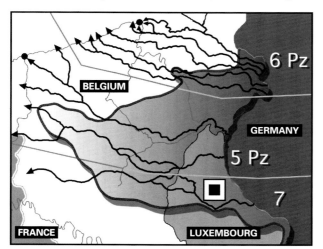

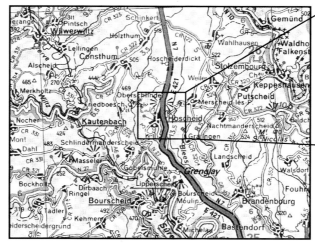

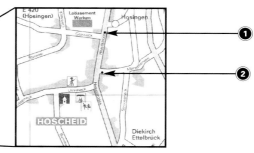

Hoscheid: **Michelin 214, Col. 9. 6° 5' East 49° 57' North. From Diekirch or Ettelbruck in Luxembourg, take the E421 (N7) north approximately 13 km to Hoscheid, which lies just off of the E421.**

Then: **With Hoscheid recaptured, American soldiers (most likely from the 11th Infantry Regiment, 5th Division) examine the spoils of war. In this particular case they are looking over a rare beast indeed — a Möbelwagen SdKfz 161/3. Consisting of a 37mm anti-aircraft 'flak' cannon mounted on the chassis of a Panzer IV tank, its single gun was no match for the Allied airpower then roaming the Ardennes skies. Note the US vehicle backed up against the house on the far right.**

Now: **After a great deal of searching, the author found the location in spite of the fact that the original caption described the place as Hosingen, some 12 kilometres further north along the E421. However, the picture was taken at the corner intersection of Haaptstrooss and Merschterwee [2] in the centre of Hoscheid, next to the Hotel des Ardennes. Though the building façade has been completely refurbished, the loft door on the left, along with the smaller window below it, act as confirmation.**

Then: **The main thrust of LVIII. Panzerkorps towards Dochamps, Beffe and Soy was led by the 116. Panzer-Division. Leading elements of Kampfgruppe Bayer maintained the offensive tempo and, in an aggressive tactical move, split between Task Forces Hogan and Orr of the 3rd Armored Division on the morning of December 21, 1944, and were soon on the outskirts of Hotton. However, the 3rd Armored occupied the area in force, and three attempts to enter the town were repulsed. Kampfgruppe Bayer, reflecting the spirited nature of the German attacks, threw several Panther and Panzer IV spearheads into the town.**

Now: **By December 23, the 116. Panzer-Division had officially disengaged from Hotton and pulled back east, the shattered remains of their efforts littering the outskirts. This is the exact spot [1] where a Panther of Kampfgruppe Bayer met its end. Today, little has changed save for silence. This is the Rue Haute in Hotton which runs beside the Ourthe river. Left to right the houses are Nos. 25 and 27.**

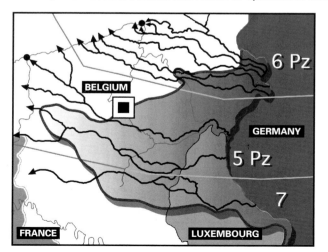

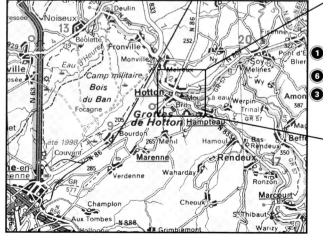

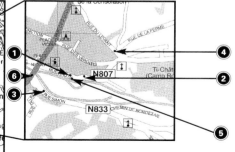

Hotton: **Michelin 214, Col. 7. 5° 27' East 50° 16' North. North or southbound on the N4 (E40), exit at Marche-en-Famenne. Head out of Marche on the N86, direction Hotton, which lies 8 km to the north-east, along the Ourthe river.**

Then: **Having seen off the attacks of the 116. Panzer-Division, this M10 tank destroyer of the 628th Tank Destroyer Battalion lurks behind a bombed-out house [2] on the eastern edge of Hotton on December 30, 1944. Kampfgruppe Bayer attempted to enter the town down the road in the distance, the smashed armour a grim testimony of its ultimate failure.**

Now: **The same location today reveals some rebuilding though the bend in the road, the stone wall on the right, and the mountain in the distance all serve to match up the comparison. This is the view looking eastwards down the Rue Haute. The road has now been widened to accommodate traffic of a decidedly more docile kind!**

Then: **By early January 1945, British XXX Corps had taken over this part of the Bulge front from the American First Army. These five Sherman 'Fireflies', possessing the potent 17-pdr gun, were pictured on January 4 lining the western bank of the Ourthe river in Hotton. They belong to B Squadron of the East Riding Yeomanry of the 33rd Armoured-Brigade.**

Now: **Over 50 years later the same stretch of road [3] along the river finds several of the original buildings remaining like the one on the right with its tell-tale stonework. This is Rue Simon (N833), looking east from the bridge which lies behind the author. The white house in the distance with the spire is No. 27.**

Then: A superb post-battle photograph which epitomises the action in and around the Belgian town of Hotton. As soldiers of the 3rd Armored Division mill about, two massive hulks representing the best efforts of Kampfgruppe Bayer belonging to 116. Panzer-Division lie defeated in front of a house on the eastern edge of the town. The tank on the left is an older Panzer IV while that in the foreground is a Panther Type G with the late-model 'stepped gun mantlet'. This 'chin' was added to prevent head-on shots against the earlier hemispherical curved versions from trapping and deflecting shots downward into the hull. These specimens met their fate in one of three German attempts to enter the town along the Ourthe river.

Now: The road now cleared for peaceful traffic, the precise location [4] of this famous photograph is pictured 50 years later. Taken on the outskirts of Hotton, this is the view looking north down Rue du Levant (the street meets the N807 behind the author). The house on the left, little changed since its adversaries came calling long ago, is No. 44. Note that the damage to the first floor above the middle window has been repaired in a manner which clearly still outlines the former destruction.

Then: With Hotton secure, the American logistical juggernaut rolls on eastwards — or does it? This 155mm M1 'Long Tom' is actually moving away from the front, which lies behind the photographer to the east.

Now: The present day view down the Rue Haute [5] in the heart of Hotton facing west along the river bank. The prominent house on the right is No. 15. Its window arrangement has changed, yet overall the scene remains much the same as it was when the last word in artillery rumbled down the street.

Then: Soldiers of the 333rd Infantry Regiment, 84th Division, enforce a checkpoint at the bridge across the Ourthe river in the centre of Hotton. Hotly contested, it was never crossed by the Germans whose forces remained on the eastern bank.

Now: Looking across the bridge [6] over the Ourthe river in Hotton today. This is the view north from the Rue Emile Parfonry which runs behind the author. Just across the bridge on the right is Rue Haute. At its junction at the foot of the bridge stands one of the 26 stone markers erected after the war to delineate the limits of the German advance, each proclaiming that the 'invaders were stopped here'.

Then: At Houffalize, a once-mighty Panther lies belly-up in the Ourthe river in the centre of the town. This specimen belonged to the 116. Panzer-Division, LVIII. Panzerkorps, 5. Panzer-Armee, which occupied the town on December 19, 1944 without a struggle. On January 3 the Allies began a major counter-attack with the VII Corps and the XVIII Airborne Corps of the US First Army striking from the north into the 6. Panzer-Armee. With the growing pressure of the US First and Third Armies converging on the German bulge from the north and south, an order was given on January 15 to pull German forces back to the east.

Now: The same day the First and Third Armies met together in Houffalize in an historic, strategic link-up. This comparison, taken 50 years later almost to the very day, shows the second of two major crossings of the Ourthe in the town, this bridge [1] being on the Rue Porte à l'Eau, where it intersects the Avenue de la Gare (behind the author).

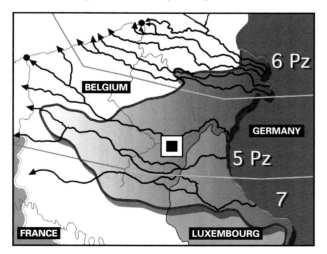

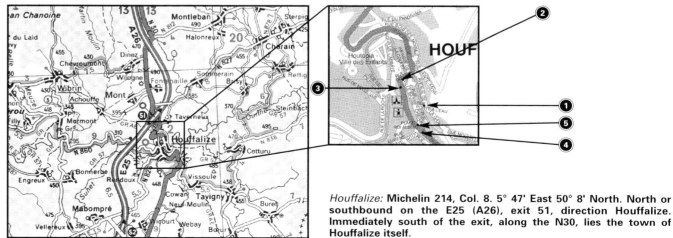

Houffalize: Michelin 214, Col. 8. 5° 47' East 50° 8' North. North or southbound on the E25 (A26), exit 51, direction Houffalize. Immediately south of the exit, along the N30, lies the town of Houffalize itself.

Then: The retreat of the 116. Panzer-Division from Houffalize on January 14 left many armoured vehicles littering the streets. Most likely taken on January 20, this USAAF photograph illustrates the final resting place of a rather rare specimen — a Panzer III. Given the battlefield attrition of earlier tank versions, and the resupply effort with more modern vehicles, it is somewhat surprising to see such an old tank still being employed in 1945.

In spite of the restored buildings, the tank's resting place [2] can be pinpointed with complete accuracy — on top of the planter in the middle of this photo which stands outside the La Vieille Auberge restaurant! The building on the left is No. 1 Ville Basse; behind the author's position runs the Rue du Pont heading to the northernmost bridge in Houffalize.

Then: In advance of the approaching American armies, Houffalize suffered terribly from repeated shelling and many of the inhabitants still have bitter memories of the damage inflicted on it by the Americans. This picture was taken on the Rue de Bastogne [3] looking south in mid-January 1945.

Now: This is the same view 50 years later. Despite the shelling, one can still match up the characteristic windowed porticos and rooflines of at least three houses in the distance. Today, the little girl would be dashing into a bank, perhaps depositing her hard-won gains.

Then: **A battered German SdKfz 250 armoured personnel carrier looking much the worse for wear lies abandoned in the centre of Houffalize in mid-January 1945. This particular specimen was almost certainly once part of the 116. Panzer-Division.**

Now: **The author pinpointed the same building [4] on the Rue de Bastogne though its facade has changed in a post-war reconstruction. This is No. 2 — fortunately without any cars parked outside to mar the view on a cold Sunday morning.**

Then: **With Houffalize back in American hands, the inhabitants re-emerge to mingle with their liberators. It was standard practice on vital road links, particularly in the face of retreating German forces, to check for the presence of mines. Here, a US soldier methodically completes his task next to the destroyed armoured personnel carrier which has now been unceremoniously pushed into a bomb crater,.**

Now: **The same location [5] today looking south up Rue de Bastogne where it joins Rue Cheravoie on the left. With buildings rebuilt and streets repaved, little remains to link this particular location with the past, save for the steepness of the street and the heights in the background. The house on the corner to the left is No. 1 Rue de Bastogne.**

Then: Attacking at first light on Christmas morning, leading elements of Kampfgruppe von Poschinger of the Panzer-Lehr-Division had captured Humain in Belgium by 9 a.m. On December 26, the 9. Panzer-Division took over this sector from Panzer-Lehr. The American attack to reconquer Humain began the following day with a devastating artillery barrage and, after a ten-hour battle, the 2nd Armored Division finally retook the town on December 27.

Now: It was here that American tankers clambered over a superb example of a Type A Panther, still heavily camouflaged, which had been abandoned outside a school in the centre of Humain. On a sleepy Sunday 50 years later, the school [1] was closed and the village at peace. This is the view looking directly north along the Rue d'Aye. Despite the addition of new windows, the building retains its original roofline.

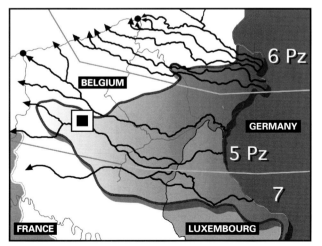

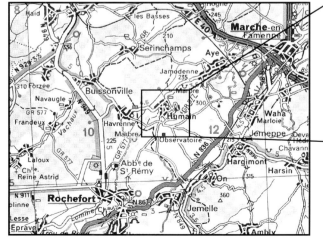

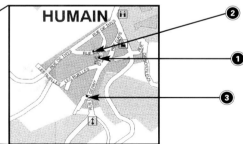

Humain: Michelin 214, Col. 6. 5° 15' East 50° 12' North. North or southbound on the E40 (N4), exit at Marche-en-Famenne and head south-west on the N836, direction Rochefort. After approximately 6-7 km, exit at On/Humain and head west towards the village of Humain.

Then: Their village having been retaken by the Americans, the inhabitants of Humain were all set to ring in the New Year though this is probably not what they had in mind! With the Panther in the previous photo having been rolled down the hill, the bell from the village church was rehung to celebrate the freedom won by the 2nd Armored.

Now: The makeshift bell-tower stood here! Alongside the new village church [2] on the corner of Rue d'Aye, the farmhouse with the same pointed roof still stands to align the comparison.

Then: The defences at Humain on Christmas Day 1944 included this 76mm anti-tank gun set up on the southern edge of the village. In the face of the overwhelming armoured might of Kampfgruppe von Poschinger, the crew abandoned their piece when the position became untenable but the tell-tale sign of shattered armour plating around its breech-block suggests that the crew possibly managed to 'spike' it before retreating.

Now: Having been rebuilt on the same site, the small house in the background, provides a perfect point of reference to the former gun position [3]. This is the view directly north from the intersection of the Rue du Gerny and the Rue de la Sapinière.

Then: **Positioned immediately east of St Vith, the Führer-Begleit-Brigade, operating in the northern sector with 18. Volks-Grenadier-Division, attacked at dawn on December 20, and succeeded in taking the villages of Nieder-Emmels and Ober-Emmels, both scarcely a kilometre north of Hünningen (Hunnange). The 7th Armored Division was forced back west of St Vith, and within two days, the area had been evacuated by the Americans. On January 23, 1945, the 7th Armored retook the area, this picture being taken by Pfc John P. Salis.**

Now: **The same location [1] is photographed by the author over 50 years later. Taken at the intersection of the present-day N670 and N62, this is the view looking south. Having long since been rebuilt, the large house is now the Café le Rustique at No. 44 Malmedyer Strasse.**

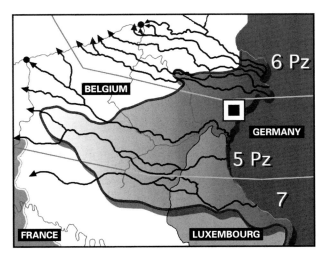

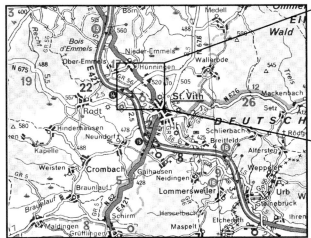

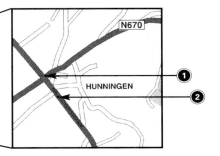

Hünningen (Hunnange): **Michelin 214, Col. 9. 6° 6' East 50° 18' North. North or southbound on the E421 (A27), exit 14 and head east on the N670. Hünningen lies directly on the intersection of the N670 and the N62 (Malmedyer Strasse).**

Then: **A scant 500 metres directly south along the N62 from where the previous photo was taken, the same day another Signal Corps photographer, Tech/5 Hugh F. McHugh, pictured other members of the 7th Armored examining a grim feature of the aftermath of war: a horse killed in the battle for the village.**

Now: **A sunny day in Hunnange along the N62 [2] heading north finds no trace of horse, cart or trees. Widened to two lanes, Malmedyer Strasse, as it is known locally, is now a vital, busy axis in and out of a well-developed St Vith. The house on the far right, matched 50 years later, is No. 27.**

Then: Taken two days into the Ardennes offensive on December 18, the famous cine sequence of pictures at the 'Kaiserbaracke crossroads' chronicles the activity of the 1. SS-Panzer-Division as it moved along Rollbahn E. It is instructive in that it unwittingly captures vehicles of several Kampfgruppen of the division, typifying the fluid nature of the rollbahns as the German spearheads sought out passable roads west. The German officer on the left, an SS-Unterscharführer (most probably Ochsner), was attached to the 1. SS-Panzer-Division's reconnaissance unit, SS-Panzer-Aufklärungs-Abteilung.1.

Now: The precise spot [1] where the Schwimmwagen halted over 50 years ago for what was probably a posed 'publicity' shot to depict the advance to the west. The wooded area around Kaiserbaracke has now been almost completely cleared, as indicated by the presence of the pipe works in the background. This small road now leads into the factory site and comes to an end in front of the woods to the left of the author. The road signs are long gone having been replaced with huge modern versions 500 metres to the right at the intersection of the present-day N659 and the N62.

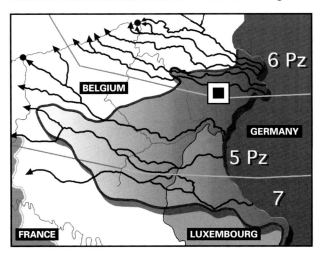

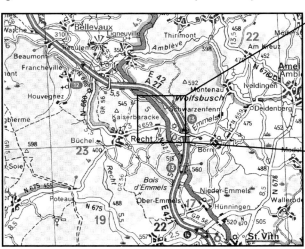

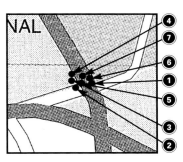

Kaiserbaracke: Michelin 214, Col. 9. 6° 5' East 50° 20' North. Travelling south on the E42 (A27), exit 13, direction Recht, along the N659. 1½ km west the N659 (Zur Kaiserbaracke) intersects the N62 running north-south. Approximately 50 meters directly north of this intersection lie the two original roads which once formed the focus of the famous cine sequence.

Then: **Elements of both Kampfgruppe Hansen and Kampfgruppe Knittel were featured in the Kaiserbaracke cine sequence. Here a German Steyr 1500A/02 of Kampfgruppe Hansen turns towards the village of Recht to the west.**

Now: **The original 'road to Recht' now leads nowhere, serving only as the entrance to a timber yard [2]. A new intersection 500 metres to the south provides the new route to Recht, a dual-lane concrete version. Once again, this photo vividly captures the development around Kaiserbaracke in the background.**

Then: **One of the most famous photographs depicting German offensive movement in the battle of the Ardennes is this King Tiger rumbling forward, laden with troops. This is in fact Königstiger No. 222 of schwere SS-Panzer-Abteilung 501, attached to the 'tail end' of Kampfgruppe Peiper. Having lost contact with the main body, Tiger 222 moved onto Rollbahn E along with Kampfgruppe Knittel.**

Now: **Incredible as it may seem, this is the exact photo comparison [3] on the road to Ligneuville. With the oak tree now felled, the author takes cover in the same ditch and captures the same angle alongside Rollbahn E — the present-day N62. The old road to Recht turns off to the right. With trees gone and industrial development spreading, it is hard to imagine the historic events which once took place here.**

Then: Crouching in a ditch along the road to Ligneuville to the north, an SS-Kriegsberichter captures a German SdKfz 250 half-track belonging to Kampfgruppe Knittel parked along the side of the road. SS-Oberscharführer Persin and SS-Unterscharführer Ochsner, both of the SS-Panzer-Aufklärungs-Abteilung 1, stroll on by after a hasty field conference.

Now: Crouching in the same ditch [4] over 50 years later, the author recreates the scene beside the present-day N62. This photograph exemplifies the extent of the deforestation around the intersection, the woods on the left being the only ones remaining. The half-track halted on this exact spot in the westward drive of the 1. SS-Panzer-Division.

Then: King Tiger 222 now approaches front and centre of the camera for a brief moment as it rumbles past the photographer on its way to Ligneuville. The paratroopers of Fallschirm-Jäger-Regiment 9 were no doubt quite happy to hitch a lift. SS-Oberscharführer Persin on the left keeps a watchful eye for other vehicles.

Now: The small road [5] that Persin once stood in front of in the wartime photo now descends to the left of the comparison, towards the new industrial site. Fifty years ago, vehicles of a different sort proceeded along the N62. What a sight it must have been, watching the king of battle thunder past this spot.

Then: Another version of the staged photograph only this time SS-Unterscharführer Ochsner grins and scowls as he checks a map aboard a German Schwimmwagen.

Now: Taken a few degrees south [6] of the previous photo location, the author turns and rephotographs the scene for posterity. In doing so, he captures his own German vehicle in the background, parked alongside a company storage area! Again, the woods have vanished to make way for industry.

Then: A better view of the small road across from the road to Recht. An SdKfz 251 stands in front of the road, as SS-Oberscharführer Persin and SS-Unterscharführer Ochsner walk past. Ochsner puffs on a cigar, a clue which, together with his dress, identifies him as the same man as the one pictured in the Schwimmwagen.

Now: Looking across the present-day Route Nationale [7] towards the same, small un-named road. From trees to industry . . . Kaiserbaracke then and now.

Then: By December 21, 1944, the tiny Luxembourg village of Kaundorf, five kilometres west of Esch-sur-Sûre had been engulfed by the LXXXV. Armeekorps of 7. Armee. The US III Corps began its counter-attack, and on Christmas Eve the 328th Regiment of the 26th Infantry Division was battling just south of Kaundorf at Bonnal. By December 26, the 104th Regiment had crossed the Sûre at Bonnal and Kaundorf was recaptured by the 101st Regiment two days later. This Signal Corps photo shows Captain Charles Kimbrell of the 6th Cavalry Group guarding German prisoners lined up along a farmhouse wall in the village after the battle.

Now: Fifty years later, Kaundorf appears deserted on a rainy Sunday afternoon with both the victors and the vanquished of long ago having passed into history. The precise spot [1] can be found behind No. 2 Um Weschbuur in the centre of the village. Here the last vestiges of German opposition were rounded up and marched off into captivity, as the III Corps advanced further through Luxembourg.

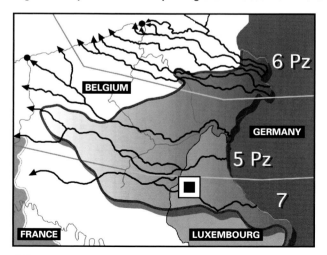

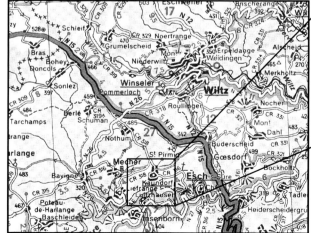

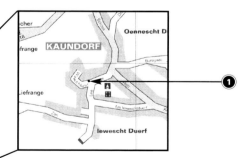

Kaundorf: **Michelin 214, Col. 8. 5° 54' East 49° 55' North. North or southbound on the N15 in Luxembourg south of Wiltz, leave the N15 at Buderscheid/Kaundorf, just north of Esch-sur-Sûre and head west for approximately 4 km into Kaundorf.**

Then: On December 16, 1944, it fell to the 277. Volks-Grenadier-Division of I. SS-Panzerkorps to clear the way west through Krinkelt-Rocherath and on to Elsenborn, to enable Kampfgruppe Müller of the 12. SS-Panzer-Division to move westward. To its left, the 12. Volks-Grenadier-Division of I. SS-Panzerkorps was to clear the road to Büllingen in the south. This entire sector, from the Monschau Forest in the north to Losheim in the south, was defended by three regiments of the green 99th Infantry Division: the 395th Infantry in the north, the 393rd Infantry around Krinkelt-Rocherath itself, and the 394th in the south.

Now: Five decades later, the same location [1] in the heart of Krinkelt is now a peaceful intersection just west of the church. House No. 14 still stands. On this spot carnage once reigned and here a Distinguished Service Cross was won for gallantry. The Panther, one of six put out of action by 1st Lieutenant Robert A. Parker of the 644th Tank Destroyer Battalion on December 18, belonged to I. Abteilung of SS-Panzer-Regiment 12.

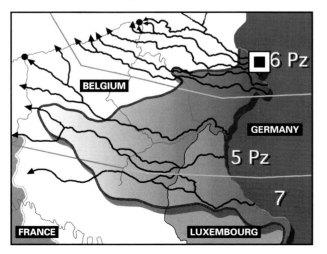

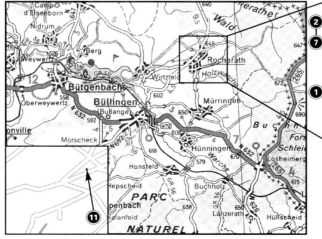

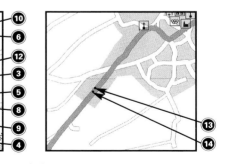

Krinkelt-Rocherath: Michelin 214, Col. 9. 6° 18' East 50° 26' North. North or southbound on the E42 (A27), exit 11 direction Malmédy. After passing through Malmédy and Waimes heading east along the N632, continue through Bütgenbach and into Büllingen, still following the N632 eastwards. In Büllingen, head north-east, direction Wirtzfeld/Rocherath. Follow the signs eastward into Krinkelt-Rocherath, approaching the twin villages from the south-west.

Then: **After the 12. SS-Panzer-Division had been halted in and around the twin villages on December 17, both sides began to shore up their efforts; the Germans with two companies of Panthers belonging to I. Abteilung, SS-Panzer-Regiment 12, the Americans with two tank destroyer battalions (644th and 612th), and an additional tank battalion (741st).**

Now: **On this spot [2] outside the Kalpers' house opposite the church in Krinkelt, two Panthers of 3. Kompanie were destroyed, almost certainly those of SS-Hauptsturmführer Kurt Brödel (foreground) and SS-Oberscharführer Johann Beutelhauser.**

Then: **This excellent shot gives another view of the disabled Panthers of 3. Kompanie, SS-Panzer-Regiment 12, in front of the Kalpers' house. This particular photograph is valuable insofar as it reveals the original positions of the Panthers before they were pushed closer to the house to clear the road. Note the Panther further down the road on the left as well as that in the immediate left foreground. A tank graveyard indeed!**

Now: **Walking the streets, the author found children laughing and playing, home-owners tending gardens and young couples sharing a drink. The powers of imagination must be strong indeed to conjure up the images and events of the past [3]. Yet the tell-tale signs remain for those willing to look hard enough . . . and remember.**

Then: The calm before the storm. Another unpublished photo captures members of the 393rd Infantry Regiment, 99th Infantry Division, in Krinkelt-Rocherath. Having arrived in Europe in November 1944, the division was sent to the Ardennes, which was considered a 'quiet' sector, but its green GIs would soon be pitted against battle-hardened SS troopers.

Now: The comparison captured over 50 years later reveals the location [4] to be outside No. 129 along an unnamed street south-west of the church. Somehow, the absence of the young soldiers, with not a trace of apprehension apparent on their young faces, gives a special poignancy to the location today.

Then: In this unpublished photo taken before the battle began, a member of the 393rd Regiment proudly poses with his trusty mount. The snow on the truck serves as a warning of conditions to come.

Now: Walking through the streets of the twin villages, the author found that the house — No. 83 [5] — had survived the war and the following half-century with very little change; save for an idol of a new age: a satellite dish!

Then: Another superb, previously unpublished photograph captures vestiges of the armoured might of the I. SS-Panzerkorps along a muddy road at the eastern outskirts of Rocherath. The two Panthers belonged to SS-Panzer-Regiment 12 of 12. SS-Panzer-Division, with the Jagdpanzer IV on the left, its spiked barrel pointing skyward, belonging to SS-Panzer-Jäger-Abteilung 12. Two of these panzers were knocked out at the beginning of the battle by a cook's helper, Isabel Salazar, while the third was put out of action by the 644th Tank Destroyer Battalion. The picture was most likely taken in February 1945.

Now: Looking down memory lane five decades later — can this really be the same street? The picture makes a contrasting match looking eastwards from Rocherath. Taken next to the Triangle d'Or restaurant [6] on the immediate left of the photo, the house in the left background is No. 67, while that opposite is No. 87. The tanks lay just east of the road intersection which led to Wahlerscheid further north. The lone 'triangular' house, standing by itself in the wartime photo, can still be seen in the distance.

Then: Another unpublished photograph taken in January 1945 reveals the full extent of the destruction on and about the Kalpers' House (see page 142). The scrap merchants have already begun to move in; the number '463' on Kurt Brödel's Panther was the designation of the company operating in Krinkelt. Most derelict Panthers and Shermans in the area bore this number.

Now: Repaired and restored. The Kalpers' house — No. 63 — taken from the exact same location [7] and camera angle over 50 years later.

Then: February 1945. The battle long over, US forces pick through the wreckage of the epic tank battle in Krinkelt-Rocherath. A hithertofore unpublished photo reveals another victim of the 12. SS-Panzer-Division knocked out in the heart of Krinkelt at a crossroads [8] west of the church. It, too, was disabled by the 644th Tank Destroyer Battalion.

Now: The same crossroads 50 years later reveals a perfect comparison. This is the scene looking directly north; the house in the distance is No. 69. The Panther has long since gone to the scrapyard; the tree on the right replaced by a modern electrical pole, and proper traffic signs direct the traveller through the narrow, unnamed streets of the twin villages.

Then: Before the battle in mid-December 1944, a little light relief for the men of the 99th Infantry Division in what was then a 'quiet sector'. This photo reveals the Dakota Dead Horse Theatre where soldiers could view movies sent from the States in a makeshift theatre set up next to the Peter Roth house on the left.

Now: Like so many of its modern counterparts, the Dakota Dead Horse Theatre is no more. On the left stands No. 73 bearing a new quilted-insulation façade, though retaining its original window configuration. This location [9] is directly south of the church in Krinkelt, again on an unnamed street.

Then: An oft-reproduced photograph depicting the battle of the twin villages, with two Panthers and a Jagdpanzer IV (the same three as in the picture on page 144) knocked out along the road leading into Rocherath from the east. The Panthers were part of SS-Panzer-Regiment 12 while the Jagdpanzer belonged to SS-Panzer-Jäger-Abteilung 12.

Now: This was the photographer's vantage point 50 years ago: the first-floor window of room No. 1 in the present-day Triangle d'Or hotel [10]. The view is looking directly to the east. The house on the far left of the wartime picture now lies directly behind the white house on the left. The farmhouse in the distance still stands in the background. The small gate beside the Panther on the right also retains its pride of place today.

Then: **East of Rocherath, in the first desperate hours of the German attack, a lone platoon of the 741st Tank Battalion moved forward to engage the armour of the newly-arrived Panther force belonging to 12. SS-Panzer-Division which had broken through the 393rd Infantry and the stop-gap 3rd Battalion, 23rd Infantry, of the US 2nd Division.**

Now: **The same road junction [11] near the forest, directly east of Rocherath. The two trees on the left, the forest line in the distance, and the curve in the road all confirm the location. This spot is approximately one kilometre east of the village at a small intersection of several roads that criss-cross the countryside east of the twin villages.**

Then: **This photo, previously unpublished, could perfectly represent the view from the turret of SS-Unterscharführer Willi Fischer's Panther, of 3. Kompanie, SS-Panzer-Regiment 12, as he moved down the main road through Krinkelt late on December 18, 1944. In fact it shows American troops clearing up in January 1945.**

Now: **The Panther graveyard 50 years on. We are looking south-west [12] towards the church in the distance. The house on the left still stands. It was most likely from the windows of this house that 1st Lieutenant Long H. Goffigon and Pfc John Welch, both of the 23rd Infantry's 3rd Battalion, using a bazooka, rained down destruction onto the panzer parade below.**

Then: **This picture of the action at Krinkelt shows Sergeant Bernard Cook of the US 165th Signal Photo Company 'capturing' a German prisoner, while Panther 126 of the 12. SS-Panzer-Division brews up in a roadside ditch. The tank was destroyed by Sergeant Stahsio Kempinski and crew of tank destroyer C-22 of Company C of the 644th Tank Destroyer Battalion at 11 a.m. on December 18, 1944, the photo itself being most likely staged some time later.**

Now: **The same stretch of road [13] immediately south-west of Krinkelt today. Moving up the hill, one enters Krinkelt, the first of the twin villages. Though few structural clues remain as to the comparison location, the curvature of the road, combined with historical knowledge of where the action took place, serves to pinpoint the spot.**

Then: **Another view of Panther 126 as it burns in a roadside ditch just south-east of Krinkelt. Note that the turret gun is fully reversed.**

Now: **The roadside is now more overgrown though the hedgeline in the wartime picture still exists today [14]. With the road now asphalted and the sun shining, it provides a stark contrast to that foggy, rainy day in December 1944.**

Then: Perhaps no single unit effort so captured the essence of the German attack in the Ardennes, both in spirit and impact, as did the battlegroup led by SS-Obersturmbannführer Jochen Peiper. Officially designated Kampfgruppe Peiper, it formed part of the 1. SS-Panzer-Division 'Leibstandarte-SS Adolf Hitler', belonging to I. SS-Panzerkorps of 6. Panzer-Armee. The manner of its failure would typify the essence of the American attack strength in the Ardennes, all the while providing scenes of high drama and ferocious fighting.

Now: And most of it would happen here — La Gleize — a tiny Belgian village perched on a hilltop overlooking the valley of the Amblève river. This comparison of a rare 'steel-wheeled' Panther, No. 221, which belonged to one of two companies with I. Abteilung of SS-Panzer-Regiment 1, was taken almost 50 years later to the very day in the centre of the village, looking directly north up the N633 while standing outside house No. 28 [1]. The building in the background, No. 23, is the hotel Aux Ecuries de la Reine.

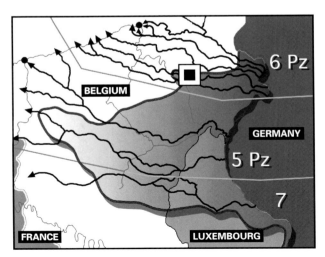

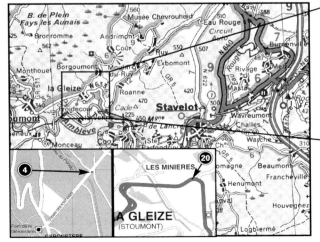

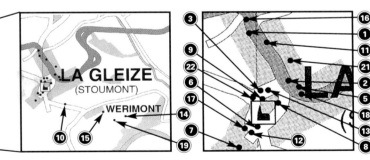

La Gleize: Michelin 214, Col. 8. 5° 52' East 50° 25' North. North or southbound on the E42 (A27), exit 11, direction Stavelot. Continue towards Stavelot along the N62, which joins the N68. Continue on the N68 through Stavelot heading west, direction Trois-Ponts. When the N68 meets the N633 just north of Trois-Ponts at the railway bridge viaduct, turn north (right) onto the N633, direction Coo. Approximately 10 km north lies the village of La Gleize.

Then: The formidable fighting force of Kampfgruppe Peiper was further supported by the three companies from schwere SS-Panzer-Abteilung 501 with its complement of 20 massive King Tiger main battle tanks. Assigned to the rear of the column due to their slow speed, they brought the tank strength of the battlegroup to approximately 100.

Now: Yet by Christmas Eve, the village of La Gleize was strewn with scores of armoured vehicles destroyed or abandoned. After the village was recaptured, men of the 82nd Airborne lined up an abandoned King Tiger on this spot [2] for bazooka target practice. The rebuilt house on the left is No. 46.

Then: After firing several rounds against the frontal area of the Tiger, the paratroopers examined their handiwork. Since the armour on the front was close to six inches thick, no commonly operated Allied field weapon could penetrate it from standard combat distances. The bazooka was no exception: none of its rocket projectiles reached the Tiger's interior though one shot managed to penetrate the side armour on the turret.

Now: Most of his Tigers were abandoned rather than destroyed when Peiper quit the village at 2 a.m. on the night of December 23/24, 1944. The final resting place [3] of this particular Tiger was pictured by the author in this exact match taken over 50 years later. The same cement cisterns and stone wall still stand, framing a timeless comparison featuring a relic of Kampfgruppe Peiper . . . all 67-tons of it!

Then: **By December 20 the battlegroup had entered and occupied La Gleize though it was desperately short of supplies, most of all, fuel. Unbeknown to Peiper, one of the largest Allied fuel depots on the European continent lay in the woods south of the town of Spa where thousands of jerrycans lay neatly stacked in endless piles through the forest.**

Now: **Often mis-captioned as the 'fuel dump north of Stavelot', it was located here on the road north of La Gleize [4]. Though it depicts neither tanks, nor soldiers, neither action nor destroyed buildings, the author considers this comparison to be one of the best. The fuel cans simply vanish on the Chemin des Fontaines, by the bridge at Ruisseau du Pendu.**

Then: **The march of Kampfgruppe Peiper was finally stopped just west of Stoumont, at mid-day on December 19 by the 740th Tank Battalion and the 119th Infantry Regiment. Falling back into La Gleize on the 21st, by the evening of the 22nd intense American artillery fire had turned the village into an explosive cauldron. Out of supplies and cut off from help, the remnants of the once-powerful battlegroup began to retreat on foot on the night of December 23/24.**

Now: **When the Americans entered La Gleize the following day, German armour lay scattered and abandoned, both within the village and in the surrounding fields. Here at the eastern entrance of La Gleize [5] a knocked-out Panther stood outside No. 54, along the present-day N633.**

Then: The battle for La Gleize over, American soldiers mill about directly behind and south of the village church [6], examining the handiwork wrought by their artillery colleagues entrenched several miles away. These men perhaps belong to the 704th Tank Battalion: a Sherman stands guard as an impromptu conference is held in front of it. The soldier on the right, close to the camera and out of focus due to his movement, wears the headgear of a US Army tank driver.

Now: Fifty years on, the devastated area about the church has been repaired; the same stone wall along its cemetery perimeter still stands as well, as does the house in the distance on the left. This is the view looking directly north from the car park next to the December 1944 museum which houses what is probably one of the most unique collections of Ardennes memorabilia and artefacts ever assembled under one roof. And, unlike those of 50 years ago, this one is intact!

Then: Another Panther belonging to Kampfgruppe Peiper lies disabled next to the Maison Communale [7]. It was perched along the ridge on the southern edge of town, its barrel pointing down towards the valley of the Amblève.

Now: With the Maison Communale having been completely rebuilt since its partial destruction 50 years ago, the author had to walk behind the chain-link fence of an adjacent tennis court to capture the precise photo comparison today. After careful examination of the distances and terrain of the present day, the author can confidently predict that the barrel of the Panther would today be firmly pressed against the chest of any unfortunate tennis player preparing to serve!

Then: In the heart of the village, the church at La Gleize suffered greatly under the incessant American artillery fire. This scene [8] was typical of the devastation which characterised the village after the battle.

Now: Looking south-west at the church 50 years later sees it completely restored, with a few newer houses replacing the older structures of the past. The modern replacement for the Maison Communale can be seen in the distance on the left. The same stone wall still stands having come through the artillery barrage in fairly good shape.

Then: Having survived the hail of steel, the inhabitants of La Gleize eventually emerged to restart their lives. All about lay the spoils of a defeated enemy. Here villagers stand on one of the disabled King Tigers of schwere SS-Panzer-Abteilung 501, knocked out along a small lane [9].

Now: Having located the exact position where the photographer took the picture in 1945, the author climbed up precariously along an adjoining stone wall next to the lane and captured the identical comparison. Though the site is somewhat overgrown, the same oak tree on the middle left of the wartime photo still stands sentinel today.

Then: **With the shell-blasted remnants of the village perched along the hill in the background, the true extent of the devastation was evident in the sloping valley on the eastern edge of La Gleize. Over 25 armoured personnel carriers that once carried the pride of the 1. SS-Panzer-Division into battle lie smashed, twisted and broken. Even the trees themselves bear testimony to the savagery of the barrage.**

Now: **The same view [10], looking west up towards La Gleize, finds a clear and untroubled field. This photo was taken just east of the village on the road leading to the Ferme Wérimont. The stillness of the present day scene belies what once happened here as the German offensive was ground into defeat.**

Then: **Another view of Panther No. 221 (see page 149) taken after the Americans had recaptured La Gleize. With the debris now cleared away, the tank becomes just another roadside attraction for the advancing Americans.**

Now: **Today Panther No. 221 would be guarding the front of a convenience store [11] on the N633! Though little remains in this photograph to identify this as the same location, other unassailable 'then and now' comparison photographs from different angles of this same Panther establish without question the site's accuracy.**

Then: **This picture which had been taken in the early summer of 1945 in front of the Maison Communale [12] in La Gleize, shows a Tiger II being salvaged from where it had been disabled (see page 154).**

Now: **The Tiger was moved and restored in the early 1950s, to be given pride of place in front of the village hall. Today the Tiger sports a new camouflage scheme and a repaired 88mm gun barrel, although true armour aficionados will note that its current muzzle brake is that of a Panther!**

Then: **A pose for the camera from a grateful yet curious inhabitant of La Gleize. This Tiger II bears the frontal scars of also having been used as target practice by the 82nd Airborne. The prize armour souvenir —the muzzle brake — has long gone and another popular item — its bow machine gun — is likewise missing.**

Now: **The 'King of Battle' once lay here on this lane [13], well and truly blocking it to passing traffic. Fifty years later, its presence is but a memory. What a pity to have destroyed such a magnificent specimen!**

Then: As the Kampfgruppe sought to establish a defensive perimeter in its doomed struggle to survive, another Tiger II, its barrel lowered in a position of supplication, was disabled in a field on the Ferme Wérimont just east of the village. This tank was No. 221 commanded by SS-Untersturmführer Georg Hantusch.

Now: Exploring Ferme Wérimont over 50 years later, the author pinpointed the precise spot [14] next to the row of trees where the magnificent beast shuddered in it death throes. The three trees and the horizon in the distance line up the comparison perfectly.

Then: After the battle. In the middle of the farm itself [15] lay this abandoned Panther, its barrel still pointing in the direction of its last shot. All around the farm lay armoured vehicles — two Tiger IIs, two Panthers, and a Panzer IV.

Now: Once permission had been granted, the author was able to walk about and take comparison photographs at will. In this particular shot it can be seen that the barn door has been filled in, as well as the shell hole, yet close inspection of the stonework still reveals the damage caused as the shell smashed into the building.

Then: **Having been recaptured by American forces on Christmas Day 1944, the centre of La Gleize was badly damaged with the fighting continuing to rage east, north and south of the village. As New Year's Eve approached, a light dusting of snow amidst the ruins seemed to be nature's way of softening the scene. Panther No. 221 (see pages 149 and 153 top right), an armoured remnant of the 1. SS-Panzer-Division, lies silently amongst the carnage and destruction.**

Now: **A similar silence greeted the author 50 years later. This is the view [16] looking south down the present-day N633 from the centre of the village. The house on the left, unchanged over the decades, is No. 31. The Panther lay just off the road directly in front of the author. The sun attempting to break through the grey clouds of a wintry day seems almost a link between yesterday and today. Now, La Gleize prospers, hosting tourists from many countries who seek out this tiny village to visit the local military museum which is simply and aptly named 'December 1944'. It happened here. They came this way.**

Then: **American GIs inspect the battlefield. This Panther sought futile cover behind a monument to First World War standing in front of the town hall. Its disabled opponent, a Sherman, lies off to the right.**

Now: **Where the Panther once sat outside the remodelled town hall, a Christmas tree, complete with decorations, celebrates festivities at the 50th anniversary of the battle [17]. The war memorial still exists but has been moved against the wall of the museum just off to the left of the photo.**

Then: **The spring of 1945 found Panther No. 202 still standing guard along the main road at the eastern edge of La Gleize [18], albeit looking decidedly the worse for wear. Sagging tracks speak of its immobilisation, while the muzzle brake has long disappeared to a souvenir hunter!**

Now: **With a new white façade hiding the shrapnel scars and a new portico awning, the inhabitants of No. 54 get on with life. The Panther once sat here, its barrel pointed down the small, gently sloping hill as one approaches La Gleize from the east. Just imagine the sight which would greet drivers along the N633 today should it reappear!**

Then: A rare post-battle photograph taken in the spring of 1945 on Wérimont farm shows King Tiger No. 213 lying in front of the tree line along the southern end of the farm. Operating in the area with No. 221 and two other Panthers, 213 was commanded by SS-Obersturmführer Rudolf Dollinger.

Now: The author photographs the precise spot [19] where 213 came to rest. Despite substantial damage — its gun was severed half-way down the barrel — this King Tiger is the same one which now stands outside the museum in La Gleize, one of only six which have survived in Europe out of nearly 500 produced.

Then: With the village now in American hands, patrols are sent down the road to Trois-Ponts. As they return to the village, they came upon yet another King Tiger at the side of the road. This particular tank was abandoned on December 19 due to a thrown track as Kampfgruppe Peiper was approaching La Gleize.

Now: The exact spot along the present-day N633 where the Tiger was disabled. Looking directly west, the tank came to a halt on the bend in the road [20] next to a small hamlet called Les Minières, just over a kilometre east of La Gleize. The tree line has grown substantially though the house on the hill on the far right of the wartime photograph still stands behind the row of trees.

Then: **Yet another armoured monster from Kampfgruppe Peiper, King Tiger No. 204, draws an admiring audience of American soldiers as engineers work to try to get it running. Surprisingly, they succeeded and it was eventually driven out under its own steam towards the railway station at Spa.**

Now: **This picture shows the small orchard [21] behind house No. 43, where King Tiger No. 204 once sat. One can only imagine the shock of looking out of the cellar door to see the bulk of the monster, with its two-foot-wide tracks, crushing everything before it.**

Then: **A small, unnamed lane in La Gleize reveals yet another disabled Tiger II. This particular tank is the same one used as target practice by the 82nd Airborne Division on page 150. When seen from the rear, the reason for its demise now becomes obvious: with a track-link broken, it quickly ran out of road!**

Now: **A long, last look finds the same wall, the same trees and the same houses [22]. On this sunny, yet cold day over 50 years later, we finally leave La Gleize and move on . . . though this tiny Belgian village will long be remembered for the part it played in the last great effort of the Third Reich against the Western Allies.**

Then: **By December 20, 1944, lead elements of the 116. Panzer-Division had nearly reached La Roche-en-Ardenne but, surmising that the streets would be inappropriate for rapidly advancing armour, the division detoured north towards Dochamps and Samrée. After subsequent unsuccessful attacks on Hotton on December 21, the division then fell back into La Roche the following day to resume its westward advance. Two weeks later, the tide had swung in favour of the Allied forces and La Roche was retaken on January 11, 1945, by the 154th Brigade of the British 51st Highland Division.**

Now: **The Hotel de Liège [1], outside which the M4A1 Shermans belonging to the 1st Northamptonshire Yeomanry (33rd Armoured Brigade) once parked, is still in business 50 years later, with a small café area now added to the front of the building. It stands on the Rue d'Echavées at the junction of the Rue de la Gare, the railway station in the background and the descending hills in the distance serving to make a perfect comparison.**

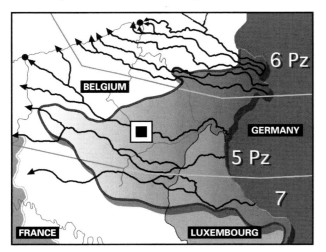

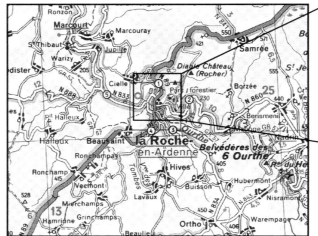

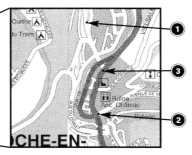

La Roche: **Michelin 214, Col. 7. 5° 35' E, 50° 11' North. North or southbound on the E25 (A26), exit 50, direction La Roche. La Roche-en-Ardenne lies 17 km to the west along the N89. Alternatively, north or southbound along the N4, exit at Barrière de Champlon, direction La Roche, which lies 13 km to the north along the N89.**

Then: In the effort to retake La Roche, the centre of town suffered horribly under incessant artillery shelling and bombardment from the air. Most likely taken in early January 1945, a Jeep slowly picks it way down a narrow street winding through the ruins. Over 120 people were killed as a result of the shelling.

Now: The same street 50 years later. With the heart of La Roche completely rebuilt, it would be difficult to match the photo if it were not for a single tell-tale building [2] which survived. Its windowed portico can just be made out in the centre of the wartime picture just above and to the left of the Jeep. Today, looking down the Rue Clerve, it still survives as part of the Capero Restaurant.

Then: Walking through war-torn La Roche in January 1945, US soldiers turn and pose in Rue Chamont [3] with the Hotel du Luxembourg in the background — though this is Belgium! Despite the snowy blanket covering the town, the destruction is self-evident.

Now: Looking south today, the Hotel du Luxembourg no longer stands on Rue Chamont; only the stately building on the far right survives. In a rare reversal, the original street dimensions have since been narrowed, not widened. The intersection with Rue de la Gare lies just behind the camera position.

Then: **Spearheaded by the Kampfgruppen of Peiper and Hansen, 1. SS-Panzer-Division's efforts were to be supported by a reinforced reconnaissance battalion, Kampfgruppe Knittel, under the command of SS-Sturmbannführer Gustav Knittel (left). This assistance was to include the capture of bridges across specific rivers. On December 18, 1944, as Peiper moved towards Stavelot and Hansen remained stuck at Recht, SS-Oberführer Wilhelm Mohnke (the commander of 1. SS-Panzer-Division) ordered Kampfgruppe Knittel north in support of Peiper's efforts.**

Now: **The picture was taken just as Kampfgruppe Knittel entered the hamlet of La Vaulx-Richard, south of Stavelot, where Knittel held an impromptu conference with his staff commander, SS-Obersturmführer Goltz [1]. In the small hamlet 50 years later, the author replaces the German photographer and captures the identical comparison. The house on the left, with its characteristic chimney and roofline, is No. 1.**

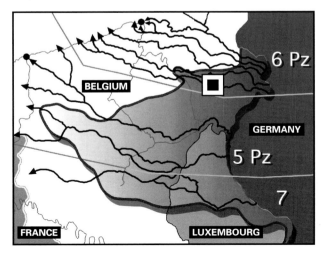

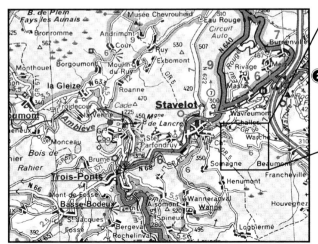

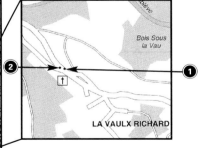

La Vaulx Richard: **Michelin 214, Col. 8. 5° 58' East 50° 23' North. North or southbound on the E42 (A27), exit 11, direction Stavelot. As N62 meets the N68 heading west, exit at the town of Stavelot off the N68, direction town centre. Pass through the town heading south, cross the bridge over the Amblève, and turn left onto the Chemin du Château, heading east. La Vaulx-Richard is approximately 2½ km east of the southern outskirts of Stavelot.**

Then: **Monday afternoon, December 18, 1944 — another shot of SS-Obersturmführer Goltz (left) conferring with the battlegroup's leader, SS-Sturmbannführer Gustav Knittel, in the hamlet of La Vaulx-Richard. Two SdKfz 251 armoured personnel carriers, both heavily camouflaged, can be seen in the background. At this stage, Kampfgruppe Knittel, 1. SS-Panzer-Division's reinforced reconnaissance battalion, was approximately three kilometres east of Stavelot, supporting Kampfgruppe Peiper further to the west.**

Now: **Over 50 years later, the two divergent roads in the upper left background serve to frame and align the comparison [2]. The house on the upper left is No. 6; that on the right No. 4. The pole carrying the power line on the right in the wartime photo has now been replaced with a more modern variety. La Vaulx-Richard consists only of about a dozen houses and farmyards. Nonetheless, after traversing the Ardennes for over four years and consulting scores of maps, the wartime photograph holds a place near and dear to the author's heart; even the most powerful of travellers occasionally has to consult the map . . . where are we?**

Then: The beginning of the end for Kampfgruppe Peiper was signalled by Kampfgruppe Hansen being stopped at Trois-Ponts to the south; an event which completely cut off Peiper from further supplies. With Cheneux having fallen to the 504th Parachute Infantry Regiment on December 22, a concerted attack on La Gleize began from the south through La Venne. On December 23, at precisely 8.30 a.m., the 119th Infantry Regiment, supported by Task Force Jordan (3rd Armored Division) and the 740th Tank Battalion, moved up past the crossroads where they were engaged by a Panther and a Panzer IV, each well hidden in the local terrain.

Now: Both German tanks were eventually silenced, but not before several of the Shermans were put out of action. The wartime photograph illustrates one of the Shermans on this stretch of road [1], virtually unchanged in spite of the passage of 50 years. With the same house, metal electric pylon and bend in the road (the Rue de l'Eglise), the scene is almost timeless. This location is approximately 500 metres before one reaches the intersection with the Gare de la Gleize. (Some time later the author passed the spot and noticed that the metal pylon has since been removed.)

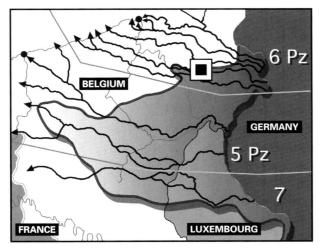

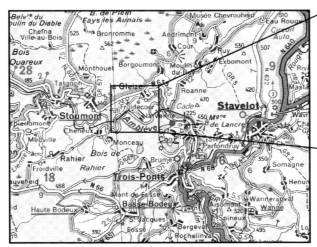

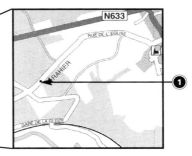

La Venne: Michelin 214, Col. 8. 5° 51' East 50° 24' North. On the E42 (A27), exit 11, direction Stavelot. Continue along the N62 which joins the N68, then on through Stavelot west to Trois-Ponts. When the N68 meets the N633 turn north (right) to Coo. Approximately 10 km north of Trois-Ponts directly on the winding N633, lies the village of La Gleize. Pass through heading south-west on the Rue de l'Eglise.

Then: **With the Allies having brought the westward thrust of the three great German armies to a standstill, by mid-January the US First and Third Armies linked up in Houffalize and the effort was now directed inexorably eastward. This classic wartime photograph typifies the spirit of the time. Taken in Langlir, Belgium, north-east of Houffalize, a Sherman of the 703rd Tank Destroyer Battalion, (3rd Armored Division) rumbles past a defeated Panzer IV, once part of Panzer-Abteilung 115, operating in the Langlir area with the 15. Panzergrenadier-Division.**

Now: **The German tank lay just beyond the house on the left (No. 3). While investigating the location, the author drove back and forth along this road numerous times, the lack of features making it difficult to pinpoint the spot [1] . . . that is, until the owner of No. 3 stepped out, marched up to his car, and angrily accused him of being a thief casing his house for a future burglary! After frantically showing him the wartime shot, the householder's attitude completely changed and he happily assisted the author in pointing out exactly where the tank once lay! The house in the far distance down the road confirms the location.**

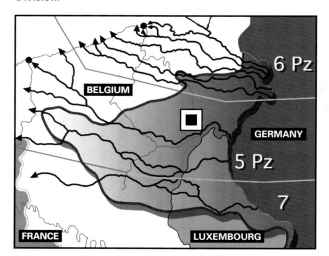

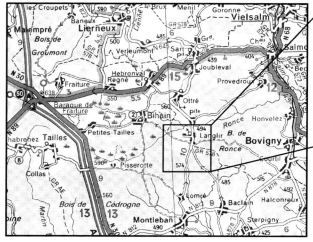

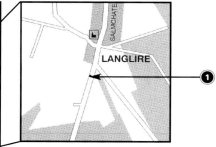

Langlir: **Michelin 214, Col. 8. 5° 51' East 50° 14' North. From north or south, exit E25(A26) at exit 50 onto the N89, heading east towards Vielsalm/Salmchâteau. Approximately 5 km east of the E25 lies Hebronval. Turn right at Hebronval, direction Ottré/Bihain. Follow unnamed road to Ottré, proceeding south through the village, direction Langlir. Enter Langlir from the north.**

Then: On December 16, 1944, Kampfgruppe Peiper finally got underway in force around 2.30 p.m. By nightfall they had crossed the Belgian border and were proceeding through Merlscheid. Peiper entered Lanzerath near midnight, the long panzer spearhead rolling through the village into the morning of the 17th. Bringing up the rear were the Tiger IIs of schwere SS-Panzer-Abteilung 501. As dawn broke, a German cameraman took one of the most famous photographs of the entire battle: a Tiger II cresting a small hill south of Lanzerath as soldiers of the 99th Division march in the opposite direction to captivity.

Now: At one of the author's favourite locations, the small hill below Lanzerath is captured on film 50 years later. The road [1] is unnamed, but the house in the distance is numbered 15. The farmhouses of Merlscheid in the distance confirm the comparison. Standing on the road today, one is struck by how narrow, unassuming and short it is, yet up this very hill once rolled the armoured might of the 1. SS-Panzer-Division . . . on past hundreds of dejected American infantrymen.

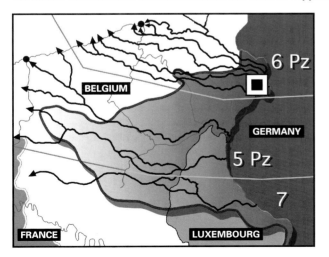

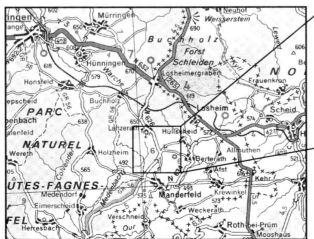

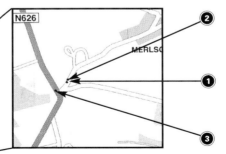

Lanzerath: Michelin 214, Col. 10. 6° 20' East 50° 22' North. North or southbound on the E42 (A27), exit 11, direction east to Malmédy. From Malmédy and Waimes, continue east along the N632 into Bütgenbach. Turn right continuing on the N632 to Büllingen. Then continue east along the N632 to Losheimergraben. Immediately before the German border, turn right onto the N626. Lanzerath is approximately 3 km south.

Then: Turning about to face up the same hill, the German photographer now shoots the rear-end of the same King Tiger seen on the previous page. Following are two German motor-cyclists. At this point, the Tiger is barely ten metres from the top of the hill whereupon it will bear right and enter Lanzerath from the south.

Now: Standing in the shoes of the German war photographer, the author looks west up the same hill [2] west of Merlscheid over 50 years later. This road and the adjoining intersection are slowly becoming more developed as housing creeps southward down from Lanzerath along the N626.

Then: Walking north behind the Tiger II, and having reached the top of the hill, the German photographer pictured more prisoners of the 99th Infantry Division who had been captured in Honsfeld earlier in the day. The Americans had marched east back into and beyond Lanzerath where they met up with the tail-end of the Kampfgruppe. They are guarded here by a member of the 3. Fallschirm-Jäger-Division.

Now: The identical stretch of road [3] leading into Lanzerath is now the present-day N626. Past this very spot tramped the tired and beaten men of the 'Checkerboard' division. The house on the left is No. 8; though its façade has been considerably changed, the roofline of the farmhouse just to the right of it in the distance is identical. Exactly 500 metres further down this road lies Lanzerath.

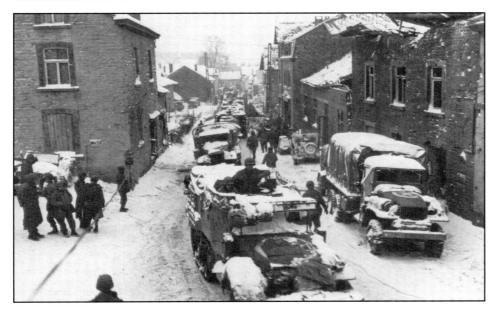

Then: **By December 24, the 2. SS-Panzer-Division had taken the crossroads at Baraque de Fraiture and was moving on Manhay, while to their right the 9. SS-Panzer-Division had just moved through Lierneux. Thus the stage was set for the epic battle of Manhay. Begun on Christmas Eve and lasting until December 27, in the intense battle the II. SS-Panzerkorps was finally stopped in its tracks, and by the dawn of the New Year, the Americans were well on the offensive again in the area. This US Army photograph reveals the depth and breadth of the logistics behind the American effort.**

Now: **Where transport of the 3rd Armored and the 83rd Infantry Divisions once pushed eastwards through the narrow streets of Lierneux, Belgium, on January 9, 1945. This is the view 50 years on looking north out the second-floor window of No. 91 along the Rue du Centre [1]. Though substantial reconstruction has taken place on the right-hand side of the street, the house on the left remains unchanged and now houses a patisserie.**

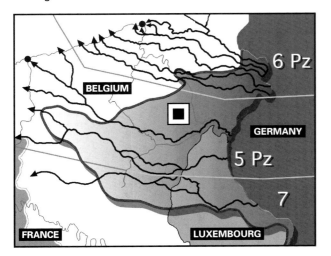

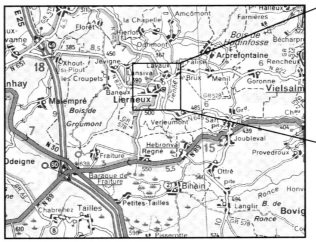

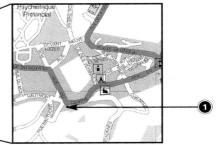

Lierneux: **Michelin 214, Col. 8. 5° 48' East 50° 17' North. North or southbound on the E25 (A26), exit 50, direction east to Vielsalm on the N89. Approximately 3 km east of Baraque de Fraiture, turn left at Regné, direction Lierneux. This unnamed road becomes Rue Marcadenes as it approaches Lierneux from the south, which is 4½ km north of the N89/Regné turn-off.**

Then: After passing through Honsfeld and Büllingen along Rollbahn D on December 17, Kampfgruppe Peiper passed through the crossroads at Baugnez, (site of the Malmédy massacre). Having learned earlier that Ligneuville was the headquarters of the US 49th Anti-Aircraft Artillery Brigade under Brigadier General Edward W. Timberlake, Peiper turned his column south to capture his prize. Forward panzer elements of his battle group entered the town from the north, while support elements moved in from the south.

Now: The same view today, [1] matching the US Army photo taken after Ligneuville was eventually recaptured, with the Hotel du Moulin on the left, which both the US and German commanders had used as headquarters. We are looking up the Grand Rue (N62) in a northerly direction. The village church remains unchanged; only the trees have been felled to make way for a more modern, two-lane paved road.

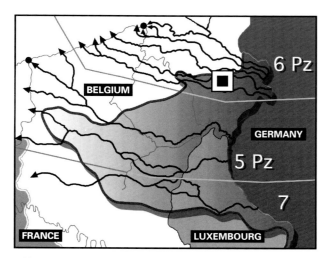

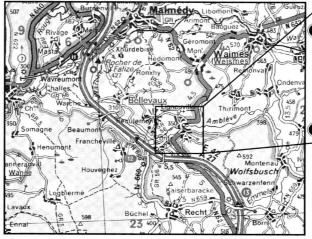

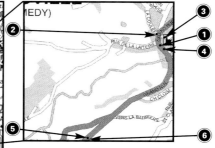

Ligneuville: Michelin 214, Col. 9. 6° 4' East 50° 23' North. Southbound on the E42 (A27), exit 12, onto the N660. Turn left (north-east) under the highway, direction Ligneuville. The N660 joins up with the N62 just south of Ligneuville. Enter the village from the south along the N62.

Then: **After the battle for Ligneuville was over, this picture was taken looking down the main street. Now occupied by vehicles of the 1st Battalion, 117th Regiment of the 30th Infantry Division, it was recaptured on January 16, 1945. SS-Obersturmbannführer Otto Skorzeny was wounded by shrapnel fire in Ligneuville, possibly when using the Jeep in the foreground.**

Now: **Looking southwards down the Grand Rue (N62) the comparison was taken standing on the intersection of La Coulée and the Grand Rue [2], with the Hotel du Moulin off to the right. The cars on the left are parked outside No. 33.**

Then: **Having taken Ligneuville, SS-Unterscharführer Paul Ochmann of the 1. SS-Panzer-Division selected eight American prisoners to dig graves for his fallen German comrades. When they had finished, Ochmann executed them one-by-one, their bodies rolling down a small hill where members of the 30th Division found them in January 1945. Point-blank head wounds indicated the manner of death, as did the testimony of Belgian eyewitnesses.**

Now: **On a snowy day 50 years later, the author revisits the precise location [3] where the frozen bodies of the executed Americans once lay. The prisoners were lined up along the N62 in the upper distance and shot beside the road, the bodies ending up in the foreground. Though a memorial stands today in the centre of Ligneuville remembering the dead, this spot is the real memorial — a small patch of empty ground across from the Hotel du Moulin.**

Then: Moving from Baugnez in the north, Kampfgruppe Peiper had entered Ligneuville at approximately 2 p.m. on December 17. In the lead was a Panther commanded by SS-Untersturmführer Arndt Fischer, the adjutant of I. Abteilung of SS-Panzer-Regiment 1. Unbeknown to Fischer, two Shermans and a 76mm anti-tank gun of the 14th Tank Battalion's Service Company (9th Armored Division) had already targeted the Germans and the first round from the 76mm set Fischer's Panther on fire. However, return fire quickly knocked out the American gun. When Ligneuville was retaken on January 16, 1945, Fischer's burned-out tank was pictured in front of the Hotel des Ardennes.

Now: From the Hotel des Ardennes to the Hotel Georges . . . the names may have changed but the buildings and location [4] remain the same. Hotel Georges — No. 37 on the Grand Rue — lies just north of the bridge over the Amblève river in the southern part of the village. A restaurant and bar have since been added on the right. On this very spot, the lead tank of the German battlegroup was put out of action — without even having time to check in!

Then: **By the afternoon of December 17, these Fallschirmjägers aboard King Tiger No. 222 of schwere SS-Panzer-Abteilung 501, were the leading lights of the German propaganda machine. Having already appeared in cine film sequences earlier in the day in the villages of Deidenberg and Kaiserbaracke, Tiger 222 takes a 'studio' break just south of Ligneuville. Filmed passing through Kaiserbaracke, Tiger 222 was attempting to rejoin both Kampfgruppe Peiper and the original Rollbahn D route. Despite the jovial atmosphere with cigarettes all round these fellows are armed to the teeth; they must be, for difficult fighting lay ahead in Stavelot, their next 'photo call'.**

Now: **Along the present-day N62, just south of Ligneuville, the author stops and records the same location [5] of the 'cigarette break' of 50 years ago. The accuracy of the comparison has been confirmed with the aid of the photo below taken from directly behind the tank.**

Then: **As the photographer moves further to the rear to expose a second frame, a subtle, yet tell-tale clue now enters the picture — the stand of trees on the left. Tiger 222 never entered Ligneuville itself choosing instead to turn left at the junction just ahead in order to pick up Kampfgruppe Peiper's route to Stavelot.**

Now: **And this is the same place [6] along the present-day N62, just south of the town, with the same line of trees on the left. Further down the road the N62 becomes the Grand Rue as it turns left across the bridge over the Amblève, and on into Ligneuville itself.**

Then: Having recaptured the area around Baraque de Fraiture by January 6, elements of the 3rd Armored Division continued to advance southward towards Houffalize. In Lomré, Belgium, just south of Langlir, US artillery fire set fire to this small house [1].

Now: Following its ordeal of 50 years ago, the identical house — No. 5 — in Lomré today seems none the worse for wear.

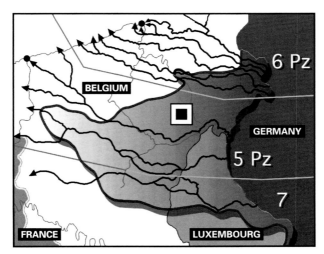

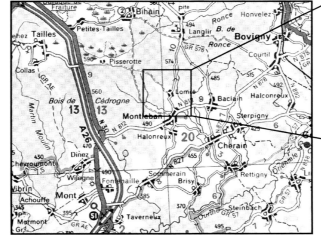

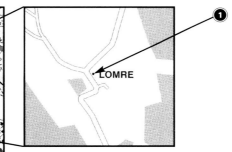

Lomré: Michelin 214, Col. 8. 5° 50' East 50° 12' North. North or southbound on the E25 (A2), exit 51, onto the N30 heading north (away from Houffalize). Just after the N30 passes under the E25, head east along the N812, direction Montleban. On the north-eastern end of Montleban, turn north towards Lomré, entering it from the south.

Then: Spearheading the 5. Panzer-Armee's thrust westward were two powerful forces, the 2. Panzer-Division and the Panzer-Lehr Division, both part of XXXXVII. Panzerkorps. Three American blocking forces opposed the 2. Panzer-Division along the Allerborn-Longvilly-Mageret road leading into Bastogne; Task Forces Rose and Harper (both of the 9th Armored Division) at Antoniushaff and Fetch respectively and Team Cherry (10th Armored Division) at Longvilly. Task Forces Rose and Harper were quickly overrun on December 18, and Team Cherry was surrounded by Panzer-Lehr and the 2. Panzer-Division the following day.

Now: Standing at position [1] on the map looking east down the present-day N874 at the spot where Team Cherry was cut to pieces by intense German artillery and panzer attacks at 1 p.m. on December 19. The wartime photo was taken in the spring of 1945 when some of its tanks still littered the area. Longvilly can be seen in the distance.

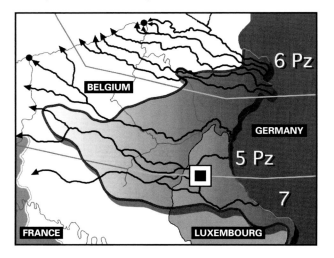

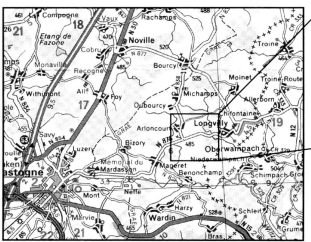

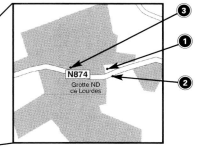

Longvilly: Michelin 214, Col. 10. 5° 50' East 50° 2' North. North or southbound on either the E25 (A26) or the N4, exit 54 and head direction city centre, Bastogne. At the major intersection at the city square, head north-east (turn left) onto the N85, towards the Mémorial du Mardasson, where the N85 becomes the N874 as it leaves Bastogne. Continue east on the N874 past Neffe, Mageret and into Longvilly.

173

Then: **Another photo taken nearer the end of the battle in January 1945 looking down the same stretch of road towards Longvilly. Wrecked vehicles from Team Cherry lay all about though by this time many had already been cleared from the road and fields. Having retaken the area, American traffic now resumed between Mageret and Longvilly, east of Bastogne.**

Now: **The author sights down the N874 looking directly east to capture the comparison photo. In spite of the foliage, this stretch of road [2] maintains its place in history. On this spot, the last of the three US blocking forces met its fate at the hands of the XXXXVII. Panzerkorps.**

Then: **With Longvilly back in American hands, the show must go on. Yet more destroyed vehicles of Team Cherry have now been unceremoniously pushed off the road to make way for the resumption of traffic. This time the picture has been taken looking back westwards towards Mageret.**

Now: **Fifty years later the author turns round and frames the same stretch of the N874 heading up the hill towards Mageret [3]. Where destruction once reigned, only the noise of an occasional passing vehicle can be heard today.**

Then: On December 26, 1944, the 4th Armored Division entered Bastogne from the south, so lifting the siege. The so-called 'Bastogne Corridor' became the first open route to the city which the Germans, in turn, sought to cut and on December 30 the counter-attack began. Led by the 1. SS-Panzer-Division and the 167. Volks-Grenadier-Division, it was directed straight at the 35th Infantry Division at Lutrebois. After ferocious fighting, the Germans captured the village and nearby Villers-la-Bonne-Eau. However, by the time the New Year dawned, the tide had turned and the Americans had retaken the area.

Now: The medical corpsmen carried their wounded this way up an unnamed road across from the village church. With appropriate snowfall framing the scene, the passing of 50 years reveals that the house in the distance [1] has been completely rebuilt. Today walking through small peaceful villages like Lutrebois, it is difficult to imagine the intensity of the fighting which once raged through the area.

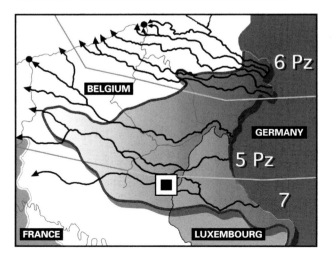

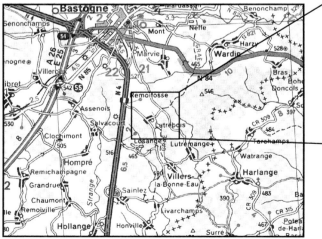

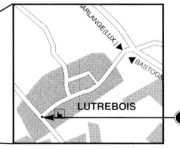

Lutrebois: Michelin 214, Col. 8. 5° 44' East 49° 57' North. Southbound on the N4, south of Bastogne, exit the N4 at Remoifosse. At Remoifosse, continue south, direction Lutrebois.

Then: After its failure to take Hotton, and having eventually been driven out of the Dochamps-Samrée sector, the 116. Panzer-Division (LVIII. Panzerkorps) turned to the defensive. Falling back through La Roche, it was eventually withdrawn from the area on January 9, 1945, as the Germans sought to reduce the vulnerability of their forces in the exposed salient. Left behind was this Panzer IV belonging to Panzer-Regiment 16 which was abandoned in Maboge, Belgium, just east of La Roche.

Now: Fifty years have passed and the centre of Maboge, situated along the picturesque Ourthe river, looks decidedly more upmarket. The farmhouse which once stood on the left is now a café, appropriately named 'Café La Ferme'. The house on the right, next to the church, is No. 6. The small incline in the foreground, where the Panzer IV once sat, is now built up with a low wall. This little road connects Maboge with the present-day N860 running east out of La Roche towards Houffalize.

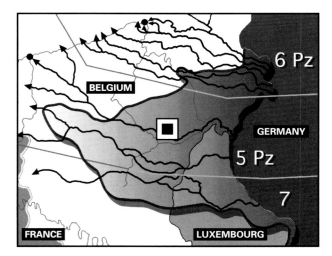

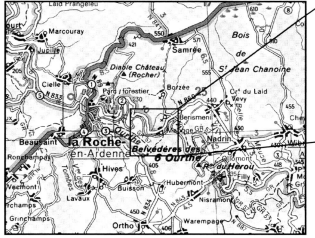

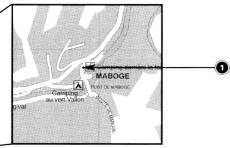

Maboge: Michelin 214, Col. 7. 5° 38' East 50° 10' North. North or southbound on the E25 (A26), exit 50, direction La Roche which lies 17 km to the west along the N89. Alternatively, north or southbound along the N4, exit at Barrière de Champlon, which lies 13 km to the north along the N89. Once in La Roche, head east out of the city on the N860 towards Houffalize. Approximately 5 km east lies Maboge, directly on the N860.

Then: **During the first two weeks of January, the 116. Panzer-Division retreated eastward from La Roche to Houffalize and beyond. As part of the covering defence, this 75mm PaK 40 gun was situated on a hill overlooking the village of Mabompré, just south of Houffalize, and it was credited with knocking out two American tanks before being put out of action. The twin pincers of the US First and Third Armies finally closed in on January 16, 1945 at Houffalize — though not around the 116. Panzer-Division!**

Now: **The same hill overlooking the modern N826 near Mabompré finds an empty farm field. This is the view looking west with the main road behind the photographer and the village on the right.**

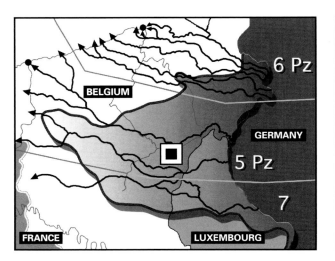

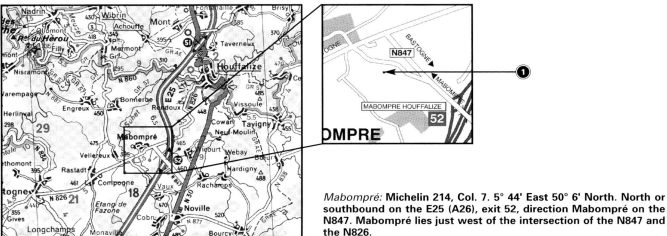

Mabompré: **Michelin 214, Col. 7. 5° 44' East 50° 6' North. North or southbound on the E25 (A26), exit 52, direction Mabompré on the N847. Mabompré lies just west of the intersection of the N847 and the N826.**

Then: Bastogne having been technically relieved by December 26, US forces organised a strong offensive drive out of the city north-east towards St Vith by the 6th Armored supported by the 35th and 26th Infantry Divisions. After a half-hearted yet successful attack on Neffe, east of Bastogne, on December 31, a larger attack was carried out and Bizory fell to American forces on New Year's Day, 1945. However, pressing onwards east, the attack was soon halted by Grenadier-Regiment 78 (26. Volks-Grenadier-Division) whereupon the fighting around and for the village of Mageret intensified.

Now: Along the present-day N874, which runs east past Mageret to Longvilly, a small line of houses stands on the southern edge of the village. The destroyed Sherman sat directly in front of No. 24A. Though the houses themselves have been completely rebuilt, previous historians, with local support, have established this site as the correct location.

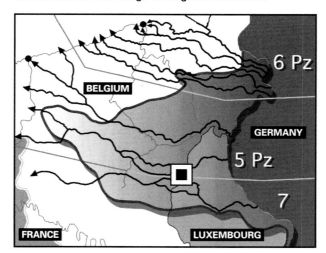

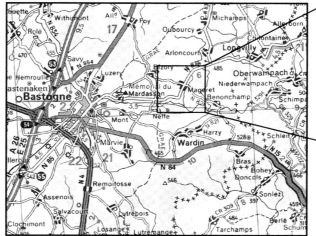

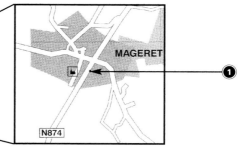

Mageret: Michelin 214, Col. 8. 5° 47' East 50° 1' North. North or southbound on either the E25 (A26) or the N4, exit 54 and head towards the centre of Bastogne. At the major intersection at the square, head north-east (turn left) onto the N85, towards the Mémorial du Mardasson, where the N85 becomes the N874 as it leaves Bastogne. Continue east on the N874 past Neffe and into Mageret, which lies at the intersection of the N874 and the N821.

Then: In 1945, after the battle of the Ardennes was over, a young Belgian named Jean Collignon rode the battlefield on his bicycle, making drawings of the weapons of war which still lay scattered all about the area. This quite rare Jagdtiger (Hunting Tiger) was sketched alongside a farmhouse in the Belgian village of Maldingen. The Jagdtiger was the heaviest armoured vehicle in operation during World War II weighing a massive 75 tons and possessing an enormous 128mm gun mounted in a fixed, slab-sided turret.

Now: As with young Collignon's earlier drawing matched by the author 50 years later in Fontenaille (see page 91), his sketch proved remarkably accurate though perhaps a little bit generous on the depth of the house. This is No. 53 just along the N827 as it winds it way through the village. The farmhouse is directly adjacent to the village church.

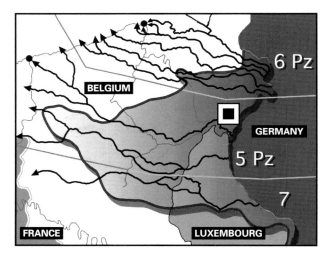

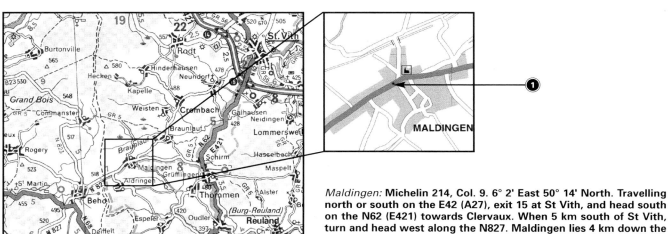

Maldingen: Michelin 214, Col. 9. 6° 2' East 50° 14' North. Travelling north or south on the E42 (A27), exit 15 at St Vith, and head south on the N62 (E421) towards Clervaux. When 5 km south of St Vith, turn and head west along the N827. Maldingen lies 4 km down the road.

Then: Malmédy's introduction to the battle came on December 16, 1944 by way of artillery fire from a K5 (E) 280mm long-range railway gun situated in Germany east of Monschau over 50 kilometres away! The town was also a prime strategic target for forward operations of SS-Obersturmbannführer Otto Skorzeny's Panzerbrigade 150 (Operation 'Greif'). On December 17, a special advance commando team led by Korvettenkapitän von Behr unintentionally entered the town early, and reported that it was only lightly held with a few roadblocks.

Now: In fact, Malmédy was occupied by the 120th Regiment of the 30th Infantry Division plus the 99th Infantry Battalion (a unit composed of Americans of Norwegian descent). These soldiers — Sergeants Greene and DeMott and Pfc Mozzani — perhaps from one of those units, relax on the corner of Rue du Châtelet at Rue Malgrave [1] on December 29, 1944, in one of the author's favourite comparisons. The house in the background is No. 6, Rue Malgrave. The fallen stone column, which once served as a seat for Mozzani, has been re-erected.

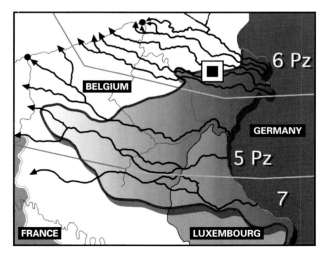

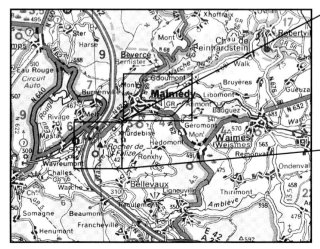

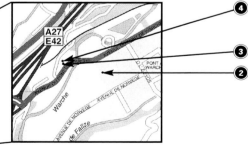

Malmédy: Michelin 214, Col. 9. 6° 2' East 50° 25' North. North or southbound on the E42 (A27), exit 11, direction Malmédy. The town is 2 km east on the N62.

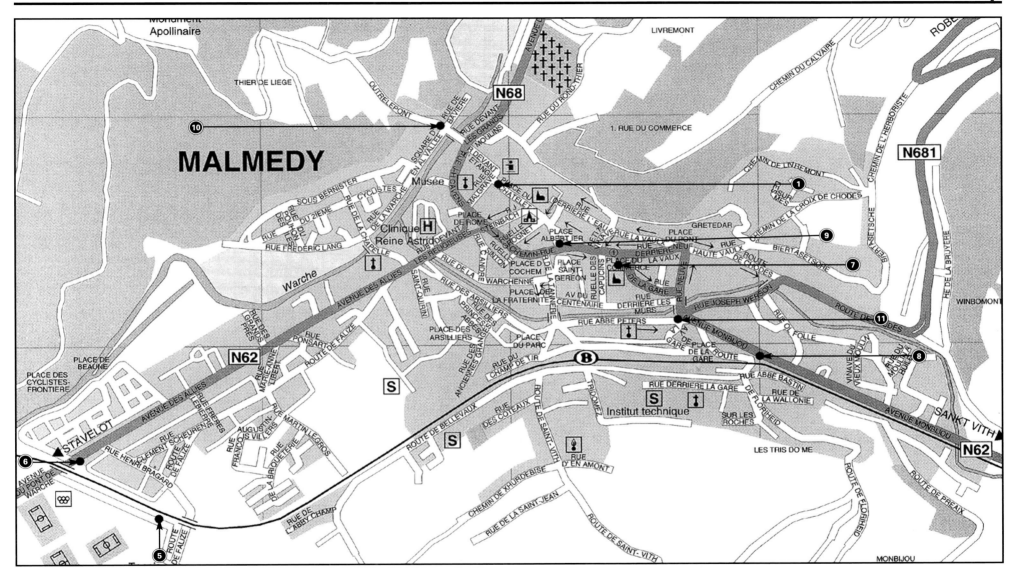

Then: **A scene of spectacular heroism. On December 21, 1944, Private Francis S. Currey of Company K, 120th Infantry, single-handedly halted the attack of Panzerbrigade 150 on Malmédy from the west. Using in turn a bazooka, an automatic rifle, anti-tank grenades and a machine gun on a half-track, he enabled many trapped US soldiers to escape from a house next to a paper mill.**

Now: **The open field [2] in front of the same paper mill where one of the Panther tanks was pictured next to the house, still wearing its' 'US' disguise. Though the building is long gone, the chimney of the paper mill and the small roof on the extreme left provide points of similarity.**

Then: **In the confusion of the attack by Kampfgruppe X of Panzerbrigade 150 on American forces at the mill, one of the leading Panthers managed to continue westwards in spite of the barrage. Crossing the small bridge over the Warche river, it halted next to a house holding the trapped Americans. It then began to fire back onto the house killing several of those inside.**

Now: **The American counter-bombardment soon found its mark and the disguised Panther (lettered B7) was hit and disabled. The passage of 50 years has seen both the tank and the house [3] swept away but the same small bridge over the Warche river remains on the right. The paper mill also still stands in the distance.**

Then: **A frontal view of the same Kampgruppe X Panther, B7. Its false Allied star can clearly be seen, as well as the fake metal sheeting added in an attempt to mimic the shape of an M10 tank destroyer. Given the hasty preparation, it was a passable ruse, yet the result was the same —defeat and death in Malmédy.**

Now: **The author found a few pieces of slate and stonework from the original house, along with the rough outline of its foundation just west of the Warche river bridge [4].**

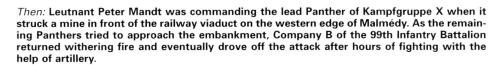

Then: **Leutnant Peter Mandt was commanding the lead Panther of Kampfgruppe X when it struck a mine in front of the railway viaduct on the western edge of Malmédy. As the remaining Panthers tried to approach the embankment, Company B of the 99th Infantry Battalion returned withering fire and eventually drove off the attack after hours of fighting with the help of artillery.**

Now: **After the battle, GIs examine Mandt's Panther: brushing off the snow, they reveal the bogus white star on the equally fake sheet metal around the turret. Over 50 years later the author visited the same spot [5] on what is today a small service road running parallel to the railway along the top of the embankment. The road links the main Avenue du Pont de Warche with the Route de Falize, the very road the Panthers drove down so long ago.**

Then: Following a German attack on Malmédy on the morning of December 22, 1944, the commander of the 120th Regiment, 30th Infantry Division, made the decision to blow both the bridge over the Warche river and the railway viaduct [6] closer into town. After being wired with over a ton of dynamite, the viaduct disintegrated.

Now: The same railway viaduct on the western edge of the town over 50 years later. Fully repaired and none the worse for wear, it looks like it would require another ton of explosive to bring it down once again! Today, it stretches out over the main road running in and out of Malmédy: the Avenue du Pont de Warche.

Then: Mounted up in Jeeps and ready to move out, elements of the 30th Infantry Division assemble in the heart of Malmédy in December 1944.

Now: This is the same narrow street corner [7] in Malmédy at the intersection of the Rue de la Gare, with the Place du Commerce, looking east.

Then: Hurry up and wait. Soldiers of the 30th Infantry Division, moving out of Malmédy towards Baugnez, line up along the main road leading east, adjacent to the rail tracks.

Now: The same view today, looking east along the railway line. This is the Avenue Mon-Bijou [8] as it leaves Malmédy as the present-day N62 towards Baugnez. The houses on the left provide the match alignment, Nos. 33 and 35 respectively.

Then: The dawn of December 28, 1944 reveals the shortcomings of US intelligence. On successive days, December 23 and December 24, US air forces bombed the town of Malmédy, despite it being continually held by American forces. The second raid was the most destructive after which the centre of the town lay in ruins.

Now: Such was the devastation, the new town square — the Place Albert Premier [9] — is largely unrecognisable with the wartime photo. This is, however, the exact comparison.

Then: An American soldier stands guard midst the destruction of Malmédy wrought by his own countrymen on the city they occupied. Mistaken intelligence led the Americans to bomb Malmédy believing it had been overrun by the Germans. A blanket of snow cannot hide the shame; nor the suffering of Malmédy's civilian inhabitants.

Now: With the same church in the background, the author matches the view looking east down the Rue devant l'Etang [10] towards the château in the centre of town. The photo was taken standing on a small bridge over the Warche river, with the Rue de la Warche behind the author.

Then: Reacting to several attacks on Malmédy by Panzerbrigade 150, the 30th Division issued orders that all the bridges and railway spans in the town be blown. The railway viaduct to the west (see opposite page) was demolished but this bridge over the Warchenne river, though wired with 850 pounds of dynamite, was not as the town itself was never substantially threatened.

Now: The bridge [11] lives to tell the tale. This is the largest of six bridges in Malmédy looking north at Rue Neuve and Rue Abbé Peters. The altered building on the right is No. 51 but most of the buildings in the street remain unchanged. The triple set of pointed roofs in the upper left centre of each photo line up perfectly, confirming the match and location.

Then: With the capture of the road junction at Baraque de Fraiture on December 23 by SS-Panzer-Grenadier-Regiment 4 (2. SS-Panzer-Division), the stage was set for the assault on Manhay to the north. The attack by 4. Kompanie, of SS-Panzer-Regiment 2, began late on Christmas Eve, the fighting quickly deteriorating into a desperate tank battle between the aggressive Panthers of 2. SS-Panzer and the confused Shermans of the 7th Armored. Accurate fire from the Panthers took a heavy toll of American tanks, and Manhay was in German hands on Christmas Day.

Now: Under similar snowy conditions 50 years later, the author rephotographs the Panther graveyard of long ago. All told, over a dozen Panthers were knocked out in the area, this one [1] lying beside the present-day N651 (Rue du Pré des Fosses). The driveway in the foreground leads to the Athénée Durbuy-Manhay school.

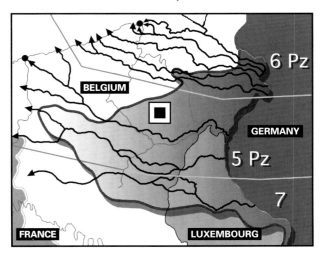

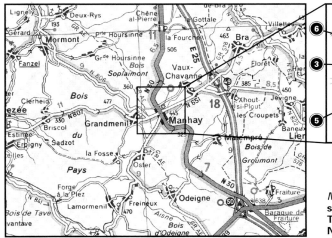

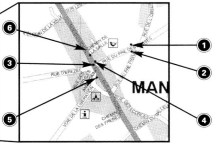

Manhay: Michelin 214, Col. 7. 5° 41' East 50° 17' North. North or south on the E25 (A26), leave at exit 49 in the direction of Manhay. The village lies 4 km west on the N651 at the intersection with the N30.

Then: The cold logistics behind the previous photo: the vital roads leading away from Manhay must be cleared for forward progress. American engineers had a busy time in and around Manhay at the end of 1944, clearing up the finest of the 2. SS-Panzer-Division.

Now: Standing beside No. 10 on the Rue du Pré des Fosses [2] facing north-west, the scene of long ago is revealed with the shoulder of the road now filled in to form a car park for the school. The house and the long farm building in the distance serve as points of comparison.

Then: US Signal Corps photographer Tech/5 Hugh McHugh captures more handiwork by the US engineers beside the crossroads in Manhay on December 30, 1944. Another disabled Panther of 2. SS-Panzer-Division lies undignified on its side while farm animals mill about in the snow and cold.

Now: Several new buildings have since been erected around the crossroads [3] including the large house rebuilt in a somewhat smaller style. Manhay is seen under the blanket of a cold foggy day. This is the view looking directly south; to the left, the Rue du Vicinal (N30) heads towards Houffalize; to the right, the Voie de la Libération leads to Dochamps.

Then: The strategic crossroads in Manhay, after the battle. No single photograph so captures the devastation and tenacity of the fight for the village as this shot taken after it had been recaptured. Manhay suffered terribly under American artillery fire, bombing and strafing. The ferocious nature of the tank battle is typified by the mixture of German and American armour in this photo alone; two Shermans and one Panther, along with sundry other destroyed vehicles.

Now: Having been rebuilt with clean, widened roads and brand-new buildings, one can scarcely imagine the scene of 50 years ago. The view [4] is looking south with the Rue du Vicinal (N30) running up to the left towards Houffalize; the Voie de la Libération, heading for Dochamps in the centre, and the Rue d'Erezée on the right leading to Grandmenil. Special thanks to Micheline Cornet, who allowed the author into her second-floor living room to take this picture looking out over the crossroads; her husband even had to move a Christmas tree in front of the window to give the author access to it!

Then: In an attitude of supplication and defeat, one of the Manhay Panthers (the same one as on page 187 bottom) [5] lies beside the main road covered with a blanket of snow.

Now: The 2. SS-Panzer-Division Panther once lay here, alongside the present-day N30 which heads south to Houffalize. The house on the left, across the Rue du Vicinal, has had its façade completely remodelled though the positions of the window and door remain. Further confirmation of the location can be seen in the houses on the right.

Then: With the signpost indicating the many directions possible from the crossroads, a wartime photographer captures Allied aircraft in the skies over Manhay, Belgium.

Now: Cloud-matching? Tongue-in-cheek, the author looks wistfully skyward in hopes of glimpsing Allied aircraft but alas, they are long gone. Though the cloud patterns are vaguely similar, there is no trace of the road sign which has been replaced with one of the functional blue-and-white versions of modern-day Belgium. The roofline belongs to No. 29 Rue du Vicinal [6].

Then: By dawn of December 16, the 2. Panzer-Division had crossed the Our river at Dasburg, and its Panzer-Grenadier-Regiment 304, was attacking the division's first objective: Marnach in Luxembourg. Later that day, it was joined by Panzer-Regiment 3 and by December 17 the village was in German hands. Just over a month later the Americans were back: on January 25, 1945, the 26th Infantry Division retook Clervaux, and pursued the retreating Germans through Marnach and back into Germany. This German 12-ton Zugkraftwagen, used to pull artillery pieces as well as ferry soldiers, was left behind.

Now: The precise parking bay [1] for the German prime mover pictured over 50 years later in the bright sunshine. The large farmhouse in the centre has gone though its gate remains on the right. Otherwise, the view is identical with the same characteristic roofline of No. 18 Haaptstrooss and even the foliage on the wall! The main road in the centre is the N18, which runs from Clervaux to the west to join the N7 in the east, where it then becomes the N10 to Dasburg, Germany.

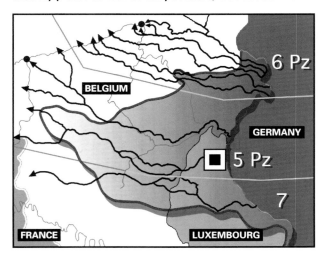

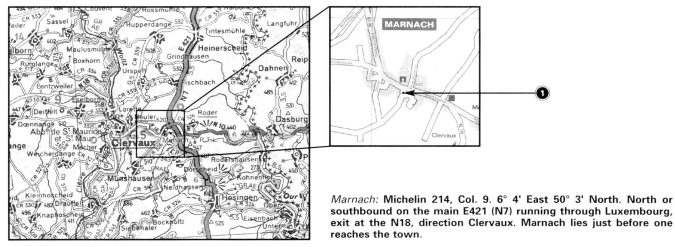

Marnach: Michelin 214, Col. 9. 6° 4' East 50° 3' North. North or southbound on the main E421 (N7) running through Luxembourg, exit at the N18, direction Clervaux. Marnach lies just before one reaches the town.

Then: The stretch of road running between Dasburg in Germany and Marnach in Luxembourg constituted the first six kilometres of the Rollbahn attack route assigned to 2. Panzer-Division. Making rapid progress, the vanguards reached Marnach on the evening of the first day of the Ardennes hostilities. A month later the road itself, once the conveyor of German armoured might, would become its graveyard. Here an American soldier peeks inside a gutted Jagdpanzer IV.

Now: The same road and same location 50 years on finds a peaceful field. This is the view [1] looking north-west from the N10, exactly 500 metres east of the N18 junction at Marnach. The hill in the distance with its deeply cut road can be matched today, along with the copse of trees on the right as the road runs off right to left in the distance.

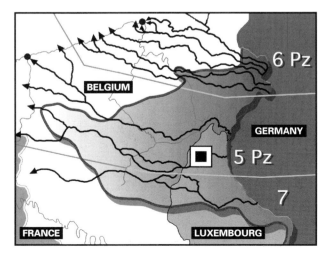

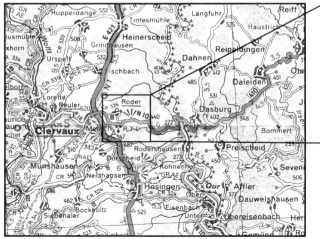

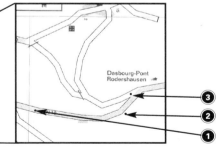

Marnach-Dasburg: **Michelin 214, Col. 9. 6° 5' East 50° 3' North. North or southbound on the main E421 (N7) running through Luxembourg, exit at the N18, direction Dasburg. On reaching Dasburg, take the N10 east. The stretch of road photographed begins 500 meters along the N10.**

Then: Hidden behind a copse of trees along the road to Dasburg lay this Panther tank, a remnant of the failed German assault. Though more than likely belonging to the 2. Panzer-Division, by the time the fighting finished, the German effort had become so confused and disintegrated that divisional integrity had collapsed.

Now: Fifty years having passed on the Dasburg road, the author stands alongside the same copse of trees [2], hoping to find the Panther still in place! But alas, the Panther is long gone and today no vehicles lurk behind the trees.

Then: With the same copse of trees on the far right that hid the Panther in the previous photo, another fighting alongside it on the same road lost its head. Turretless tanks were usually the result of strikes by either bombs or artillery and, though the precise cause of this Panther's demise remains unknown, the Allies did mount a bombing run on the nearby bridge over the Our river on January 22, 1945, catching many fleeing German vehicles.

Now: The precise spot [3] in the road to Dasburg as it is today. Off to the right stands the same copse of trees though grown denser with the passage of time.

Marvie

Then: **With Bastogne secured and the battle won, soldiers of the 101st Airborne Division march out through Marvie, Belgium. They are headed east towards Luxembourg and Wiltz — the first large town over the border.**

Now: **Looking down the N84 (the Rue de Wiltz) east of Bastogne as it passes Marvie, the author captures the same route [1] that the 'Screaming Eagles' took 50 years ago. This photo reveals the extent of the suburbanisation which has since taken place all around Bastogne.**

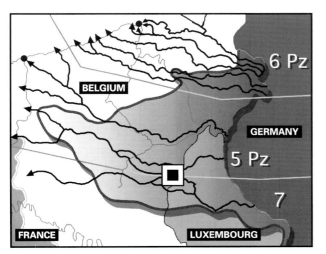

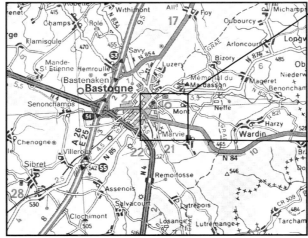

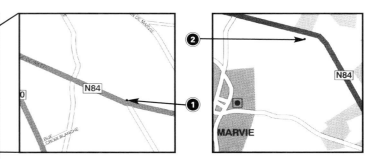

Marvie: **Michelin 214, Col. 8. 5° 44' East 49° 58' North. North or southbound on either the E25 (A26) or the N4, exit 54 and head direction town centre, Bastogne. At the major intersection at the town square, head east on the N84 towards Wiltz. Marvie lies 2 km east of Bastogne.**

193

Then: **By December 20, Bastogne and its outskirts were technically an American island in a German sea. With the 2. Panzer-Division flowing north of Bastogne and Panzer-Lehr to the south, the Germans began a series of probing attacks on the town itself. On the morning of the 20th, Kampfgruppe 901 of the Panzer-Lehr attacked the village of Marvie on the eastern outskirts of Bastogne only to run smack into Team O'Hara which was supported by the 2nd Battalion of the 327th Glider Infantry Regiment. Repulsed, Kampfgruppe 901 tried again on December 23, this time capturing half the village in heavy fighting. Taken in the spring of 1945, this grainy photo reveals a Panzer IV belonging to the Panzer-Lehr rusting away in a field next to a farmhouse.**

Now: **Over 50 years later, Bastogne and the surrounding villages have spread out and this is the view along the N84 just north of Marvie, looking west back into Bastogne. When the author began to search for this location [2], knowing that Panzer-Lehr came down this very road, he was dismayed to find row upon row of houses, many newly-built or being built. Incredibly, however, the same farmhouse with its twin chimneys stood out amid the other houses as did the smaller house to its right. The photo was taken next to No. 7 on the N84 — the Panzer lay just to the left of the car parked on the right and today would be right in the front garden!**

Then: By late evening on December 20, 1944, Kampfgruppe Bayer of the 116. Panzer-Division had taken the Belgian village of Dochamps. Moving quickly under cover of darkness, Oberst Johannes Bayer led his forces through Devantave to the west, into and beyond Beffe, through the villages of Trinal and Melines to reach the road from Soy to Hotton. In doing so, he had inadvertently slipped between the US task forces of Hogan to the west and Orr to the east. The road now lay open to attack Hotton. Along the route between Melines and Trinal, this Panther belonging to Panzer-Regiment 16 struck a mine and threw a track.

Now: In another of the author's favourite 'then and now' comparisons, the lonely stretch of road [1] where the Panther once sat matched up perfectly over 50 years later. Helping frame the location is the fact that this small stretch of road is bounded on both sides by forests and has the Roumière hills in the background. The fact that flowers bloom where panzers once rolled makes the comparison all the more poignant. They came this way — yet life moves on.

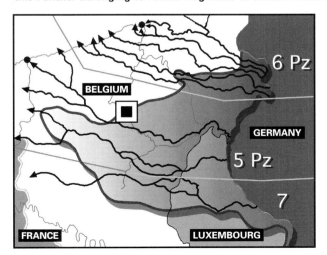

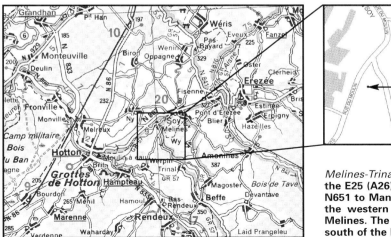

Melines-Trinal: **Michelin 214, Col. 7. 5° 30' East 50° 16' North.** From the E25 (A26) north or southbound exit 49, then head west on the N651 to Manhay. Then take the N807 west past Erezée to Soy. At the western edge of Soy, turn off onto the Rue du Moulin to Melines. The location between Melines and Trinal is exactly 1.7 km south of the N807 (Rue Grand Mont) in Soy.

Then: Having disengaged from the area around Hotton on December 23 after their failed attack, a tired Kampfgruppe Bayer nevertheless went on to attack Verdenne, south-west of Hotton, in an attempt to cut the March-Hotton road. Though it seized Verdenne on the 24th, elements of the Kampfgruppe were cut off from the remainder of the division, and over Christmas and the following day, the position became untenable. As a result, it was forced to fight its way out to German lines.

Now: The wartime photograph shows some of the vehicular casualties of a diversionary attack on Ménil, a village just to the east of the Verdenne pocket, on December 26 though the picture was most likely taken in January 1945. These two SdKfz 251 armoured personnel carriers belonging to the 116. Panzer-Division lay shattered and still in the snow south of the village which can be seen in the distance. The present-day view was taken standing on a small rise in the road. This is the Rue du Bois leading into Ménil from the south.

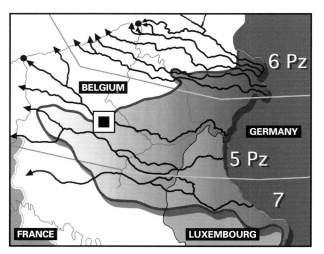

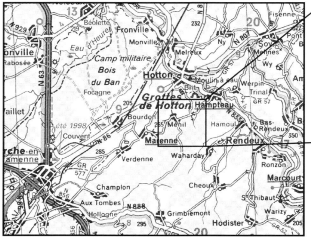

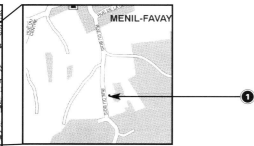

Menil: Michelin 214, Col. 7. 5° 27' East 50° 15' North. North or southbound on the N4 (E40), exit at Marche-en-Famenne. Head out of Marche on the N86 towards Hotton and 4 km east of Marche lies Bourdon. Turn right to Marenne. Continue through Marenne towards Ménil. You will enter Ménil from the west; continue through the village, exiting to the south where the location lies.

Then: The attack route utilised by Kampfgruppe Peiper in the battle of the Ardennes has been well-documented. On December 17, 1944, after crossing the German border at Losheim, the battlegroup turned north before reaching Berterath and entered Hüllscheid. From there, the group moved through Merlscheid, a very small Belgian village south-east of Lanzerath. Despite its small size, the road was defended by the Americans — this 76mm anti-tank gun being knocked out opposite the village church.

Now: The author walks in the footsteps of the German war photographer. The anti-tank gun sat right here in front of a small farm [1]. The house on the right, No. 12, has been completely rebuilt but, the tell-tale roof on the farmhouse to its left, complete with its unique three white patches, clearly identifies the location.

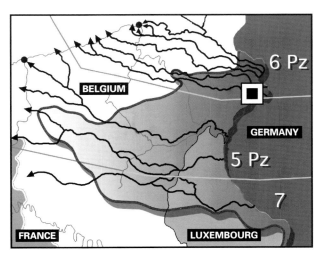

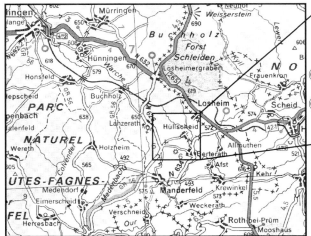

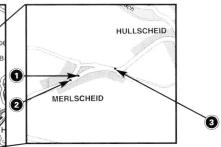

Merlscheid: Michelin 214, Col. 10. 6° 22' East 50° 22' North. North or southbound on the E42 (A27), exit 11, direction east to Malmédy. From Malmédy and Waimes, continue east along the N632 into Bütgenbach. Turn right to Büllingen, then east to Losheimergraben. Cross the German border then turn south onto B265 to Losheim, and 2 km to the south turn right onto the Belgian N634 to Berterath. Go right into Hüllscheid and arrive at Merlscheid.

Then: After picturing this scene from in front of the American anti-tank gun, the German photographer walks behind the gun, turns, and photographs members of 1.SS-Panzer-Division rolling past. The chapel of Merlscheid [2] stands in the background.

Now: A timeless comparison 50 years later. Past this small chapel moved one of the most notorious battle divisions ever assembled in SS military history. The photo was taken standing next to No. 12.

Then: As lead elements of the battlegroup began moving out of Lanzerath, the Americans, desperate to stem the tide of the advancing spearhead, began to call in fighter-bombers. While in Merlscheid, a German photographer must have heard the approach of a P-47 whereupon, turning to his left, he snapped the approach run of the Thunderbolt diving to strafe the column, the head of which now stretched past Buchholz and into Honsfeld.

Now: The wartime shot must certainly be one of the earliest photographic records of American aircraft responding to the German attack around about noon on December 17. Fifty years later, despite the absence of a droning Pratt & Whitney R-2800-59, the author photographs the same patch of sky, with the corner of the same house (No. 9, along the unnamed street through Merlscheid).

Then: January 6, 1945, found the British 29th Armoured Brigade occupying the tiny village of Mesnil-St Blaise, just south of Dinant in Belgium. This formation was tasked with defending the Meuse river sector from Namur to Dinant. As the tide of the battle turned, the brigade moved east in support of the British 6th Airborne Division. Here a British soldier walks past a Daimler 'Dingo' scout car belonging to a medical unit on the main street.

Now: With both the snow and history having melted away, Rue d'Hastière [1] basks in bright sunshine. This is the view looking directly south, the house on the left being the rear of No. 1 on the Rue des Écoles.

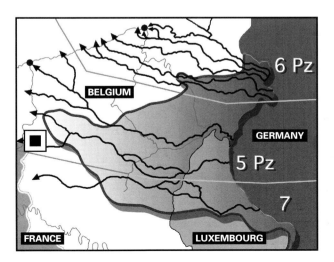

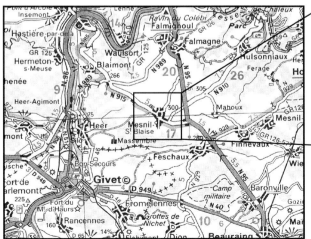

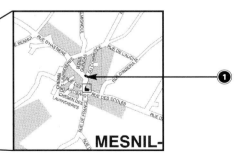

Mesnil-St Blaise: Michelin 214, Col. 5. 4° 53' East 50° 10' North. North or southbound on the E411 (A4), exit 22 onto the N94, heading south. At the village of Vignée, turn right (west) onto the N911, direction Beauraing. Enter Beauraing, then bear north out of the town along the N95, direction Dinant. 1.5 km past Feschaux along the N95, turn west onto the N915, direction Mesnil-St Blaise, entering the village from the east.

Then: **During the first three days of the Ardennes offensive, Grenadier-Regiment 914 of the 352. Volks-Grenadier-Division operating with its sister regiments 915 and 916 to its left, pushed deep into American-held territory north and east of Diekirch. The strategic heights around Michelau, manned by the 687th Field Artillery Battalion, had to be given up under the pressure of the attack and the village was overrun, as was Diekirch to its south. After heavy fighting, Diekirch was retaken by the Americans on January 19, 1945, whereupon the 5th Infantry Division moved northwards towards Michelau and Lipperscheid.**

Now: **The same street [1] in Michelau, Luxembourg, where soldiers of the 1st Platoon, 5th Cavalry Reconnaissance Troop, once descended into the picturesque village. We are looking up the Rue de la Chapelle at the point where it intersects the Rue de Flebour. With the buildings to the left and right having been demolished, the farmhouse in the distance (No. 11, Rue de Flebour) is the sole survivor to help marry up the comparison.**

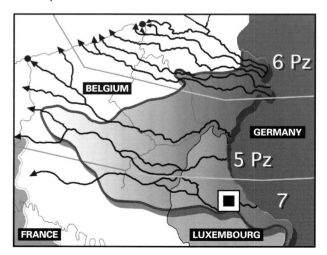

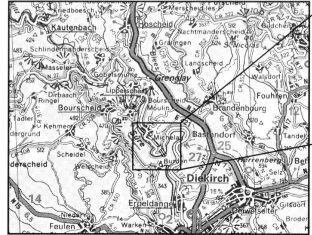

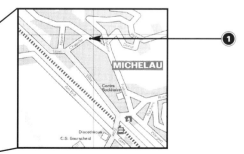

Michelau: **Michelin 214, Col. 9. 6° 5' East 49° 54' North. From Bastogne to the west, take the N84/N15 west direction Wiltz/Ettelbruck. Ettelbruck lies 41 km to the south-east of Bastogne along the N15. Immediately east of Ettelbruck, on the city outskirts, take the N27 (not the N27a) north to Erpeldange. Follow the N27 through Erpeldange north as it twists and turns along the Sûre river. Approximately 11 km north of Erpeldange lies the village of Michelau.**

Then: After capturing Büllingen on the morning of December 17, 1944, Kampfgruppe Peiper, in the lead on Rollbahn D for the 1. SS-Panzer-Division, then turned towards Moderscheid, Belgium. Rolling through the tiny village around 10.30 a.m. meeting only token US resistance, Peiper continued on towards Schoppen to the north-west. Yet while at Büllingen, Peiper had missed a golden opportunity to outflank both the 99th Infantry and the 2nd Infantry Divisions which were providing very stubborn resistance in the Krinkelt sector to the north.

Now: After the battle. Then, seven dead Germans lay under a blanket of snow at the edge of a small hill overlooking the tiny village; now, 50 years later, the same spot is identified. Though the trees block the view of houses in the distance, the road directions remain the same. The final confirming clue can be seen in the upper right of the photo: the same farmhouse, though built-up, retains the original divided window. The hill [1] which once bore the graves is directly opposite the village church.

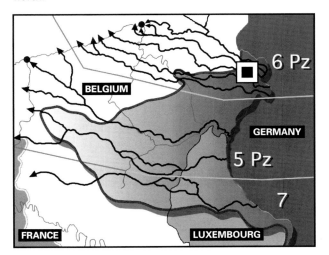

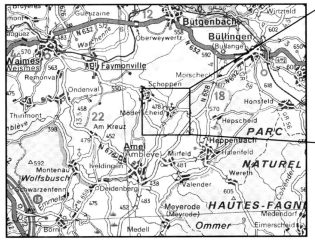

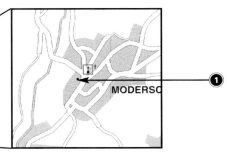

Moderscheid: Michelin 214, Col. 9. 6° 12' East 50° 23' North. North or southbound along the E42 (A27), exit 11, direction Malmédy along the N62. Continue towards Waimes then head east along the N632 into Bütgenbach. In the centre, turn right continuing to Büllingen. Approximately 2 km before the village, turn right (south) onto the N658 to Amel (Amblève). In 4 km turn right to Moderscheid and enter the village from the east.

Then: **Moestroff, a small village in Luxembourg lying peacefully on the Sûre river east of Diekirch, was attacked and overrun by elements of Grenadier-Regiment 915, 352. Volks-Grenadier-Division, on December 16, 1944. American forces managed to reverse the situation by the end of December and, by January 18, 1945, the 8th Infantry Regiment (9th Division), having massed three battalions along the river, attacked in force. Two makeshift bridges were built near Moestroff; US forces swept into the area and the village was taken on January 19.**

Now: **The same location [1] over 50 years later looking east towards the N19 in the distance. It was here that the 1st Platoon of Company G, 2nd Battalion of the 8th Infantry, stormed the bridge across the river again two days later — this time staged for the camera. In fact, the troops are attacking in the wrong direction, west into Moestroff itself! The new bridge replaced the temporary one built by the Americans during the war. Though the distant view is obscured by trees, the same houses still stand, as does the one on the far right.**

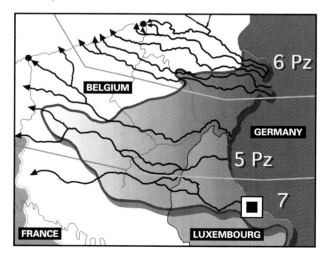

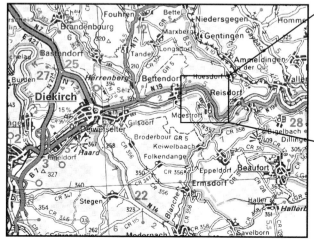

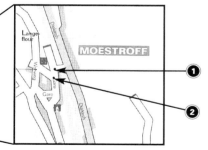

Moestroff: **Michelin 214, Col. 9. 6° 15' East 49° 52' North. From Bastogne in the west, head east along the N84, which becomes the N15 at the Luxembourg border. Continue along the N15 to Ettelbruck. In Ettelbruck, head towards Diekirch. Heading east out of Diekirch, Moestroff lies 3 km east of Bettendorf along the N19. Cross a small bridge over the river to enter the village from the east.**

Then: Members of the 2nd Battalion, 8th Infantry, 4th Division, move through the Luxembourg village of Moestroff having recaptured it on January 19, 1945. They are marching south, parallel to the Sûre river which lies off to the right of the photo. Ahead lies Echternach.

Now: An accurate photo comparison captures the scene 50 years on. This is the view looking north; the photo was taken at the intersection [2] of Rue de la Gare and Am Wohwee in the middle of the village. The farmhouse in the left distance is No. 2, Am Wohwee.

Then: **With Bastogne having been relieved on December 26, the 6th Armored Division continued to drive north-eastwards yet tenacious opposition by the 12. SS-Panzer-Division delayed their progress. After heavy fighting, this elite force had retaken Arloncourt, Mageret and Bizory from the Americans but by January 6, 1945 the division's strength was spent and it was ordered into reserve with 5. Panzer-Armee. In vain support, armoured elements of schwere Panzer-Abteilung 506 sought to shore up the fading effort, this King Tiger meeting its fate in the small village of Moinet.**

Now: **Over 50 years later, on a similar snowy day, the author seeks out the same location [1] where the king of battle was finally disabled by no less than eight armour-piercing shells fired by armour of the 15th Tank Battalion, 6th Armored Division. The same house on the right in the wartime photo still stands behind the newer home in the present-day picture. The corrugated metal barn is a recent addition.**

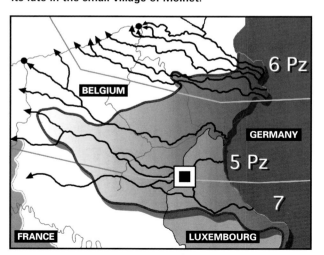

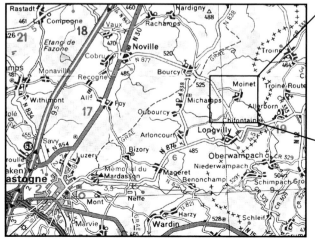

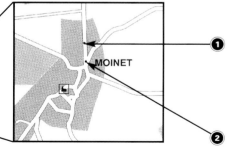

Moinet: **Michelin 214, Col. 8. 5° 51' East 50° 3' North. North or southbound on the E25 (A26), exit 52, heading south on the N847 a short distance to the N30. Head south on the N30 direction Noville. At Noville, turn left heading east on the N877 to Bourcy. Continue east past Bourcy approximately 2 km to Moinet.**

Then: **Morale is everything in battle. On January 4, 1945, General George S. Patton, Jr. commanding the Third Army commented on the quality of the opposition he continued to face north-east of Bastogne: 'They are colder, hungrier and weaker than we, to be sure. But they are still doing a great piece of fighting.' Compliments indeed to SS-Panzer-Grenadier-Regiment 25 of the 12. SS-Panzer-Division facing the 6th Armored Division. After the battle, a US soldier, walking through the small farm village of Moinet, Belgium, encounters written testimony of their spirit; graffiti on the side of a farmhouse [2] proclaims: 'Our Führer orders us, we will obey'.**

Now: **Fifty years later, the author drove slowly through the snow, stopping alongside No. 33 — the same house seen in the picture opposite — and history. The characteristics of the wall are still there with the two windows on the left and the rectangular slot in the wall on the centre right. A vent on the centre left has been added, along with a door on the right. Despite these changes, the scene is timeless and with snow on the ground and the same peeling white paint, it seems like only yesterday. Immediately after this photo was taken, the owner of the house, an old lady, cheerfully called out. She then walked the author to the centre of the village, sweeping her hand left to right. 'They came this way', she said. 'First the Germans, then the Americans.'**

Then: **By December 26, 1944, the entire effort of XXXXVII. Panzerkorps was spent, and its units forced onto the defensive, the Panzer-Lehr taking up positions between St Hubert and Remagne. On December 30, VIII Corps launched their attack in this sector, led by the 11th Armored and the 87th Infantry Divisions. Forward elements of the 345th Regiment of the 87th reached Moircy only to be driven back by Panzer-Lehr but, after sustained attacks, the village was taken the same day only to be lost again the following day. The 87th Division finally secured the area between St Hubert, Moircy and Bonnerue on January 2.**

Now: **Walking in the footsteps of the 87th Infantry. This is the view looking west up the Rue de Vesqueville [1]. The house on the far right is No. 28; those along the upper left and centre in the distance are Nos. 27, 29 and 31.**

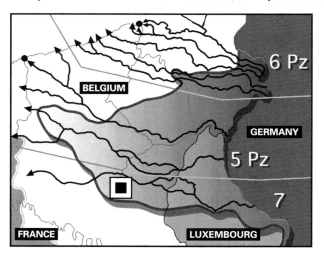

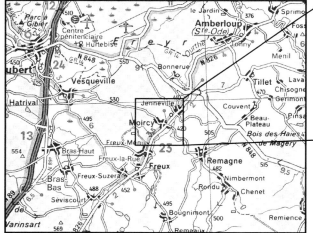

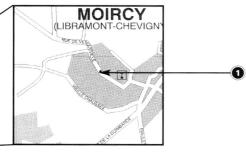

Moircy: **Michelin 214, Col. 7. 5° 28' East 49° 59' North. North or southbound on the E411 (A4), exit 26, heading north on the N40 into Libramont/Recogne. Leave Libramont heading north-east along the N826 — Moircy lies approximately 16 km away.**

Morhet

Then: Moving west from Drauffelt, Luxembourg, on December 18, 1944, the Panzer-Lehr-Division advanced through Eschweiler, Derenbach, Oberwampach, Niederwampach and on to Mageret. After an attempt to capture Neffe immediately east of Bastogne was repulsed, Kampfgruppe 902 (Major Gerd von Fallois) swept south of the besieged town and moved on St Hubert via Morhet to its east. Following the VIII Corps counter-attack, Panzer-Lehr was pushed back east through Morhet. In their retreat, they left behind this Bergepanther, a specially-equipped armoured recovery vehicle built on a Panther chassis.

Now: With the farmhouse on the right and the house on the left providing the perfect frame, this is the same place [1] photographed 50 years later. The location lies on the N848 running through Morhet, the view looking west. The house on the left is No. 97; the farmhouse on the right now consists of two separate dwellings, No. 97A and No. 97B. The photo was taken standing in front of the Café de la Jeunesse, No. 101.

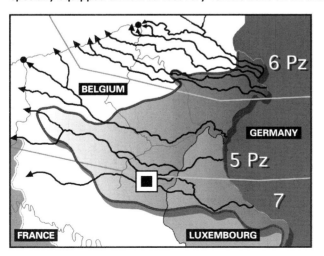

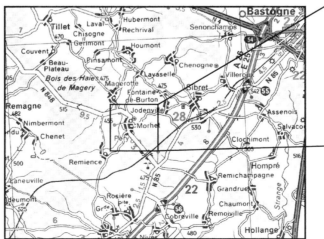

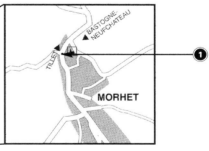

Morhet: Michelin 214, Col. 7. 5° 35' East 49° 57' North. North or southbound on the E25 (A26), exit 56 near Cobreville, heading north on the N848 to the intersection with the N85. Turn right (north) on the N85 to Sibret. After 2 km turn left (west) onto the N848 to St Hubert. Morhet lies 3 km further on.

Then: Within three days of the launch of the Ardennes offensive, Bastogne was already under threat of becoming completely surrounded and cut off. The two powerful spearheads of the XXXXVII. Panzerkorps (2. Panzer-Division and the Panzer-Lehr-Division) had literally blasted their way through the screen provided by the American task forces. Approaching the town, each force began a series of probing attacks and on December 19 the 5. Kompanie of Panzer-Lehr-Regiment moved on Neffe, immediately east of Bastogne, taking the village the same day after a brief fire-fight. This Panther 533 was disabled by a mine.

Now: Visiting Neffe today, just down the road from Bastogne, one is struck by how close the Panzer-Lehr penetrated towards the town before being stopped. No. 93, where the Panther from 5. Kompanie of the Panzer-Lehr-Regiment was knocked out [1], has been completely rebuilt on its original foundation.

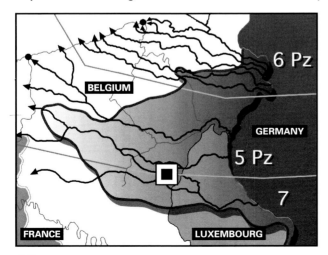

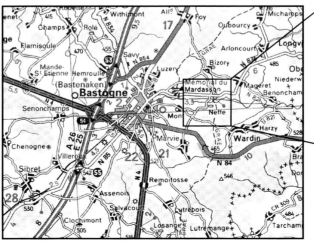

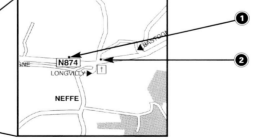

Neffe: Michelin 214, Col. 8. 5° 46' East 50° 1' North. North or southbound on the E25 (A26), exit 54, Bastogne towards the city centre along the N84. At the town square in the centre of Bastogne, turn left onto the N874 to Clervaux. Approximately 3 km east out of Bastogne along the N874 lies the village of Neffe.

Then: **After the battle for Neffe was over, the 'calling cards' of two nations lie disabled outside the village church [2]. For the Panzer-Lehr-Division an armoured personnel carrier; for the 6th Armored Division, a Sherman tank, ostensibly knocked out by a German panzerschreck missile fired from the church. Given the snowy conditions, the photograph was most likely taken in early January.**

Now: **Without the photographers having recorded the events of long ago, it would be hard to imagine what once transpired on this spot. Fifty years have passed and the church lives on, minus the trappings of war. The church itself lies directly alongside the N874; the view is looking south. Today Neffe is just another peaceful village along the busy road linking Bastogne with Mageret and Longvilly to the east.**

Then: **By the evening of December 19, 1944, St Vith and its outskirts was confronted by 5. Panzer-Armee's attack by the 18. and 62. Volks-Grenadier-Divisions. Operating in the northern sector with 18. Volks-Grenadier-Division, the Führer-Begleit-Brigade attacked at dawn on December 20, and succeeded in taking the village of Nieder-Emmels, just north of Hünningen (Hunnange). The 120th Infantry, 30th Division, recaptured Hünningen on January 20, 1945, and several days later, soldiers of the 'Hickory Division' were pictured marching through the village towards Hünningen in the distance.**

Now: **Looking south-east down the N62 towards Hünningen, the author photographs the same stretch of road 50 years later. The picture was taken immediately north of the village standing in the drive of No. 85. Today, the dead German grenadier would be lying just off the road to the right of the entrance.**

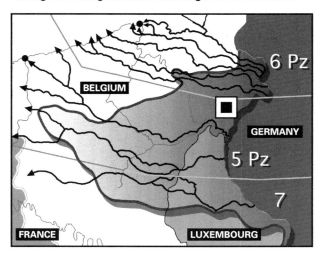

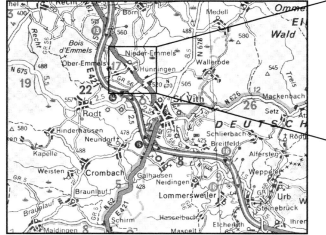

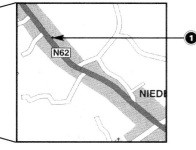

Nieder-Emmels: **Michelin 214, Col. 9. 6° 5' East 50° 18' North. North or southbound on the E421, exit 14, heading east on the N670, direction Hünningen. At the intersection of the N62 and the N670, turn left (north) onto the N62, direction Malmédy. Approximately 2 km north of the intersection lies Nieder-Emmels.**

Then: **By December 30, 1944, the battle situation in Luxembourg immediately south-west of Wiltz had become so precarious for the Germans that the 9. Volks-Grenadier-Division was committed to assist LIII. Armeekorps in defence of the area around Nothum yet by early January the area fell to the advancing US Third Army. This Signal Corps photograph, taken on January 9, shows soldiers of the 90th Division marching through the village. They have just passed a line of armoured vehicles belonging to the 773rd Tank Destroyer Battalion. Lying at the foot of the M10 tank destroyer in the right foreground is the commander of the 712nd Tank Battalion, Lieutenant Colonel George B. Randolph, killed by shrapnel as he jumped from his Jeep which can be seen in the distance.**

Now: **Walking the streets of Nothum 50 years later, on a similar snowy day, the author pauses to capture the identical photo comparison. The view is looking south-west down Duerfstrooss [1], where it intersects Um Knupp. The houses on the right are Nos. 2 and 4. With the house in the left distance still standing unaltered, the scene of a former tragedy is complete. With tracks in the snow, it almost seems as though the tanks have just departed — along with the body of Colonel Randolph.**

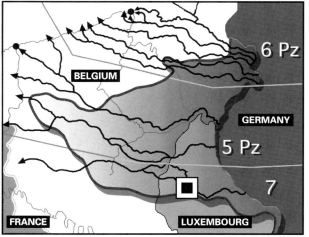

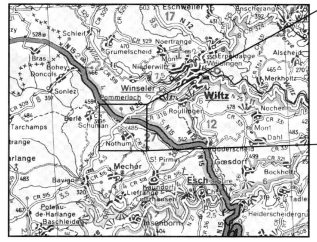

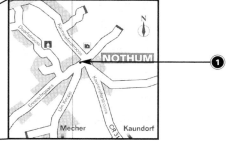

Nothum: **Michelin 214, Col. 8. 5° 53' East 49° 56' North. North or southbound on the E25 (A26), exit 54, Bastogne, direction city centre along the N84. Leave Bastogne travelling east along the N84, towards Wiltz. On reaching the Luxembourg border the N84 becomes the N15. Continue east on the N15 to the intersection of the N26, which leads into Wiltz to the north. Nothum lies just south of this intersection.**

Then: **As the German noose tightened around Bastogne on December 19, 1944, several key villages on the outskirts began to be contested as the 2. Panzer-Division fought its way into the area. At dawn, Oberst Meinrad von Lauchert's forces attacked Noville but were initially repulsed by Team Desobry and the 506th Parachute Infantry Regiment. After heavy fighting, the village fell on December 20. On January 5, 1945, the 12. SS-Panzer-Division was closing on Bastogne yet the deteriorating situation on the northern front forced it to pull back and by the second week of January Noville was back in American hands.**

Now: **Fifty years later the town hall [1] stands completely restored, and with time and history having long since swept away the German armour, private and commercial transport now pass down the N30 into Bastogne. Despite the rebuilding, the small house on the left of the wartime photo stills stands, behind the town hall. Here, a Sturmgeschütz once lay shattered in a bomb crater.**

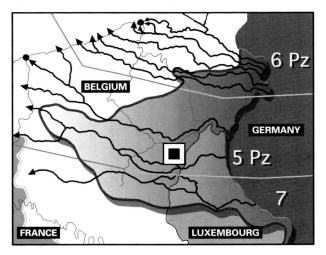

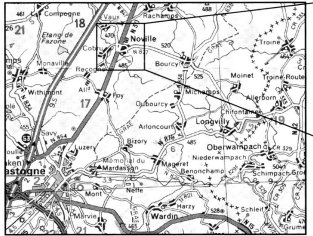

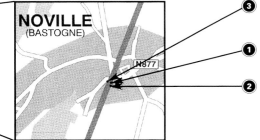

Noville: **Michelin 214, Col. 8. 5° 45' East 50° 4' North. North or southbound on the E25 (A26), exit 52, heading east on the N847. At the intersection of the N30, turn right (south) towards Noville which is 2 km south.**

Then: **Amidst the devastation of a recaptured Noville, the Americans plan their advance to the east. On January 16, 1945, an impromptu roadside meeting was held in the rubble of Noville, with Major General Maxwell D. Taylor, commander of 101st Airborne Division and his deputy, Brigadier General Gerald J. Higgins, conferring with Colonel Robert F. Sink (506th Parachute Infantry Regiment), Colonel Joseph H. Harper (327th Glider Infantry Regiment) and Major James J. Hatch (CO of the 2nd Battalion 502nd Parachute Infantry). The 101st played a significant part in the defence and break-out from Bastogne. The extent of the destruction is clearly evident; the village suffering tremendously as it lay along a strategic transit route.**

Now: **They met on this spot [2] 50 years ago. Now the tidy intersection is pictured under a steady drizzle of wintry rain, with the traffic light indicating that once again all is clear for car and lorry. The photo was taken with the church wall directly behind the author looking north down the N30.**

Then: **Noville paid the price of total war. After the battle, destroyed vehicles from both sides lay about the crucial intersection [3] in the centre of the village. In the left foreground, the same Sturmgeschütz shown on the previous page lies half buried in a bomb crater. Virtually all the houses in Noville were gutted by artillery and bombardment. American soldiers can be seen walking through the devastation, taking stock of the damage.**

Now: **With houses restored and roads cleared, Noville is a thriving village. This is the view looking north-west along the N30. The large house on the right, completely rebuilt, is No. 45 Rue du Général Desobry, which street joins the N30 from the right. It was named after (then) Major William R. Desobry who gallantly fought for Noville on December 19, 1944. Hit by a shell fragment, he was evacuated to Bastogne during the night only to be captured en route.**

Then: Oberwampach, Luxembourg, saw armoured elements of Kampfgruppe 902 (Oberst Joachim von Poschinger) of the Panzer-Lehr-Division rumble through on December 18, 1944, heading for Bastogne to the west. Following the failed attempt to capture the encircled and besieged town, Oberwampach played host to American soldiers in January 1945 as the 6th Armored Division pushed the 5. Panzer-Armee back. Seemingly oblivious to the massive hulk of a Tiger I, Private Virgil McWilliams and Sergeant Glenn Keller of the 358th Infantry, 90th Division, gaze down the hill to assess the situation.

Now: As we travel through time, the temporal passes away leaving bricks and mortar to match the comparison taken at position [1]. The corner of the farmhouse can just be made out in the wartime photograph to the far right, behind the Tiger which was numbered 411 and belonged to schwere SS-Panzer-Abteilung 501. The farm stands on an unnamed road which runs up the hill from the CR329 snaking through the village below. The view is looking south-east; Oberwampach itself lies behind the author.

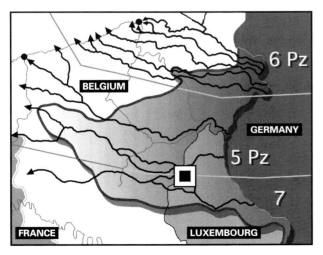

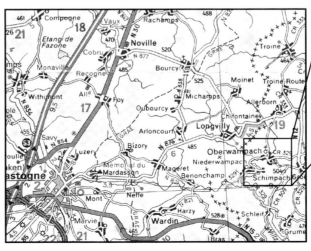

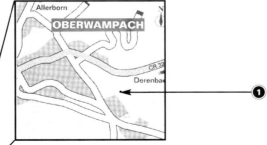

Oberwampach: **Michelin 214, Col. 8. 5° 52' East 50° 1' North. North or southbound on the E25 (A26) take exit 54 to Bastogne on the N84. Leave Bastogne to the north-east along the N874, direction Longvilly/Clervaux. Across the border into Luxembourg, the N874 runs into the N12. Head south for approximately 4 km and turn right on the CR329 to Oberwampach which lies 2 km to the west.**

Then: **Lying some ten kilometres due south of La Roche, Ortho in Belgium had been overrun by the 5. Panzer-Armee by December 20, 1944. However, on January 11, 1945, La Roche was retaken by the 1st Black Watch, a battalion of 154th Brigade of the British 51st Highland Division, and two days later, on January 13, Ortho was entered by the 5th/7th Gordons of the same division. The 116. Panzer-Division lost a variety of vehicles in the battle; pictured here is an SdKfz 251 armoured personnel carrier disabled in the centre of the village.**

Now: **Fifty years later the author stops on the same street [1] to capture the comparison. The view is directly east down the N843 looking towards Nisramont. The intersection with the N834 running north to La Roche is immediately behind the author. The building on the left is in fact the town hall and, despite some modernisation, the roofline and window arrangement provide the historical match, as does the corner stonework on the house to the far left. The houses down the road on the right still stand as well.**

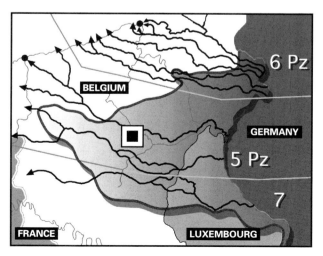

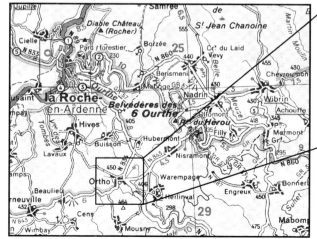

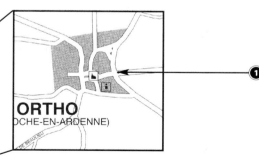

Ortho: **Michelin 214, Col. 7. 5° 37' East 50° 7' North. North or south-bound on the E25 (A26), exit 52, heading north to Mabompré on the N847. At the intersection of the N826, turn left (west) to Bertogne. At Bertogne, head for Ortho which lies 10 km further north.**

Then: **With Kampfgruppe Peiper having advanced as far west as Stoumont, Kampfgruppe Sandig attacked Stavelot from the south-east while Kampfgruppe Knittel moved on the town from the west via Trois-Ponts. On December 19, Knittel's forward elements captured the hamlets of Ster, Renardmont and Parfondruy but the following day they were driven out by the Americans. Then on December 22 elements of Kampfgruppe Hansen recaptured Parfondruy only to be ejected again the following day.**

Now: **Five decades later, along the same N68 west of Stavelot, the author rephotographs the final resting place [1] of Tiger II No. 003 near the Antoine Farm. This was the exact spot where it made its last stand in a futile attempt to move on Stavelot from the west. The house is a new construction. The angle is directly south looking into the valley of the Amblève river. The same oak tree, now much larger, still stands in the left distance of both photos.**

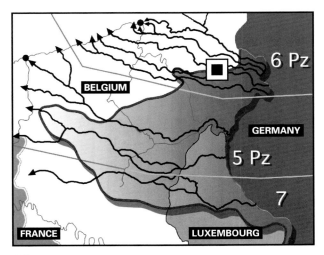

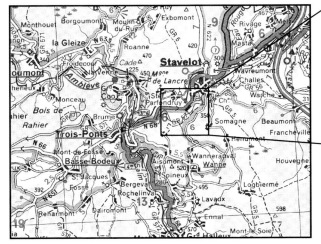

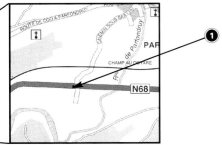

Parfondruy: **Michelin 214, Col. 7. 5° 55' East 50° 24' North. North or southbound on the E42 (A27), exit 11, heading west on the N62, direction Stavelot. At the intersection of the N68, turn left towards Stavelot. Approximately 3 km west of Stavelot along the N68 lies the village of Parfondruy.**

Then: With Bastogne becoming increasingly cut off by elements of XXXXVII. Panzerkorps, on December 19, 1944, Patton's Third Army was ordered to swing northwards in an attempt to prevent its total encirclement. After hasty and often confusing corps and sector responsibility rearrangements, the relief attacks towards Bastogne began in earnest. Throughout the following week, elements of the III Corps moved on the city from the south. Pictured here is a Sherman belonging to Combat Command A of the 9th Armored Division thundering through the small village of Petite Rosière, some 11 kilometres from Bastogne.

Now: They came this way to break the siege of Bastogne. This is the view 50 years later, looking south at the intersection [1] of the N85 with the unnamed road to Nives on the left. Note the unusual roof of the house in the left distance in the wartime photo, partially visible in the haze of a sunny dawn. This house (No. 80) can be seen in the upper left background of the present-day photo.

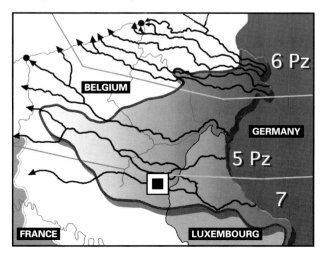

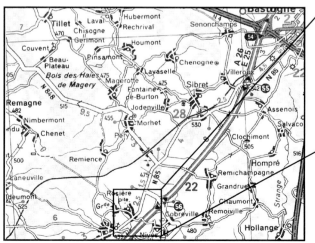

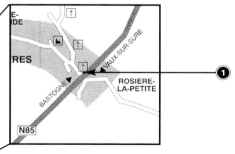

Petit-Rosière: Michelin 214, Col. 7. 5° 35' East 49° 55' North. North or southbound on the E25 (A26), exit 56, heading west to St Hubert on the N848. At the intersection of the N85, turn left (south), direction Vaux-sur-Sûre. 1.5 km along the N85 lies the small village of Petite-Rosière.

Then: By December 19, 1944, Kampfgruppe Peiper had fought its way into and beyond La Gleize, Belgium, where it was eventually cut off and surrounded. Bringing forward the remainder of the 1. SS-Panzer-Division to try to relieve Peiper, Kampfgruppe Hansen moved north from Wanne to reach the road towards La Gleize on the north side of the Amblève river. With three bridges having already been blown in the area (two at Trois-Ponts and one at Stavelot) Hansen was desperate to push his forces over any bridge still standing. Unfortunately the one at Petit-Spai proved too much for a 25-ton Jagdpanzer IV/70.

Now: The modern-day replacement at Petit-Spai [1] just east of Trois-Ponts along the current N68 (Route de Trois-Ponts). Walking along the small, narrow bridge today, one can appreciate the desperate nature of Kampfgruppe Hansen's attempt to cross the Amblève as the bridge is scarcely wide enough for a small car, let alone a Jagdpanzer! The new span is still supported on the original abutments.

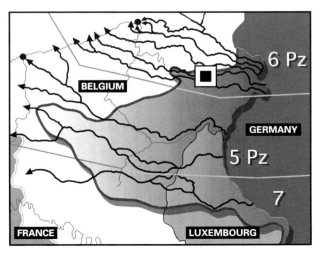

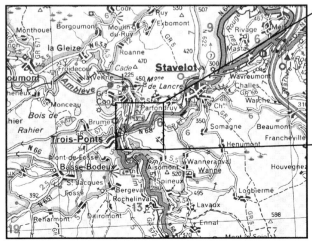

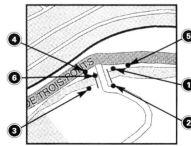

Petit-Spai: Michelin 214, Col. 7. 5° 53' East 50° 23' North. North or southbound on the E42 (A27), exit 11, heading west on the N62, direction Stavelot. At the intersection of the N68, turn left towards Stavelot. Continue past Stavelot on the N68. Approximately 1 km before the N68 meets the railway underpass at Trois-Ponts lies the small bridge over the Amblève river.

Then: **With the small bridge at Petit-Spai down, Germans engineers of the 1. SS-Panzer-Division go to work on a snowy December 21, 1944, to try and ford the river. During the attempt a US artillery barrage halted work and night fell with the river still unbridged.**

Now: **Fifty years later, the same spot [2] just south of the current bridge at Petit-Spai lies under an identical blanket of snow. The Amblève still flows along to the west while the N68 road runs east towards Stavelot.**

Then: **Another view [3] of the collapsed bridge at Petit-Spai, now looking east. The attempt to cross the river using a K-Gerät engineers' bridge was unsuccessful. One of its girders can be seen behind the drowned Jagdpanzer IV in the centre.**

Now: **A sunny, summer's day in Belgium belies the drama that once took place here over 50 years ago. Today, only the occasional hiker or farmer crosses the small span while canoeists and kayakers on the river pass beneath it.**

Then: **River of the damned. Along the Amblève the wrecks of Kampfgruppe Hansen lay all around the Petit-Spai river crossing. This is an SdKfz 251.**

Now: **With a similar blanket of snow 50 years later, the author looks south from the shoulder [4] of the N68 immediately west of the new bridge.**

Then: **A headless Tiger II lies on the bank of the Amblève just east of the fallen span at Petit-Spai. Taken after the war's end, this photo reveals the final resting place of Tiger II No. 133, commanded by Werner Wendt of schwere SS-Panzer-Abteilung 501. Returning from an aborted attack on Stavelot to the east, its transmission seized and it had to be abandoned on the river bank.**

Now: **Believe it or not, this is the precise location [5] where Wendt's Tiger ended its days over 50 years ago. In the distance, hidden by the new row of trees, lies the bridge.**

Then: **A post-war, close-up view of the German Jagdpanzer IV/70, whose weight brought down the small bridge at Petit-Spai. Though cold and fast, the river at this location [6] is not very deep.**

Now: **Before leaving the Petit-Spai, the author could not resist searching for any trace of the Jagdpanzer . . . but alas to no avail.**

Then: In one of the most reproduced sequences depicting the battle for the Ardennes, panzergrenadiers of SS-Panzer-Grenadier-Regiment 1 dash across the vital road linking Recht to the north-east with Poteau to the south-west. Their compatriot nonchalantly strolling through the ditch on the left implies the action has been staged. Part of Kampfgruppe Hansen, this regiment took Recht on December 18, 1944, and, departing from their assigned Rollbahn E, technically moved into 5. Panzer-Armee's sector by taking the Poteau crossroads later the same day.

Now: This photo and those that follow are provided as a documentary update to the superb analysis of this site carried out by Jean Paul Pallud in the late 1970s and early 1980s for his book *The Battle of the Bulge Then and Now* published by After the Battle in 1984. Since then the birch trees, which then still existed along the road, have been felled, and the entire 'stage' of the Poteau-Recht cine film sequence [1] is once again under attack: this time from progress!

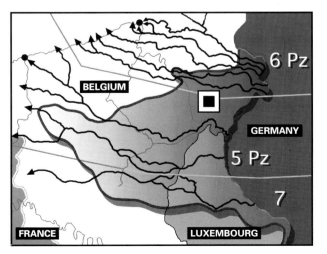

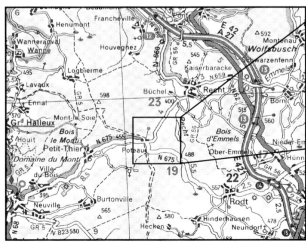

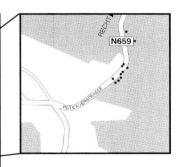

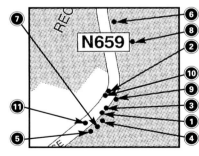

Poteau: Michelin 214, Col. 7. 6° 1' East 50° 18' North. North or southbound on the E42 (A27), exit 14, heading west on the N675 towards Rodt. Continue west to the village of Poteau at the intersection of the N675 and the N659. Head north-east out of Poteau on the N659 and 500 meters down the road lies the famous curve.

Then: **After the surprise attack on Task Force Mayes of the 14th Cavalry Group, panzergrenadiers found American vehicles abandoned and ablaze along the road, the perfect backdrop for propaganda footage. Careful analysis of the order, type and condition of the vehicles by Jean Paul Pallud enabled the author to determine the direction the various photos were taken.**

Now: **Serving as a 50th anniversary update of Jean-Paul's publication, the author pictures the same stretch of Poteauer Strasse (N659) looking north-east [2].**

Then: **Several M8 armoured cars belonging to the 14th Cavalry Group lay abandoned along the road. Careful analysis of vehicle markings identify these vehicles as belonging to the 18th Cavalry Reconnaissance Squadron. The panzergrenadiers found the pickings amongst the vehicles to be rich indeed, including prized American cigarettes and rations.**

Now: **Direction south-west [3]. The tree is long gone though the telegraph pole in the distance remains. The armoured cars were abandoned on this very spot but today, traffic moves unimpeded between Recht and Poteau, much of it no doubt oblivious to the events which took place here 50 years ago.**

Then: Another staged photo finds panzergrenadiers marching along the verge of the raised road while the smoke of burning vehicles obscures the background. The long coats betray the cold; they must have been very tiring to march and fight in.

Now: Direction west-north-west [4]. Standing in the field looking back towards the road.

Then: As panzergrenadiers mill about, the German cameraman inadvertently captures a significant landmark in the distance — a small farmer's shed surrounded by a few small trees.

Now: Direction now south-west [5]. In a rather amazing comparison, the same shed still stands on the same spot although the rapidly-growing conifers now tower over and block it from view. With over 50 years of growth to their credit, they stand as one of the few indications that time has indeed moved on.

Then: **Support for the regiment arrived around noon on December 18, 1944 in the form of a massive Jagdpanzer IV/70 from SS-Panzer-Jager-Abteilung 1. It has just entered the area, leaving the road and rolling into a broad field.**

Now: **Direction south [6]. The Jagdpanzer left Poteauer Strasse at this precise spot, proceeding down the slope to the left. Most of the cine film was taken further down the road at the curve in the distance. Today the small farm track still joins the road but it is obscured in this picture by the tall brush.**

Then: **With the wreckage of the American armoured column as a backdrop, an SS soldier and two Fallschirmjägers pause for a smoke.**

Now: **Direction north-west [7]. Standing in the same field off the road 50 years later, the author looks back towards the edge of the road.**

Then: **Cut and print! The officer 'actor' walks with his adjutant away from the 'film set' with the vehicles still burning in the background. One can only speculate on their conversation: discussions of past successes or the inherent futility of 'Wacht am Rhein'?**

Now: **Direction south [8]. With the post of the power line in the distance providing a point of alignment, the field where the officer and his ADC once strolled is rephotographed 50 years after the battle.**

Then: **Clearly staged, but with points earned for dramatic content an SS-Rottenführer 'shows the way' to further battles ahead. Technically, however, he is pointing away from both Poteau and Vielsalm.**

Now: **Direction now south-west [9] 50 years later. With no one to lead the way, the author nonetheless captures the Rottenführer's stage of long ago. The pylon remains as a point of reference**

Then: **Burning Jeeps and half-tracks are all that remain of Task Force Mayes of the 14th Cavalry Group, which was a mixture of vehicles belonging to the 18th and 32nd Cavalry Reconnaissance Squadrons. Given that they still look fairly intact, they were probably hastily abandoned in the face of the advancing SS-Panzer-Grenadier Regiment 1.**

Now: **Direction north-east [10]. Today, the same stretch of the Poteauer Strasse is free of stalled traffic, the modern variety rapidly passing between Recht in the distance and Poteau which lies a few hundred yards behind the author.**

Then: **A captured German photograph taken on the road to Recht which illustrates the variety of equipment left behind by the retreating Americans: a Stuart light tank in the immediate left foreground, an M8 armoured car on the right, and astride the road in the distance, a 76mm anti-tank gun and several half-tracks and Jeeps.**

Now: **Looking north-west [11]. Now completely passable and sporting the ubiquitous white line, the paved Poteauer Strasse today runs off towards Recht. Just down the road to the right is the spot where the panzergrenadiers dashed across, as depicted in the photo on page 221.**

Then: Having fought westwards along Rollbahn D through Stavelot, Trois-Ponts and La Gleize, Kampfgruppe Peiper found an intact bridge across the Amblève at Cheneux, and crossed it on the afternoon of December 18, 1944. Now attempting to gain Rollbahn E, Peiper pressed on through Rahier and Froidville, but was stopped by a blown bridge at Habiémont and was forced to pull back to La Gleize. By December 19, US forces were moving to contain Peiper's group, with the 82nd Airborne Division pushing west on to Cheneux. This photo depicts men of the 504th Parachute Infantry Regiment marching east through Rahier.

Now: The road [1] through Rahier, 50 years later, looking west. Now tarmacked and minus its electricity poles on the left, this is the same stretch of unnamed road running east out of the village which lies in the distance. The house on the far right is No. 62. The white house in the centre of the photo remains.

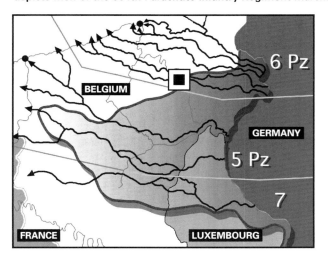

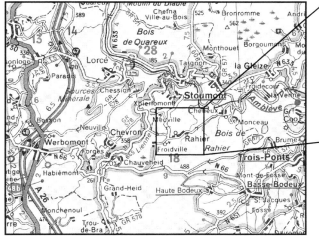

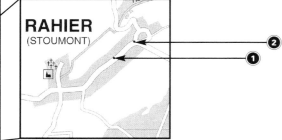

Rahier: Michelin 214, Col. 8. 5° 47' East 50° 23' North. North or southbound on the E25 (A26), exit 48, heading east on the N66, direction Trois Ponts. Approximately 9 km east along the N66, turn left, direction Froidville/Rahier. Pass through Froidville to enter Rahier from the west.

Rahier

Then: December 21, 1944. Pausing in the small Belgian village of Rahier, Company D of the 2nd Battalion, 504th Parachute Infantry, 82nd Airborne Division, listen as their chaplain delivers a 'prayer for the day'. The village of Cheneux to the east had been retaken in heavy fighting the day before so perhaps the men were more than aware of the ferocity of the fighting which still lay to the east. Despite this, they appear to be fairly calm and sanguine . . . another day . . . another battle . . . another village.

Now: The bright sunshine along an unnamed road east of Rahier [2] illuminates the former meeting place. The house (No. 30) provides the perfect link with the past as it still sports the same small circular window. Likewise the hedgerow still runs along the road though the pole has been replaced with a modern concrete version.

Then: Following the loss of St Vith on the evening of December 21, American forces withdrew into the Vielsalm/Salmchâteau area. However by the end of the year, substantial defences had been reorganised both north and south of Vielsalm and, as part of a larger attack eastwards by the First Army which began on January 3, 1945 the 82nd Airborne Division attacked towards Vielsalm. On January 9, the 505th Parachute Infantry captured Rencheux, just north of Vielsalm, being relieved there two days later by the 75th Infantry Division. This picture was taken on January 17.

Now: The GIs of the 75th Infantry met here over 50 years ago. This view is looking due east at the corner intersection [1] of Rue de Veze (from the left), Rue du Vivier (to the right) and Rue des Chasseurs Ardennais. Vielsalm itself lies down the road in the distance. The prominent house is No. 2, Rue de Veze; apart from the new addition to the left and a modernised roof, the rest of the building remains virtually untouched, as do the buildings in the background.

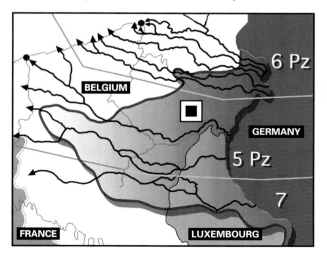

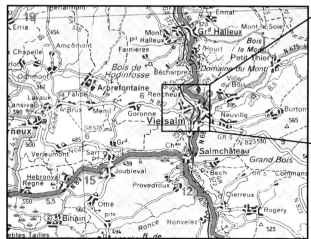

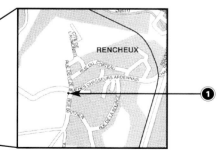

Rencheux: Michelin 214, Col. 8. 5° 54' East 50° 17' North. North or southbound on the E25 (A26), exit 50, heading east on the N89, direction Salmchâteau/Vielsalm. At Salmchâteau, head north along the N68 to Vielsalm. In Vielsalm, exit west along the N822 (Rue des Chasseurs Ardennais). Rencheux is 1 km to the north-west.

Then: The fall of St Hubert to the Panzer-Lehr-Division on December 22 cleared the way west to the vital road centre of Rochefort. Defended by the 84th Infantry Division, Rochefort was attacked in force at 2 a.m. on December 24 by Panzer-Lehr and by late afternoon, the Americans were forced to withdraw. On Christmas Day sustained attacks on Humain and Havrenne by American forces, backed by massive artillery support, pushed Panzer-Lehr to the bridgehead south of Rochefort. This still from a German cine film shows a Panther from the division moving through the main crossroads in the centre of town.

Now: The same crossroads [1] in the heart of Rochefort photographed over 50 years later. Looking south through the major intersection of the Rue de Marche (left), Avenue du Forest (lower right) and Rue de France (upper right), the author finds the same buildings framing the scene today. Only the traffic markings and modern signposts betray the passage of time.

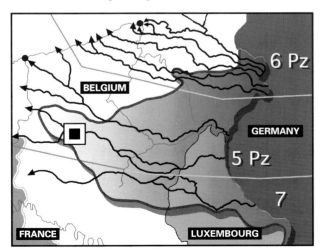

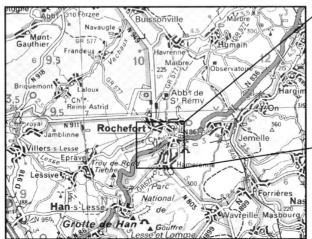

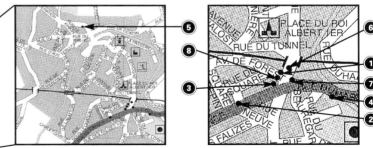

Rochefort: **Michelin 214, Col. 6. 5° 14' East 50° 9' North. North or southbound on the N4, exit at Marche-en-Famenne, heading southwest on the N836, direction Rochefort. Rochefort lies 12 km to the south-west.**

Then: **This Jagdpanther of schwere Panzer-Jager-Abteilung 559 (the unit which replaced the II. Abteilung in Panzer-Lehr's Panzer-Regiment 130 during the Ardennes offensive) threw a track in Rochefort, just off of the road leading to Han-sur-Lesse.**

Now: On a sunny Sunday afternoon, the author tracks down the final resting place of the great beast along the present-day N86 (Rue de France) at the intersection with Rue Neuve to the left [2]. Over 50 years later, little has changed in this corner of Rochefort; the view is looking directly south with the same house (No. 6) on the right.

Then: **Heads down! The action intensifies in the battle for Rochefort on December 24, 1944. Crouching in a small café area off the main intersection, a German war reporter raises his camera to capture this Panther of Panzer-Lehr-Division negotiating the crossroads in the centre of the town. Though it would appear that the tank is thundering past at speed, viewing the complete cine film sequence reveals that it is in fact turning in place on its tracks to gain a better firing position.**

Now: Crouching down in the same location [3] today, the author records the same scene exactly half a century later. From this position, the entire crossroads can be covered. The view today is looking south-west down the Rue de Marche, the photo being taken in front of the Foxy Pub.

Then: **Passing a knocked-out American anti-tank gun, grenadiers of the Panzer-Lehr-Division march through Rochefort across the bridge [4] over the River Lomme.**

Now: **The Rue de Marche (N86) heads south out of Rochefort towards Jemelle to the east. In spite of the passage of over 50 years, the houses in the distance remain virtually identical; the white building on the right being the Hotel Troumaulin. The picture was taken in front of No. 9.**

Then: **A destroyed SdKfz 251 of Kampfgruppe Holtmeyer lies next to an equally destroyed house in the northern part of the city of Rochefort. It rode with the 2. Panzer-Division, operating in the area with Panzer-Lehr.**

Now: **The same location [5] today outside of No. 17, on the aptly named Rue de la Libération in modern-day Rochefort. Though the façade of the house has changed somewhat, the others in the upper-right distance remain almost unchanged.**

Then: **After the battle, the streets of Rochefort were clogged with defeated American vehicles and guns.**

Now: **Despite the intensity of the battle, the houses along this stretch of the Rue de Behogne [6] have changed little in 50 years.**

Then: **With Panzerfausts at the ready, weary resignation seems apparent on the faces of these grenadiers of the Panzer-Lehr-Division as they move through Rochefort. Behind them lay the battles with the 84th Infantry Division.**

Now: **The same view today [7] in a decidedly more modern and well-kept Rochefort. The photo was taken looking west across the Rue de Behogne towards the Hotel Le Limbourg on the left. Despite a new café area built out from the hotel along the street, the original arched windows still exist.**

Then: **After the battle for Rochefort had turned in the Germans' favour, the armoured shield of a knocked-out American 76mm anti-tank gun serves as an impromptu message board for this grenadier of the Panzer-Lehr-Division. 'Aus der Traum' — the dream is over. The division had come a long way since December 16 but little did this grenadier know that Rochefort would be as far as they would advance in Belgium; the following day, Panzer-Lehr would forever be on the defensive.**

Now: **Another of the author's favourite comparisons. The view is across the present-day Rue de Behogne, looking at the Hotel Le Central [8]. The anti-tank gun stood on this exact spot. Despite the rather extensive alterations that have taken place on the buildings in the background, other photos showing the gun from different angles confirm the precise location.**

Then: With the evacuation of the St Vith area on December 22, a defensive perimeter was established north of Vielsalm along the Salm river by the 504th, 505th, and 508th Parachute Infantry Regiments of the 82nd Airborne Division. Approaching this line on December 24 were the 1. SS and 9. SS-Panzer-Divisions. Lying in wait for their attack, paratroopers of the 505th are pictured huddling on top of the railway embankment. However, on this same day, after reviewing the overall military situation, Field-Marshal Montgomery ordered a further pull-back and consolidation to the west to shore up the overall US perimeter.

Now: Now heavily overgrown with undergrowth and trees, the same embankment [1] is pictured over 50 years later along the railway line east of Rochelinval. The hills in the distance, as well as the direction and distant curvature of the line itself helps to align the comparison. The photo was taken from a small bridge which crosses the tracks as it heads west into the village.

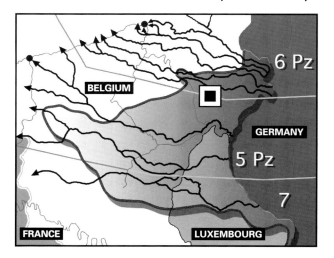

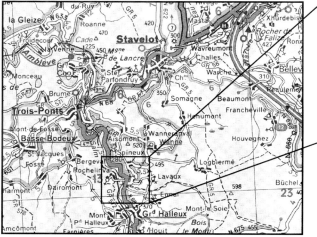

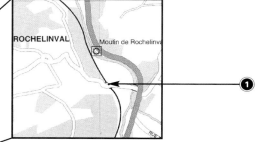

Rochelinval: Michelin 214, Col. 8. 5° 54' East 50° 21' North. North or southbound on the E42 (A27), exit 11, heading west on the N62 towards Stavelot. At the intersection of the N68, turn left. Continue past Stavelot on the N68 to Trois-Ponts. At Trois-Ponts, take the N68 southbound, which runs parallel to the Salm river; Rochelinval lies 6 km further on. Just past the Moulin de Rochelinval is the small bridge over the Salm.

Then: In a famous photograph which has come to symbolise German defeat in the battle for the Ardennes, American GIs clamber over a King Tiger of Kampfgruppe Peiper. After its abandonment by the Germans and subsequent capture by the Americans in La Gleize, Tiger 204 was restarted and driven along the road east of La Gleize and then to a point north of Ruy where it finally gave up the ghost. Though US engineers attempted to bring it back to life, it was eventually pushed off the road and down the hill to the right.

Now: Though the tree on the left has been felled, and a new tree-line planted on the right-hand side of the Rue de Neuville, this is where Tiger II No. 204 breathed its last. The same concrete post on the right, and the tree-line running up the hill in the distance on the left all match. The picture was taken looking south-west back into Ruy. To further confirm the precise location [1], the author searched for — and found — the remains of the large tree on the left.

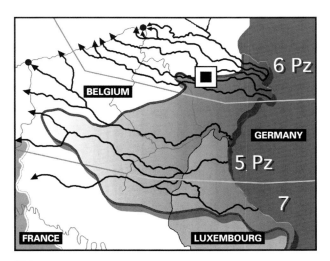

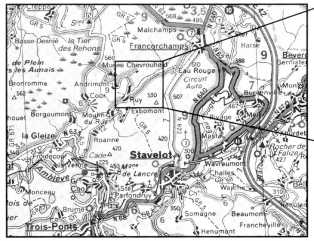

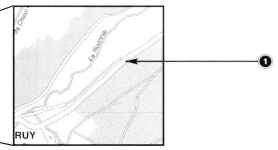

Ruy-Neuville: Michelin 214, Col. 8. 5° 55' East 50° 26' North. North or southbound on the E42 (A27) take exit 11 for Stavelot. On the N62, which joins the N68, continue through Stavelot heading west to Trois-Ponts. Just north of Trois-Ponts at the railway bridge viaduct continue right onto the N633 towards Coo. In 6 km, turn right onto the Roanne road to Ruy. Approximately 1½ km north of the village is the site where the Tiger II came to rest.

Then: With the 2. SS-Panzer-Division having been halted in the Manhay-Grandmenil area, II. SS-Panzerkorps sought to maintain westward momentum by bringing the 12. SS-Panzer-Division into the fray. On the evening of December 27, 1944, its SS-Panzer-Grenadier-Regiment 25 attacked Sadzot east of Erezée to be met immediately by the 509th Parachute Infantry Battalion. After an intense two-day battle, the village was recaptured by the Americans on December 29. Shown here are medical corpsmen of the 3rd Armored Division looking over a casualty of a different kind — their own Jeep!

Now: Driveway to history 50 years later in the Belgian village of Sadzot — referred to as 'Sad Sack' by the Americans after the famous cartoon character. The corpsmen's Jeep sat on this spot [1] in front of No. 3. The view is looking south down the main road. The white house with the pointed roof in the right distance remains as it once did in the wartime photo, helping to complete the comparison.

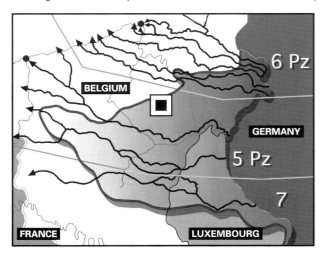

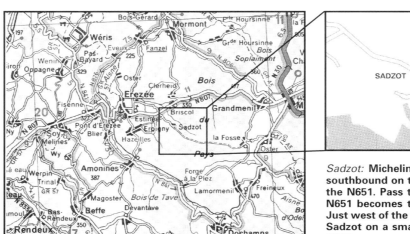

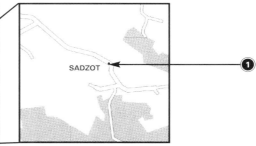

Sadzot: Michelin 214, Col. 7. 5° 35' East 50° 17' North. North or southbound on the E25 (A26) exit 49, direction west to Manhay on the N651. Pass through both Manhay and Grandmenil, where the N651 becomes the N807 (Rue d'Erezée) west out of Grandmenil. Just west of the village of Briscol along the N807, turn left direction Sadzot on a small unnamed road. Sadzot lies 1½ km south of the N807.

Then: By dawn on December 20, 1944, the 116. Panzer-Division had passed Houffalize and was moving on La Roche. However, before reaching the town, the division turned north towards Samrée-Dochamps. Supported by the 560. Volks-Grenadier-Division on their right flank, they attacked Samrée that same morning, capturing the village along with 30,000 gallons of gasoline. Later, after being halted at Hotton and Erezée, the Germans were driven out by the 2nd Armored Division. This picture shows GIs drawing water from a well in Samrée.

Now: A small, innocuous driveway [1] leading to a house (No. 6) in Samrée reveals its secrets when it is compared to the wartime photo of 50 years ago. The house on the right, with the small stone shed attached to it, still remains though it now sports a layer of insulation. The well where the soldiers once drank sat in the middle of the driveway; its patched-up hole still being visible on the ground. Sadly, shortly after this comparison was taken, a new house was built in the drive, so destroying the comparison forever.

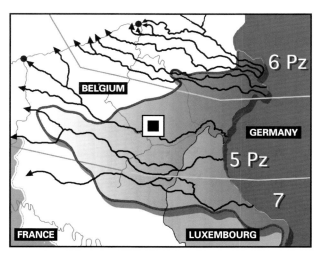

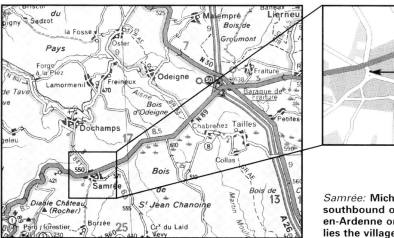

Samrée: Michelin 214, Col. 7. 5° 38' East 50° 13' North. North or southbound on the E25 (A26) exit 50, direction west to La Roche-en-Ardenne on the N89. Some 8.5 km west directly along the N89 lies the village of Samrée.

Then: With Bastogne having been completely surrounded by December 22, 1944, the only means of resupply to American forces was from the air. On the morning of December 23 a resupply operation was begun by the US IX Troop Carrier Command using over 240 C-47 transport planes. Supplies were parachuted into the Bastogne perimeter for six days during which time 19 planes were lost, including this C-47 which crash-landed in a field at Savy.

Now: The place [1] where *Ain't Misbehavin* came to grief pictured over 50 years later southwest of the hamlet of Savy. The direction of view is east; with the N854 running along the top of the photo from right to left. Today, the road has been considerably widened. Combined with the loss of the roadside trees, the comparison looks empty, yet the houses on the far left match the ones immediately to the right of the tail of the C-47.

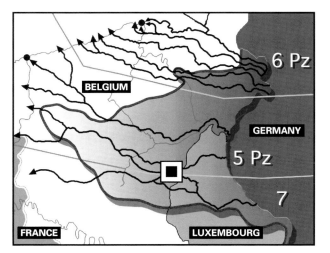

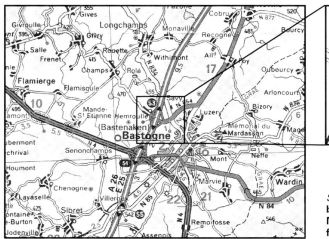

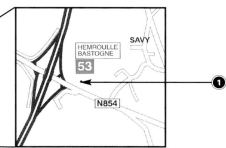

Savy: Michelin 214, Col. 8. 5° 42' East 50° 2' North. North or southbound on the E25 (A26) exit 53, direction east to Bastogne on the N854. Only 200 meters east of the E25 exit along the N854 lies the field off to the left, before the hamlet of Savy.

Then: On December 21, 1944, in the advance of the 7. Armee past Bastogne, the village of Sibret fell to Fallschirm-Jäger-Regiment 14 of 5. Fallschirm-Jäger-Division forcing the 28th Infantry Division to withdraw. However, by December 30, thanks to the counter-attack by the US Third Army, a corridor had been opened to the city from the south and Sibret had been retaken, but not without cost. Here, an M18 tank destroyer from the 4th Armored Division lies destroyed itself along the main road leading from Sibret towards Bastogne in the distance.

Now: On a sunny day 50 years later, it is difficult to believe that tanks once burned on this spot [1]. This is the view on the N85 looking north-east towards Bastogne on the northern outskirts of the village of Sibret; the M18 lay directly in front of the author. The electrical pylon through the trees on the right of the wartime photo still stands. The N85, called the Chaussée de Bastogne, curves right in the distance as it crosses over the E25 autoroute.

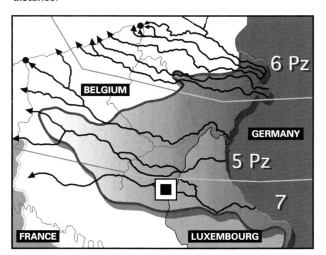

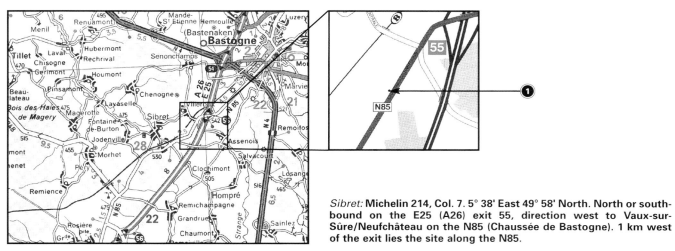

Sibret: Michelin 214, Col. 7. 5° 38' East 49° 58' North. North or southbound on the E25 (A26) exit 55, direction west to Vaux-sur-Sûre/Neufchâteau on the N85 (Chaussée de Bastogne). 1 km west of the exit lies the site along the N85.

Then: **By December 21, 1944, the rapidly moving Kampfgruppe Bayer of 116. Panzer-Division had moved past Houffalize, Samrée and Dochamps and, dashing between Task Forces Hogan and Orr of the 3rd Armored Division, made it as far as Soy, before turning on Hotton. Despite an unsuccessful attack on Hotton by the Germans, Task Force Hogan found itself completely cut off from American lines. On Christmas evening, under cover of darkness, the task force marched for 14 hours north along the Ourthe river to freedom, arriving in Soy in the late afternoon of December 26.**

Now: **Fifty years later, silence is golden on a rainy Sunday afternoon in a Belgian farmyard at Soy. This is the view looking north from the same farm gateway where happy members of Task Force Hogan once celebrated their good fortune with rations and Lucky Strike cigarettes. The farmyard [1] lies right on the intersection of the Rue St Roch and the main Rue Grand Mont (N807) in the centre of the village. The steeple of the village church can just be made out in the far upper left corner of both photos.**

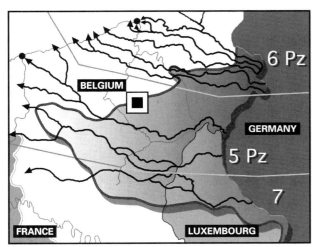

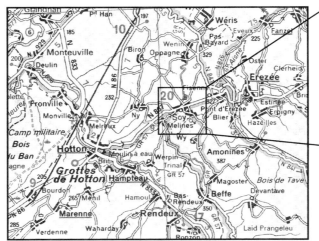

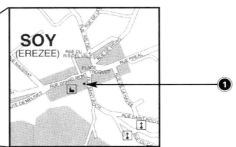

Soy: **Michelin 214, Col. 7. 5° 31' East 50° 17' North. From the E25 (A26) north or southbound exit 49, then head west on the N651 to Manhay. From Manhay, take the N807 west past Erezée to Soy which lies directly along the route.**

Then: **Dwarfed by a massive spoil of war, men of the 740th Tank Battalion listen in as their commander, Lieutenant Colonel George K. Rubel, points out the operational niceties of a captured Tiger II. This particular example No. 332, was abandoned along the N633 just outside Coo in Belgium and moved by the 463rd Ordnance Evacuation Company to the railway at Spa for eventual shipment to the States. It now resides, beautifully restored, in the Patton Museum at Fort Knox, Kentucky.**

Now: **Fifty years later the car park outside the station at Spa no longer plays host to vehicles with curb weights exceeding 67 tons! Only mere cars gather for journeys east and west. Today the town is a popular tourist and relaxation centre for its name is the original!**

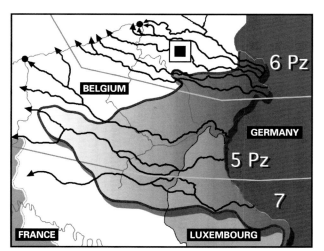

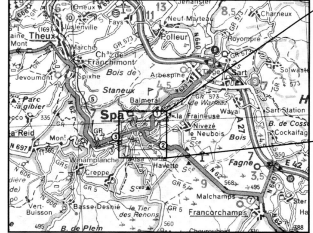

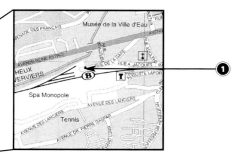

Spa: **Michelin 213, Col. 11. 5° 53' East 50° 29' North. From the E42 (A27) north or southbound exit 10, heading south on the N640, direction Francorchamps. At the intersection with the N62, take the N62 directly into Spa.**

Then: **Upon reaching Bastogne alongside the 2. Panzer-Division, Kampfgruppe 902 (von Poschinger) of the Panzer-Lehr-Division bypassed the city to the south following a series of failed probing attacks. Passing through Villers-la-Bonne-Eau, Assenois, Sibret and Morhet, Kampfgruppe 902 captured St Hubert on the evening of December 22, 1944. The town was to remain in German hands until the second week of January when the 87th Infantry Division of the US Third Army recaptured it. A snowy day in January 1945 finds men of the division marching through the streets, towards battles which lie ahead.**

Now: **Looking north [1] down the present-day Rue de la Fontaine, with the prominent abbey of St Hubert on the right, one finds only traffic lanes 50 years later. This is the junction with the Rue St Gilles running off to the left. The house on the left, No. 18, is a rather nice hotel and restaurant. While having lunch therein, the author was pleased to find the very same wartime photo hanging above his table!**

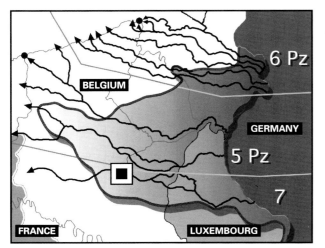

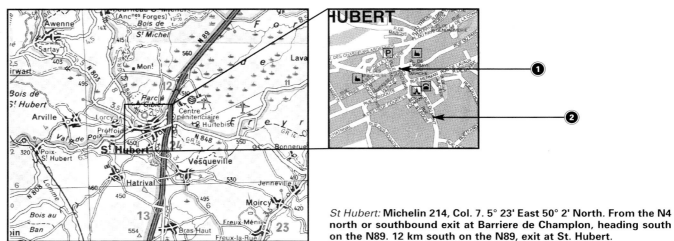

St Hubert: **Michelin 214, Col. 7. 5° 23' East 50° 2' North. From the N4 north or southbound exit at Barriere de Champlon, heading south on the N89. 12 km south on the N89, exit at St. Hubert.**

Then: **On January 11, 1945, GIs of the 87th Infantry Division spill over the main street of St Hubert having just recaptured the city from the Panzer-Lehr-Division.**

Now: **The street of liberation, 50 years later. Looking north down the present-day Rue du Mont, near the intersection [2] with Rue St Roch (off to the left), towards the bell tower of the abbey in the distance. The house on the far left, with its decorative stone pattern about the windows, is No. 104.**

Then: Situated at a vital crossroads in Belgium, St Vith lay astride the attack boundaries of the 5. and 6. Panzer-Armees. While the 1. and 9. SS-Panzer-Divisions of 6. Panzer-Armee swept past St Vith in the north, the 18. Volks-Grenadier-Division of 5. Panzer-Armee attacked the town on the evening of December 21. A determined resistance was put up by the 7th Armored Division but St Vith finally fell into German hands as American forces were withdrawn to the west to form a new defensive line. This photo shows soldiers of the 7th Armored after they recaptured the town in January 1945.

Now: Fifty years later, a similar snowfall covers a reconstructed St Vith. This is the corner of Aachener Strasse and Hauptstrasse, in the heart of the town looking south-west. The buildings in the centre (Nos. 95, 97, 99) remain more or less as they once were but the prominent house on the left in the wartime photo was razed for a new block of apartments in the 1980s. Expanded and widened, this junction is now a bustling thoroughfare for traffic heading to all points of the compass.

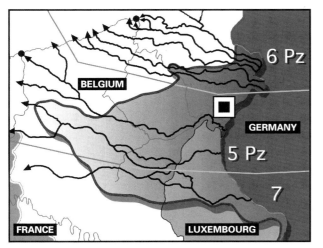

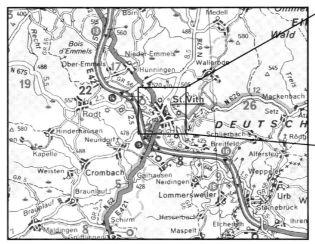

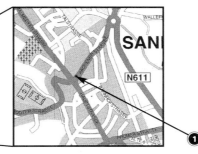

St Vith: Michelin 214, Col. 9. 6° 8' East 50° 17' North. North or southbound on the E42(A27), exit 15 at St Vith, heading north on the N62 directly into the town.

243

Then: The lead spearhead of Kampfgruppe Peiper initially moved into Stavelot on the morning of December 18, 1944, but by the early afternoon most of the unit had pushed on towards Trois-Ponts to the west. Supporting the rear of the column were the heavy tanks of schwere SS-Panzer-Abteilung 501. Amongst them SS-Obersturmführer Jürgen Wessel sought to negotiate the narrow streets of the town which was still being defended by small bodies of American soldiers. A round from a bazooka startled the King Tiger, and Wessel ordered it to reverse, where it became permanently lodged in the side of a house.

Now: The king of battle once lay ignominiously stranded here [1] alongside No. 9 on Rue Haut Rivage in the centre of town. This is the view looking south on a quiet Sunday morning with the triangular roofline of No. 5 in the background as a useful point of reference. With the houses repaired and the streets cleansed by a wintry rain, it is difficult to imagine the scene here 50 years ago but the ancient town of Stavelot will go down prominently in the annals of war between the US Army and the 6. Panzer-Armee.

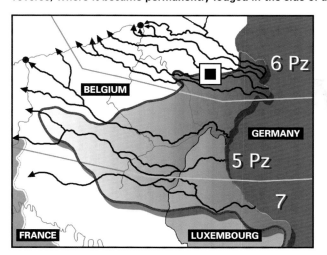

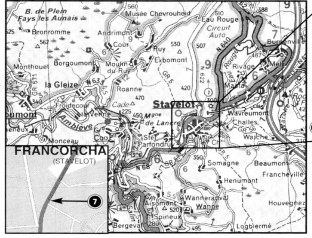

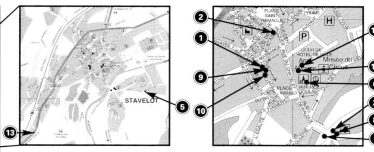

Stavelot: Michelin 214, Col. 8. 5° 56' East 50° 24' North. North or southbound on the E42 (A27), exit 11, direction Stavelot. Continue towards Stavelot along the N62, which joins the N68. On the N68, head west approximately 2 km into Stavelot from the east.

Then: **Kampfgruppe Knittel followed Peiper in support but during the late afternoon of December 18, the 1st Battalion, 117th Regiment of the 30th Infantry Division, together with the 843rd Tank Destroyer Battalion, fought to regain control of the town and by the evening Stavelot was back in American hands.**

Now: **The battle for the market square was particularly tense; after the battle, a fallen German soldier lay lifeless here on the south-west corner. This is the junction [2] of the present-day Rue de la Fontaine and Rue Général Jacques. The house on the left is No. 31 on the Place St Remacle — the name of the main town square.**

Then: **No sooner was the town back in American hands than a third German force, Kampfgruppe Sandig, approached from the south-east supported by Tiger IIs of schwere SS-Panzer-Abteilung 501. Sandig attacked Stavelot on the afternoon of the 19th yet stiff American resistance from positions overlooking the Amblève bridge drove back the Germans. Tiger II, No. 222 (see pages 68, 138, 139 and 171), was disabled immediately south of the bridge.**

Now: **With the river to the author's back and the bridge to his right, this is the precise location [3] where the tank was stopped. The view is directly south facing the intersection of five roads that merge into one, Rue Dewalque, before crossing the Amblève into Stavelot. Kampfgruppen Peiper, Knittel and Sandig came down the Chemin du Château which joins the Rue Belle Vue behind the tree on the right.**

Then: Another, clearer post-battle view of King Tiger No. 222 of Kampfgruppe Sandig. The extent of the destruction left in the wake of the group's effort to gain the bridgehead on December 19, 1944 can clearly be seen in the background.

Now: The well-restored site [4] in Stavelot today. This is the view looking east, the house bearing the white Tudor-style façade being No. 4. The photo was taken standing in a small commemorative area called the Place 18 Decembre 1944; on display behind the author is a US Army half-track. It is perhaps unusual that Stavelot, which saw Tigers blasting their way through the streets, does not have any surviving armour — German or American — on display.

Then: The battle for Stavelot over, the late afternoon sunshine reveals a 1. SS-Panzer-Division Panther knocked out along the road [5] leading down to the bridge at the southern end of Stavelot.

Now: With the cobble-stoned Chemin du Château still leading down the steep hill to the bridge, 50 years later the author was able to take a good comparison. The house on the upper right with typical Belgian insulation is No. 29. The Rue du Chêne on the left, along with the row of houses which line it today, was built after the war.

Then: **Stavelot, Belgium, pictured after the battle of December 18-19, 1944. Having suffered the attacks and counter-attacks of two opposing forces, followed by an intense American artillery bombardment, Stavelot lay in ruins. The town experienced house-to-house fighting in the market square, tank battles in the narrow streets, atrocities against its civilians, and multiple attempts to cross the river. Thus, Stavelot's historical place in the battle for the Ardennes is assured.**

Now: **Stavelot lives on! In a photo comparison that the author considers one of his finest, the town of Stavelot is captured 50 years later, having risen like a phoenix from the ashes of war. The author gained access to the abbey rooftop [6] via helpful Belgacom employees, whose company now occupies the enormous structure. Hanging out of a small attic window barely larger than his waist, the author slowly squeezed off the shutter. This is an exact match: the walls of the buildings in the immediate foreground still remain as they were, including a modern version of a similar playground swing! A further point of comparison is the gutted building with the sloping roofline immediately to the left of the chimney in the wartime photo which still stands today as the white structure with rectangular windows. The bridge likewise is properly aligned.**

Then: By 10.00 a.m. on December 18, Kampfgruppe Peiper had already passed through Stavelot and began to move on Trois-Ponts further west. Unbeknown to him, his forces had passed just south of this American fuel dump lining the steep road just north of the town. Comprising almost a million gallons of gasoline, the Americans began to burn it to prevent its capture. Some 145,000 gallons went up in flames before it was apparent that it would not be taken, whereupon the conflagration was extinguished.

Now: Looking south back down the present-day N622 [7]. This is now the Rue Haute Levée which becomes the Rue Albert Counson north of Amerimont as it approaches Francorchamps. Some time later, the author returned to the same location to find that enormous downhill 'runaway lorry' escape chicanes had been constructed on this stretch of road; thus marring the purity of the comparison.

Then: A side view of Tiger II No. 222 from schwere SS-Panzer-Abteilung 501 which was abandoned just south of the bridge [8] over the Amblève. The abbey can be seen across the river on the left.

Now: Pictured 50 years later almost to the very day, No. 2 on the corner of Rue des Iles and Chemin du Château stands in the rain of a silent Sunday afternoon.

Then: A different view and photo angle of SS-Obersturmführer Wessel's King Tiger II coming to rest in a pile of debris on the afternoon of December 18, 1944.

Now: The author adjusts his own camera angle and captures the precise comparison [9]. Today, the Tiger would be literally sitting on top of a crushed VW Golf!

Then: Another view [10] of Jürgen Wessel's King Tiger completes the panorama of the tank and the damage to No. 9 Rue Haut Rivage.

Now: A decidedly smaller and definitely lighter vehicle of today takes its place. The author was struck by how narrow the Rue Haut Rivage is — a classic tank trap if ever there was one!

Then: Medical corpsmen bear the handiwork of the 1. SS-Panzer-Division — one of over 65 civilians murdered in and around the town. The bodies were brought in to be buried in front of the abbey [11].

Now: Today, the manicured lawn in the courtyard belies the tragic scene. Just off to the right, a monument now stands inscribed with the names of those civilians massacred by the SS.

Then: A mass grave had been dug in the centre of the abbey courtyard. Here, a priest blesses the victims as they are laid to rest.

Now: Shortly after this photo was taken 50 years later, the author visited the same courtyard only to find the entire area being excavated in an archaeological dig, ancient ruins having been discovered on the site [12]. And, no, they did not find any bodies — those had all been moved to places of permanent burial decades earlier.

Then: This disturbing photo documents the horror which occurred just outside the Legaye home [13] on the outskirts of Stavelot. On the evening of Tuesday, December 19, 1944, at around 8 p.m., SS butchery reached its zenith. As SS grenadiers marched towards Trois-Ponts, shots were allegedly fired at them from this house. In vengeful fury, the SS rounded up eleven women, two men and ten children hiding in the cellar, marched them out, lined them up along the hedgerow to the right, and mowed them down at point-blank range with machine pistols. After the battle, a stunned American soldier finds the frozen body of a small child, no more than eight years old, lying at the foot of the gate.

Now: Site of infamy 50 years later on the Avenue Constant Grandprez on the western outskirts of the town. The Legaye house, No. 5, bears a distinctive brass plate announcing the family name. Immediately after the author took this photo, an old lady, Madam Legaye, walked out of the front door and gestured. After speaking with her about the tragedy, she took the author around the back of the house to show him the cellar. Later, as she served coffee, she called the local historian, who promptly came over and produced a hand-drawn map pinpointing the homes of those killed in the mass execution. And Madam Legaye? She said she only survived because she was away from home that night.

Then: After the battle, the snows of January became the floods of February. A US Army Signal Corps photo taken looking out over the breach of a 75mm German PaK 40 sees American supply trucks on the move in the valley of the Our river. This location is close to the border between Belgium and Germany.

Now: With the valley now lush with nature and bathed in sunshine, the author contemplates the view from the gun's position high on top of a hill on the western edge of Steffeshausen. The photo was taken next to house No. 32 overlooking the scene. The hedgerow lining the bottom of the hill remains. Today a new bridge and a widened roadway allows traffic to flow into the village unimpeded.

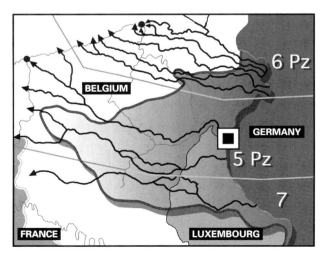

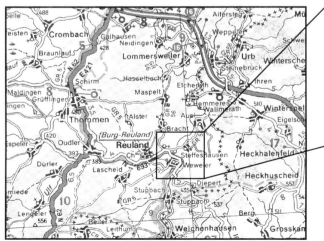

Steffeshausen: Michelin 214, Col. 9. 6° 10' East 50° 12' North. North or southbound on the E421, exit 15, direction south along the E421. 8.5 km south, turn right onto the N693 towards Reuland. Pass through the village and over the Our river. The hill is up on the right at the western edge of Steffeshausen.

Then: With the battle for St Vith at an end, American trucks roll eastwards through a destroyed rail bridge [1] south of the town. The road ran from St Vith to Steinebrück; the railway to Prüm in the east.

Now: The original scene is no more! Having survived until the mid-1980s in virtually identical condition to its wartime equivalent, the site has now been completely transformed. This is the view looking east along the N646 through the bridge which now carries the E421 autoroute on top of it.

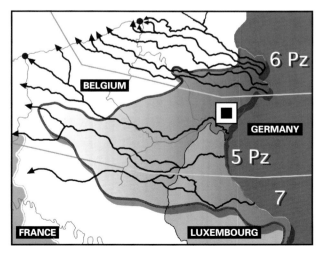

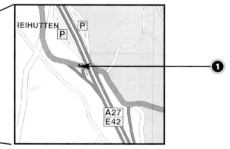

Steinebrück: Michelin 214, Col. 9. 6° 11' East 50° 14' North. Southbound on the E421, exit 16. Turn left immediately onto the N626, which then passes under the bridge in the photo.

Then: **January 20, 1945, finds a lone Panther parked serenely in the snow just outside the village church in Sterpigny, Belgium. On January 17, it fought with the 9. Panzer-Division as they attempted to extricate themselves from the advancing Americans. The US Army photo caption stated that three US tank destroyers knocked out the Panther (No. 412) by firing three rounds into its rear. To the left, two Jeeps are parked outside the bombed-out church; possibly their occupants are inside giving thanks for the battle won.**

Now: **A 'weather-match' photo comparison finds the identical scene in Sterpigny 50 years later. This is the view looking directly north along the N827 in front of the church with battle damage restored.**

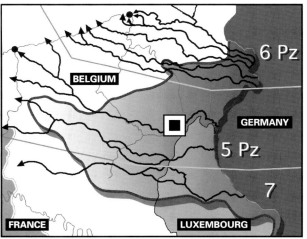

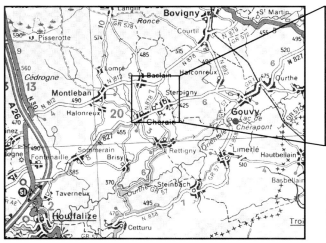

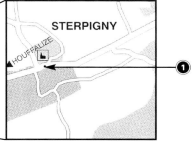

Sterpigny: **Michelin 214, Col. 8. 5° 53' East 50° 11' North. North or southbound on the E25 (A26), exit 51 at Houffalize. Continue east on the N827 direction Gouvy. Approximately 10 km east along the N827 lies the village of Sterpigny.**

Then: **Having been reinforced by Kampfgruppe Knittel's reconnaissance battalion during the night of December 18 at La Gleize, the following morning Kampfgruppe Peiper attacked Stoumont to the west in force. Supported by Panthers and Panzer IVs, the town was captured by noon from the 119th Infantry Regiment of the 30th Infantry Division. Pictured here early on the 19th, SS grenadiers of 1. SS-Panzer-Division advance towards the centre of the village.**

Now: **Fifty years ago, they came this way, moving down the Rue Village [1] just south of the local church. Despite the clouds of smoke in the wartime photo which obscures the buildings further down the street, the brick pattern of the wall to the left can be matched up perfectly; belonging to house No. 3, the one in the centre being No. 5.**

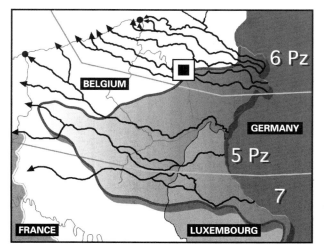

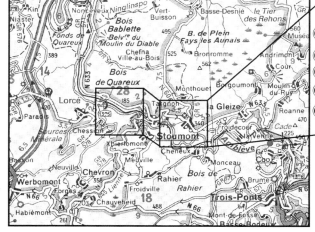

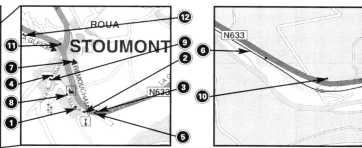

Stoumont: **Michelin 214, Col. 8. 5° 49' East 50° 25' North. North or southbound on the E42 (A27), exit 11 Stavelot. Continue towards the town on the N62, which joins the N68. Continue through Stavelot towards Trois-Ponts. When the N68 meets the N633 just north of Trois-Ponts at the railway bridge viaduct, turn north (right) onto the N633, direction Coo. Approximately 13½ km north of Trois-Ponts directly on the winding N633 lies the village of Stoumont.**

Then: December 19, 1944, 10 a.m. — action lifted from a German cine film. By now, the bulk of the Peiper battlegroup had entered Stoumont from the east. With a Panzer IV rumbling into the fray on the left, SS grenadiers huddle along a hedgerow lining the main road as reinforcements move on the centre of the village from the hilly south.

Now: Fifty years later, the field [2] where the battle took place is now home to another force, the local gendarmerie! This is the view looking north-west just south of the N633 (Route de l'Amblève) as it winds its way through the village. Still standing timeless in the background is No. 1 Rue Village: la Maison Robinson.

Then: With the cine camera rolling, a Panther of Kampfgruppe Peiper rolls into Stoumont on December 19 while another already lies burning in front of it, knocked out by a massive US 90mm anti-aircraft gun firing horizontally. Yet it was to be in vain, for by noon Stoumont had fallen.

Now: Road to invasion and attack. The present-day N633 enters Stoumont from the east. The Panther came this way down the Route de l'Amblève [3]. The Robinson house can be seen on the left just visible in the wartime photo through the trees. The photo was taken standing next to No. 22, looking west.

Then: As SS troopers look on, several American soldiers march past into captivity. They were among approximately 270 US prisoners captured at Stoumont, most belonging to the 3rd Battalion, 119th Infantry, 30th Division.

Now: The scene of surrender [4] today along the Rue Village. The roof of the farmhouse on the right in the wartime photo can just be made out through the trees on the right today. In the centre of the photo, the same long stone house.

Then: American prisoners of the 119th Infantry Regiment, 30th Infantry Division, are marched east out of Stoumont under SS guard, the village having been taken earlier that day by Kampfgruppe Peiper.

Now: Though the trees have been felled and a new gendarmerie headquarters built on the right, this is the precise stretch of the N633 [5] which the Americans soldiers once marched down. By cross-referencing the white striped tree in the wartime photo in other photos, the location can be pinpointed exactly.

Then: Moving west out of Stoumont, Kampfgruppe Peiper was finally stopped by the 740th Tank Battalion and the 1st Battalion of the 119th Regiment. Three Panthers lie destroyed along the road into Stoumont from the west.

Now: History records this precise spot [6] as the furthest penetration point west by the 1. SS-Panzer-Division. The advance was stopped here, along the N633 (Gare de Stoumont), just west of the village.

Then: After the war, US military authorities returned to Stoumont to investigate alleged war crimes committed by the 1.SS-Panzer-Division. While GIs stand in line alongside a small house, the authorities ponder what really occurred on the site.

Now: Now reconstructed with cement blocks, the small building [7] still stands, the original front façade facing the N633. This photo was taken next to No. 44 across the Route de l'Ambleve.

Then: The battle for Stoumont took its toll on structures of all kinds, including the village church [8], with the roof and steeple both suffering substantial damage from American artillery fire. Heavy and intense in the area around Stoumont and La Gleize in particular, the barrage was instrumental in halting the advance of Kampfgruppe Peiper.

Now: The restored church pictured on a misty Sunday morning some 50 years later. The restoration work is truly remarkable, incorporating the same rosette and window patterns.

Then: This cine still shows a Panther of I. Abteilung of SS-Panzer-Regiment 1 slowly negotiating the tight streets of Stoumont. With grenadiers directing traffic, Kampfgruppe Peiper moves onward.

Now: A remarkable photo comparison of a murky wartime photo. The house on the left, No. 77 Rue Village [9], now displays its new bright, white façade, yet it matches perfectly with the visage of 50 years ago. This is quite a busy corner with the junction of four narrow streets.

Then: **After the battle, Panther 211 lies abandoned beside the railway west of the village. Marking the furthest point of penetration west for Kampfgruppe Peiper, this particular specimen had its gun barrel spiked. It and two other Panthers in the area were disabled by the 740th Tank Battalion stationed at a road-block down the road to the right.**

Now: **With the dip in the hill crest in the background providing a point of alignment, this is the same spot alongside the N633, looking south [10]. This location was also aided by other photos of the same tank from different angles.**

Then: With the snows of January 1945 partially covering the relics of battle, an American war photographer frames the business end of a German 75mm PaK 40 standing alongside a knocked-out Panther. The gun was sighted to fire down the main road leaving Stoumont to the west. The Germans perhaps put it to use for covering fire as they retreated from losses west of the village. Regardless, Stoumont was retaken by American forces by Christmas Eve, 1944.

Now: Pausing on the N633 over 50 years later, the author looks south along the Route de l'Amblève [11] and takes the same photo comparison. The house on the immediate left, No. 58, is still intact. The building in the far right background is the Le Vieux Stoumont restaurant where the author then retired for a quick cup of coffee!

Then: The battle to retake Stoumont, led by Task Force Harrison of the 30th Division (the 119th Infantry supported by the 740th Tank Battalion), commenced on the afternoon of December 20, 1944. With the sanatorium of St Edouard's [12] the initial focal point of a vicious and deadly battle, Task Force Harrision lost five Shermans and over 200 men in the assault. Stoumont was finally taken late on the evening of December 21.

Now: With the trees now lining this stretch of the N633, the sanatorium is completely obscured, yet despite the advances of nature this is the exact location [12] where a Sherman and a Panther once lay in defeat. The restored sanatorium lies immediately behind the row of trees.

Then: December 15, 1944. With weeks of preparation and deception complete, and the vanguard of three German armies massed along the borders of Belgium and Luxembourg, Operation 'Wacht am Rhein' is set to begin in less than 24 hours. As the 1. SS-Panzer Division moves forward through a staging area in Tondorf, Germany, the rearguard in the form of schwere SS-Panzer-Abteilung 501 rumbles down the main street. Under the command of SS-Obersturmbannführer Heinz von Westernhagen, 501 was operating approximately 20 King Tigers in support.

Now: Fifty years have passed yet in the small village of Tondorf time seems to have stood still. On this spot [1] a German cine cameraman stood and filmed an armoured column moving forward to the battlefront, approximately 30 kilometres to the west. The houses in the distance form a perfect match.

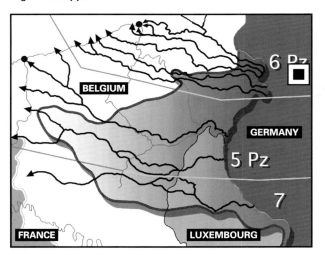

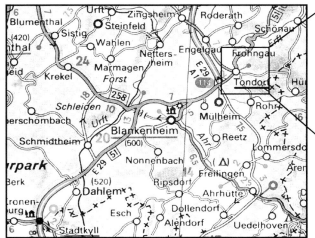

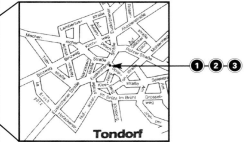

Tondorf: Michelin 417, Col. 4. 6° 43' East 50° 28' North. Southbound on the Belgian E42 (A27), exit 15 at St. Vith. Head east on the N626, direction Schonberg/Manderfeld. At Manderfeld, take the N634 east into Germany, direction Stadtkyll. N634 becomes German 421 at the border, heading west. At the intersection of the E29 just west of Stadtkyll, take E29 (E29/51) north, direction Koln. As E29 splits from 51 towards Koln, continue west on 51 and enter Tondorf from the west.

Then: One by one, the tanks move forward. Further into the film, a closer look at this particular one identifies it as number 003 — a tank of the staff company of schwere SS-Panzer-Abteilung 501. It would soon see action along Rollbahn D in the thrust to the west.

Now: Though the hotel on the right (Gasthaus zum Weissen Ross) is more or less identical to how it looked 50 years ago, nevertheless the scene has yielded to change, in particular the house and wall on the left.

Then: With a wave to the assembled locals, an SS trooper enjoys a heady ride on the back of Tiger 222. German cameramen followed this particular tank all the way along Rollbahns D and E until it was knocked out at the bridge in Stavelot (see pages 245-248).

Now: Looking up along the road [3], the author matches the same angle of the frame exposed in December 1944. Although now substantially modified, nonetheless enough is shown of the house in the wartime still to pinpoint the location.

Then: **With river crossings vital for Kampfgruppe Peiper's westward thrust along Rollbahn D, late on the morning of December 18, 1944, Peiper managed to cross the Amblève in Stavelot over an intact bridge. He immediately made for Trois-Ponts — so named in French after the three bridges in the town (over the Amblève and Salm rivers). The first of the bridges was blown at 11.15 a.m. right in front of the Germans, and a second over the Salm some hours later. Forestalled at Trois-Ponts, Peiper thereupon headed north for La Gleize — and eventual defeat.**

Now: **Now, long since replaced, the bridge and the railway viaduct [1] form a picturesque backdrop over the river. The present-day Route de Coo (N633) runs north out of Trois-Ponts from the right towards La Gleize. The wartime shot shows the bridge when it was destroyed earlier in the war when the Belgians retreated in 1940; by 1944 a temporary structure was in place.**

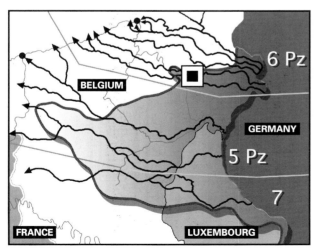

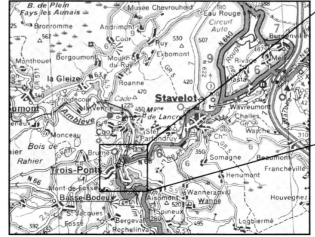

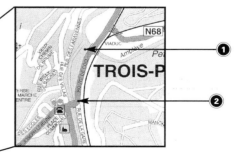

Trois-Ponts: **Michelin 214, Col. 8. 5° 53' East 50° 23' North. North or southbound on the E42 (A27), exit 11, direction Stavelot. Continue towards Stavelot along the N62, which joins the N68. Continue on the N68 through Stavelot heading west, direction Trois-Ponts. When the N68 meets the N633 just north of Trois-Ponts at the railway bridge viaduct, turn left onto the N68 and park in Trois-Ponts. The bridges are in front of and behind you.**

Then: The second of the three bridges of Trois-Ponts, this one over the Salm river, is seen in this wartime photo. Unlike the one over the Amblève, this one was not blown by the Belgians in 1940 but was destroyed by the Americans on December 18, 1944, right in the face of Kampfgruppe Peiper.

Now: The view today looking west at the intersection [2] of the Rue de la Gare and Route de Coo shows the rebuilt bridge in the centre. Though the buildings on the right have changed substantially, those on the left have not.

Then: **By December 20, 1944, Troisvierges in Luxembourg had been overrun by the 560. Volks-Grenadier-Division of the LVIII. Panzerkorps, part of the 5. Panzer-Armee. Following the evacuation of the St Vith salient in the north, Troisvierges settled into German occupancy but a month later the tide turned and the LXVI. Armeekorps retreated through the town before the advance of the First and Third Armies. Left behind on an unusual slate wall of a house was this graffiti, indicative of German morale even at the bitter end: 'Behind the last battle of this war stands our victory!'**

Now: **With Troisvierges being a fair-sized town, the author was not optimistic about finding a single wall. However, knowing the street down which the Americans entered the town, the author began his journey along the Rue d'Asselborn . . . and promptly found the wall in fifteen seconds off to the left! It stood out because of its unusual slate tile construction; it is actually the side of No. 42 [1]. The same metal piping still trims its bottom edge.**

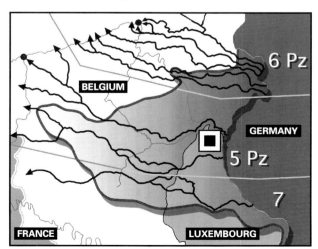

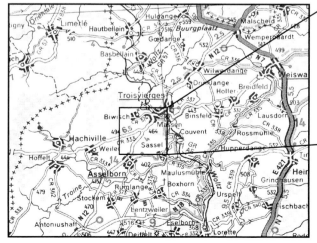

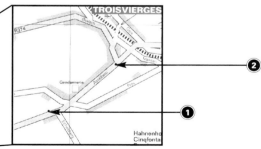

Troisvierges: **Michelin 214, Col. 8. 6° 00' East 50° 7' North. North or southbound on the E421, exit 15 at St Vith. Head south along the N62, crossing into Luxembourg after 15 km. The N62 becomes the N12 at the border. Troisvierges lies 5 km south from the border along the N12.**

Then: **A US Signal Corps photographer captures a poignant moment in Troisvierges during the heady days of September 1944 when the end of Germany seemed only weeks away. As soldiers of the 28th Infantry Division march down a street in the centre of the town, a young girl offers a flower as her parents look on in admiration.**

Now: **A similar, sunny afternoon in Troisvierges, Luxembourg, over 50 years later, finds the same street [2] deserted. The view is looking south-west up the Rue d'Asselborn. The houses to the right are Nos. 10 and 12.**

Then: **Thunder in the valley. Aiming at enemy concentrations around the village of Arbrefontaine, nine kilometres to the south-east, M4 guns of the 2nd Battalion, 32nd Armored Regiment, 3rd Armored Division, fire over the hilltops in early January 1945.**

Now: **With the great guns long gone and the trees felled, the same field [1] just north of the village of Trou-de-Bra lies still and silent beside the present-day N645. The house in the distance on the far left, just visible through the smoke in the wartime photo, is No. 36. On the right the same tree-clad hillside frames the photo.**

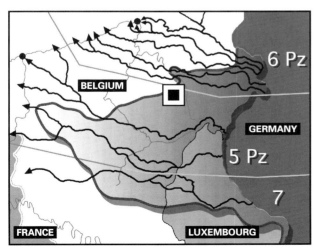

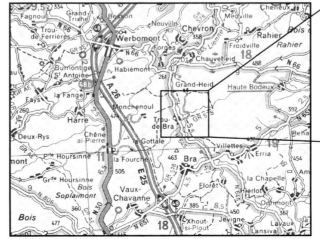

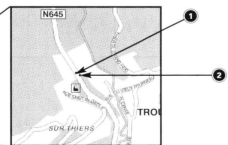

Trou-de-Bra: **Michelin 214, Col. 8. 5° 44' East 50° 21' North. North or southbound on the E25 (A26), exit 49, direction east along the N651. Some 4½ km east of the exit, through and beyond the village of Bra, lies the intersection with the N645 heading north. Turn left onto the N645. Approximately 3 km north lies Trou-de-Bra.**

Then: With gun barrels skyward, all manner of armoured vehicles get into the act in the artillery field [2] north of Trou-de-Bra. On the right, adding to the chorus from the Sherman tanks, is an M7B1 105mm self-propelled howitzer. The valley is thick with smoke from the deadly barrage.

Now: With the tell-tale backdrop to line up the comparison, this is the same field 50 years later. However, even this has now changed; upon returning to the site after this photo was taken, the author was dismayed to find that several homes had since sprung up, marring the comparison.

Then: Under the unrelenting pressure of both the 18. and 62. Volks-Grenadier-Divisions, the St Vith sector was evacuated on December 22, 1944. The 7th Armored Division withdrew east to Vielsalm where the 82nd Airborne Division had set up a defensive screen. On December 23, 7th Armored personnel set up this 76mm gun west of the town, its barrel trained on the western approach road. The defensive line was now in place, yet already the 2. SS-Panzer-Division was outflanking it to the south.

Now: A perfect comparison west of Vielsalm along the Rue des Chasseurs Ardennais [1] which runs into the town. Although 50 years have passed, with the same buildings still standing and snow on the ground, there is little to betray the passage of time. The building on the left, No. 16, houses the Café la Technique.

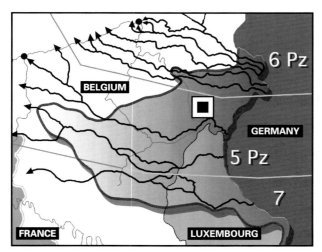

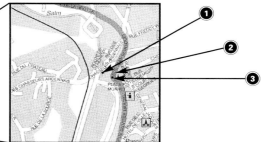

Vielsalm: Michelin 214, Col. 8. 5° 55' East 50° 17' North. North or southbound on the E25 (A26), exit 50, direction east along the N89. 15 km east of the exit lies the village of Salmchâteau. Turn left (north) onto the N68. Vielsalm lies 2½ km north of Salmchâteau.

Then: On Christmas Eve 1944, the hasty defences of Vielsalm include the wiring of the railway bridge [2] immediately west of the town. At the time, the railway line headed south to Salmchâteau.

Now: In what must surely be the most changed of all locations that the author visited, the entire railway bridge and track has disappeared but, scrambling up the steep embankment, he managed to find the remains of the bridge abutment still embedded in the side of the hill (lower left). Today the line bypasses Vielsalm on its way north towards Trois-Ponts.

Then: January 17, 1945. The tide of war having moved permanently in favour of the Allies, American troops of the 75th Infantry Division (First Army) enter Vielsalm midst the snows of the New Year.

Now: Looking east along the Rue Jean Bertholet [3] in the centre of the town, the author captures the scene, with identical January snow. The soldiers would have been marching towards the present-day Place Pauline Moxhet, which leads into Rue Général Jacques.

Then: With the siege of Bastogne lifted by the Third Army on December 26, 1944, the Germans began to try and sever the so-called 'Bastogne Corridor' which Patton had opened up from the south. It fell to the 1.SS-Panzer-Division and the 167. Volks-Grenadier-Division to attack the corridor from the east at 4.45 a.m. on December 30. The tiny village of Villers-la-Bonne-Eau, defended by the 137th Infantry Regiment, (35th Infantry Division) was eventually taken by the Germans that afternoon after heavy fighting.

Now: The same stretch of winding road [1] which leads into the tiny hamlet from the east. With the smashed wartime vehicles long since removed, this unobtrusive country road now holds no clues as to the carnage which once occurred all around it. In its place, only the silence and stillness of a cold, Sunday morning.

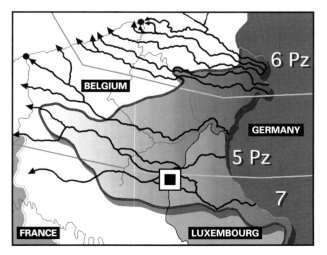

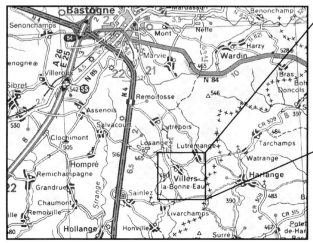

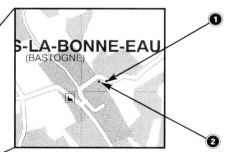

Villers-la-Bonne-Eau: Michelin 214, Col. 8. 5° 44' East 49° 56' North. North or southbound on the N4 south of Bastogne, exit at Losange, direction east towards the village. Continue through and past Losange; at the next intersection, turn right, direction Villers-la-Bonne-Eau/Lutremange. The village lies to the west of Lutremange.

Then: **January 13, 1945. In the cold afternoon, a US Army Signal Corps photographer captures the aftermath of the battle at Villers-la-Bonne-Eau. With both German vehicles and American tanks intermingled at the roadside, and the village gutted by artillery fire, only the snowy blanket attempts to soften the scene. Yet beneath the snow the fields were scarred from the incredible barrage of over 6,000 shells.**

Now: **A lovely 'weather match' comparison along the same stretch of road [2] — almost to the very day 50 years later. With barns restored and new houses built, the village can hold its head high once again.**

Then: **Moving east past Hünningen (Hunnange), Belgium, with the 7th Armored Division, US Signal Corps photographer Hugh F. McHugh of the 165th Signal Photo Company followed them into the next village to the east, Wallerode. On January 25, 1945, he was recording the activity of the soldiers of Company A of the 23rd Armored Infantry Battalion. After climbing inside an old château in the centre of the village, he leaned out a window and took this photograph of a gutted house with a burning German Hetzer next to it.**

Now: **Fifty years later, the author gained access to the same château [1]. After requesting permission from the front desk to photograph from inside a particular room on the second floor, the tenants were contacted who kindly gave their permission. While husband and wife watched, the author then hung out of the same window to take the comparison.**

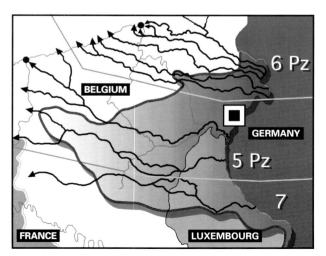

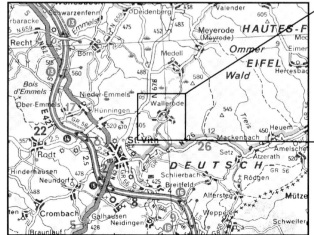

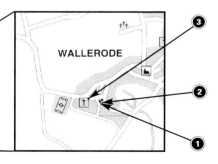

Wallerode: **Michelin 214, Col. 8. 6° 10' East 50° 18' North. North or southbound on the E42 (A27), exit 14, direction Hünningen (Hunnange) east along the N670. East of Hünningen, at the intersection with the N676, turn left (north) onto the N676. The road leading into Wallerode from the west lies a few hundred meters off to the right, just north of the intersection.**

Then: Having taken the photograph from the window of the château, Hugh McHugh left the building to take a close up of the burning tank. The Hetzer was a small fixed-turret design sporting a 75mm PaK39 L/48 gun.

Now: Today, a shed has been added to the side of the house [2]. Minutes later, McHugh was killed by a German sniper. Standing upright to take his last photo, he did not hear his fellow-soldiers' warnings to get down.

Then: Earlier that same day, Hugh McHugh pictured men of Company A cutting through a wire fence next to the château. With makeshift white sheeting to camouflage their outlines, one soldier goes to work while another stands guard.

Now: Following in Hugh McHugh's footsteps, the author walked down the road [3] leading into Wallerode. The houses on the left remain as they once were, as does the turret-like structure in the centre. Many of the trees and the fence line itself also remain today.

Warche-La Falize

Then: The full measure of deception of SS-Obersturmbannführer Otto Skorzeny's special Panzerbrigade 150 is revealed outside a small café between Warche and La Falize, Belgium. This Panther, coded 'B10', was dressed up in sheet metal and white stars to resemble an M10 tank destroyer. From the heights at La Falize, Skorzeny watched his troops in the valley below as they fought beside the paper mill (see page 182) on the western outskirts of Malmédy.

Now: Having been enlarged since the war, the present-day café-restaurant-Pension on the Route de Falize sports a new wing yet the original section on the far right betrays the location as the place where an uninvited German patron once came calling.

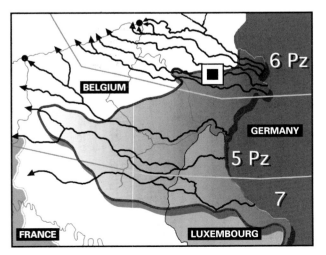

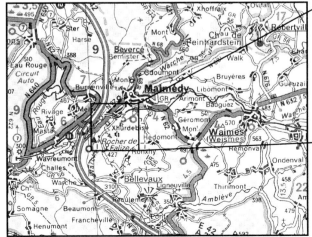

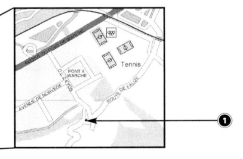

Warche-Falize: Michelin 214, Col. 9. 6° 1' East 50° 25' North. North or southbound on the E42 (A27), exit 11, direction Malmédy east along the N62. Just over the Warche river bridge and past the paper mill on the left, turn right onto Ol'Z-Eyos, direction La Falize. Continue up the hill until the Ol'Z-Eyos intersects the Route de Falize. Immediately to your right is the 'Pension' restaurant.

Wardin

Then: Two years after the battle, a lone Sherman still lies on the battlefield awaiting a Belgian scrap merchant who will soon come to destroy it. It is a shame as this particular tank was disabled near the spot where Team O'Hara fought to stop Kampfgruppe 901 of the Panzer-Lehr-Division as it moved on Bastogne from the east.

Now: The same stretch of road [1] today, just west of Wardin, is now the present-day N84 heading into Bastogne from the east. The view is looking directly west down the road, standing on the south side across from house No. 3. Though the original large trees have been felled, their replacements are making a comeback.

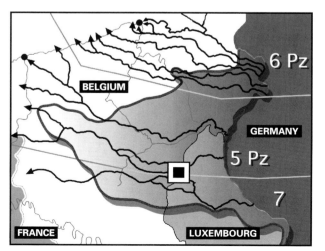

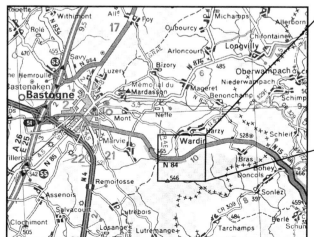

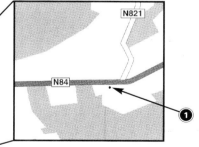

Wardin: Michelin 214, Col. 8. 5° 47' East 49° 59' North. North or southbound on the E25 (A26), exit 54 at Bastogne. Head east on the N84, direction Wiltz/Ettelbruck. Approximately 5 km east of Bastogne, just before the intersection with the N821 leading into Wardin from the south, lies the location along the N84 looking back west.

Then: December 20, 1944, Werbomont, Belgium. Bazooka at the ready, soldiers of Company C, 325th Glider Infantry Regiment, 82nd Airborne Division, await the arrival of Kampfgrupper Peiper. However, Herr Peiper was not to show up. With his leading spearhead having made significant — albeit fitful — progress along Rollbahns D and E, December 18 saw his battle-group halted by a blown bridge four kilometres east of Werbomont.

Now: The view over 50 years later now shorn of fog and smoke, the location where members of the 82nd once lay in wait is pictured again by the author. With the sun shining and flow-ers blooming, it is hard to imagine that this is indeed the same spot — yet it is. This is the view looking north [1] along the present-day N30 (Avenue Bosson), just south of the village of Ernonheid, immediately before the intersection of the Route de Paradis with the N30.

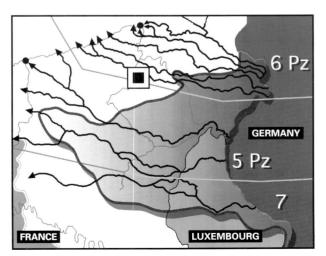

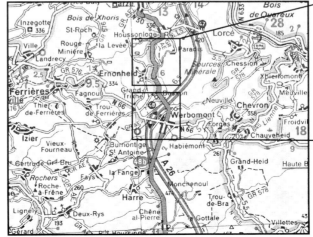

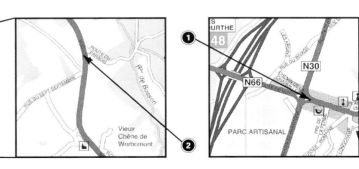

Werbomont: Michelin 214, Col. 7. 5° 42' East 50° 23' North. North or southbound on the E25 (A26), exit 48, direction east to Werbomont on the N66. Werbomont lies at the intersection of the N66 and the N30 which runs north-south.

Then: **Fleeing westward in the face of the onslaught of the 1. SS-Panzer-Division, refugees pour into Werbomont and points west. By December 18, Peiper's battlegroup had reached Habiémont four kilometres down the road, only to have a vital bridge blown in its face. They never made it to Werbomont.**

Now: **Looking east down the present-day N66 (Route de Stavelot) half a century later. The white houses [2] on the left are Nos. 1 and 2. The same old farmhouse in the background still stands as if time has stood still. Where Belgian refugees once trekked with horse-drawn carts, today the paved surface of the N66 carries modern commerce onto the E25 via exit 48, which lies directly behind the author.**

Then: For the citizens of Wiltz in Luxembourg, the second liberation (after that of September 1944) was a long time coming. After being overrun on December 19, 1944, by the 5. Fallschirm-Jäger-Division, the town remained in German hands until the arrival of the American 80th Infantry Division on January 23, 1945. With the snows of January as a backdrop, the soldiers are following the sweeping road [1] in the south of the town. Note the shell-burst in the centre of the square.

Now: On a sunny day over 50 years later, the author returns to Wiltz. This is the view looking north-west down the Route d'Ettelbruck, with the Place des Martyrs in the centre. The houses and buildings lining Rue Fontaine in the background have remained remarkably intact. A US Sherman is now displayed on the far right as a memorial.

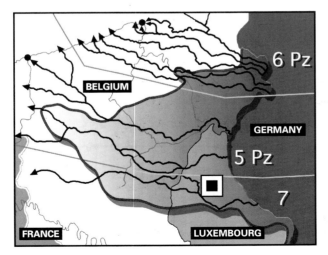

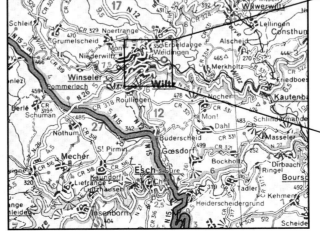

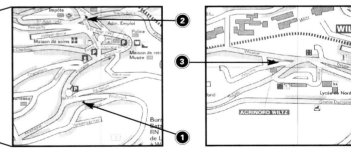

Wiltz: Michelin 214, Col. 8. 5° 56' East 49° 58' North. North or southbound on the E25 (A26), exit 54, direction east to Bastogne city centre on the N84. Continue through and out of Bastogne heading east on the N84, direction Wiltz. After 16 km east along the N84 (which becomes the N15 at the Luxembourg border) turn at Nothum onto the N26, heading north into Wiltz. The town lies 5 km away.

Then: Five wooden crosses, inscribed with the names of those that have fallen in combat, rise starkly out of the snow on a lengthening winter afternoon in Wiltz in 1945. This photograph also illustrates how the town nestles in a small valley along the river of the same name.

Now: Where German dead were once buried now stands a new park bench, the remains having been exhumed and moved to Lommel Soldatenfriedhof after the war. This is the view looking due north at the intersection of Avenue Nicholas Kreins and Route de Kautenbach [2]. The brick memorial serves to align the comparison.

Then: On New Year's Day the Luftwaffe scrounged together what little aircraft they had left and took to the skies over Belgium in a last-ditch attempt to inflict some measure of destruction. While achieving surprise, this raid cost the Germans dear in terms of experienced pilots. With Wiltz back in American hands by the third week of January 1945, soldiers of the 633rd Anti-Aircraft Artillery Battalion (80th Division) man a Bofors on a nearby hillside.

Now: Believe it or not, this is the same place [3] — the backyard of No. 10 Rue de l'Industrie. Though the trees now obscure the distant view, the stone wall enclosing the cemetery behind the gun still stands behind the clutter of today.

Then: **With the 80th Infantry Division moving through Wiltz on January 23, 1945, and then north-east into Wilwerwiltz, the LIII. Armeekorps of 7. Armee was forced to withdraw further to the east in a confused attempt to hold together the now substantially mixed-up German front. Left behind in the village while undergoing repairs inside a railway shed was this Sturmgeschütz III.**

Now: **Over 50 years later the building and its stone platform still stand. In the distance, the house with the triangular rooftop and the single window is visible, and can be seen in the wartime photo by looking through the destroyed house. Several of the stones on the platform can be matched as well.**

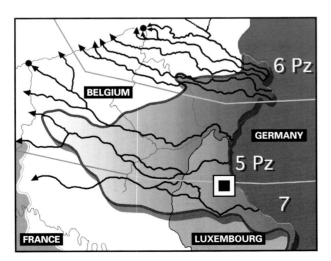

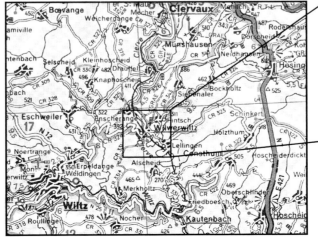

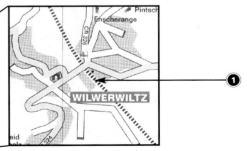

Wilwerwiltz: **Michelin 214, Col. 7. 6° 00' East 49° 59' North. North or southbound on the E25 (A26), exit 54, direction east to Bastogne city centre on the N84. Continue through and out of Bastogne heading east on the N84. After travelling 16 km east along the N84 (which becomes the N15 at the border) leave at Nothum onto the N26, heading north into Wiltz. Pass through Wiltz continuing east, now along the CR325 and thence the CR324 into Wilwerwiltz.**

Then: **Perhaps deciding that discretion is the better part of valour, soldiers of the 372nd Field Artillery Battalion, 99th Infantry Division, prepare to evacuate the village of Wirtzfeld, Belgium, on December 17, 1944. With the 277. Volks-Grenadier-Division and the 12. SS-Panzer-Division on their heels, part of the 99th withdrew to Elsenborn to the north-east of the village. Note the M10 tank destroyer covering the retreat on the right.**

Now: **A rather remarkable comparison taken 50 years later almost to the very day finds little has changed. This is the intersection [1] of three unnamed roads in the northern part of the village. Ahead lies the road to Elsenborn. The house on the far right where the tank once sat is No. 66; the white house behind No. 65. The small tree in the centre distance in the wartime photo still stands though much larger.**

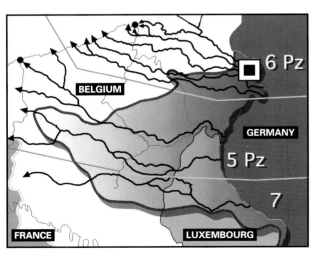

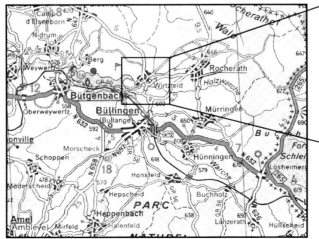

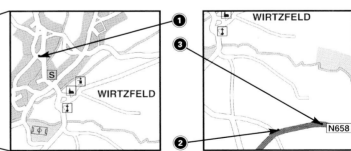

Wirtzfeld: **Michelin 214, Col. 9. 6° 16' East 50° 26' North. North or southbound on the E42 (A27), exit 11, direction east to Malmédy on the N62. Continue through Malmédy to Waimes and points east along the N62 and then the N632, passing through Bütgenbach and into Büllingen. Moving east through Büllingen, turn left immediately underneath the railway overpass, direction Wirtzfeld. You will enter the village from the south.**

Then: These Panzer IVs (the second is down the road on the extreme left) were probably a probing force from Kampfgruppe Peiper. They were dispatched by US tank destroyers just south of Wirtzfeld.

Now: The same stretch of road [2] just south of Wirtzfeld, Belgium. This is the view looking east along the present-day N658 as it approaches the twin villages of Krinkelt-Rocherath in the distance. The trees on the far left still stand in place, aiding the alignment.

Then: Having walked down the road towards Krinkelt-Rocherath, the Signal Corps photographer now turns to picture the same stretch of road looking west. This time, the other destroyed Panzer IV is nearest the camera. These tanks were knocked out by the 1st Platoon of Company C of the 644th Tank Destroyer Battalion.

Now: And a fitting end at a fitting location [3] — where once German armoured might was met and defeated, today there is only sunshine and warmth . . . and the memories of what once took place here over five decades ago. Scores of cars now pass this way every day. Do their drivers really know what transpired? We can only hope that they, like us, remember. Long ago, it happened here. They came this way.

In The Field:
Then Meets Now at Fifty Years

TUESDAY, DECEMBER 19, 1944.   TUESDAY, DECEMBER 19, 1994.

IN THE FIELD:
Then Meets Now at 50 Years.

Then Meets Now at 50 Years: **Transported through time back to its original resting place, a destroyed King Tiger II of schwere Panzer-Abteilung 506 once again lies along the road leading north out of Moinet, Belgium. Disabled on January 13, 1945, on this precise spot, the location today is shrouded once again in fog and snow. Despite the newly constructed houses and barn, the scene remains the same — and the author wills the great beast back into existence, and its rightful place in our modern world. Here it once lay, and here it rests again. Compare this composite photo to its wartime equivalent on page 204.**

Then meets Now at 50 Years: **The hills east of the city of Echternach, Luxembourg, are once again visited by Battery C of the 457th Anti-Aircraft Artillery Battalion, as the trio guard the skies with their Bofors gun. Though the tree-lines are denser, and the city of Echternach has long since spread across the valley, the field remains the same half a century later. In the identical setting, the author once again restores the gun pit to its precise location across time. With the hill range silhouette identical, and the same overcast of long ago, the barrel of the Bofors pierces the sky at the precise spot that it once did — and the ghost figures assume their place in eternity. Again, compare this composite to the original on page 78.**

Then meets Now at 50 Years: **Winter, 1994, and along the N15 just east of the Belgian border in Luxembourg, the same German Jagdpanzer IV/70 still rests in the snow — an eternal guardian put back into place today only by the author. Where the occupants of house No. 10 look out upon an empty field in the snow of the present day, the author still sees tracks in his mind's eye, and captures time on film. For the wartime shot, see page 32.**

Then meets Now at 50 Years: **On the same school playground 50 years later, members of the 393rd Infantry Regiment, US 99th Infantry Division, along with their medical detachment, reconvene across time to hand out decorations once again. In the clear, crisp setting of today, one can almost hear the accolades being announced, as the author captures the scene in 1998 in the village of Born, Belgium. Compare this composite photo to its wartime equivalent on page 48.**

Then meets Now at 50 Years: **The tragedy of January 9, 1945, in Nothum, Luxembourg, is revisited 50 years later on the precise spot. With members of the 90th Infantry Division marching through time and once again out of the village in the background, armoured vehicles of the 712th Tank Battalion still line the snowy streets of Nothum today. Its slain commander, Lieutenant Colonel George Randolph, now lies directly in front of the author in the present-day snowy setting of Nothum. No greater testimony to the power of the 'then and now' format is needed — it happened here, and this reconstructed picture reveals its impact. Look back to page 211 to compare with the original picture.**

Then meets Now at 50 Years: **Leaving its 9. Panzer-Division compatriots consigned to eternity, Panther 412 rumbles through time and stops outside of the village church at Sterpigny, Belgium. On a snowy day in 1995, villagers would be astonished to find their place of worship once again under guard —yet there it sits today, parked along the N827, waiting to take on the US Army one last time in a desperate attempt to turn the clock back. Compare the author's composite photo with the wartime equivalent on page 253.**

Then meets Now at 50 Years: **The ultimate price of war is revisited at Henri-Chapelle, Belgium. No amount of present-day debris can erase the significance of this site, as Gefreiter Wilhelm Schmidt once again hangs lifeless from the cross of retribution. With the bullet impact pock marks still present in the concrete facing behind him, the effect is timeless and powerful — and the futility of war is revealed. The original photo for comparison can be found on page 118.**

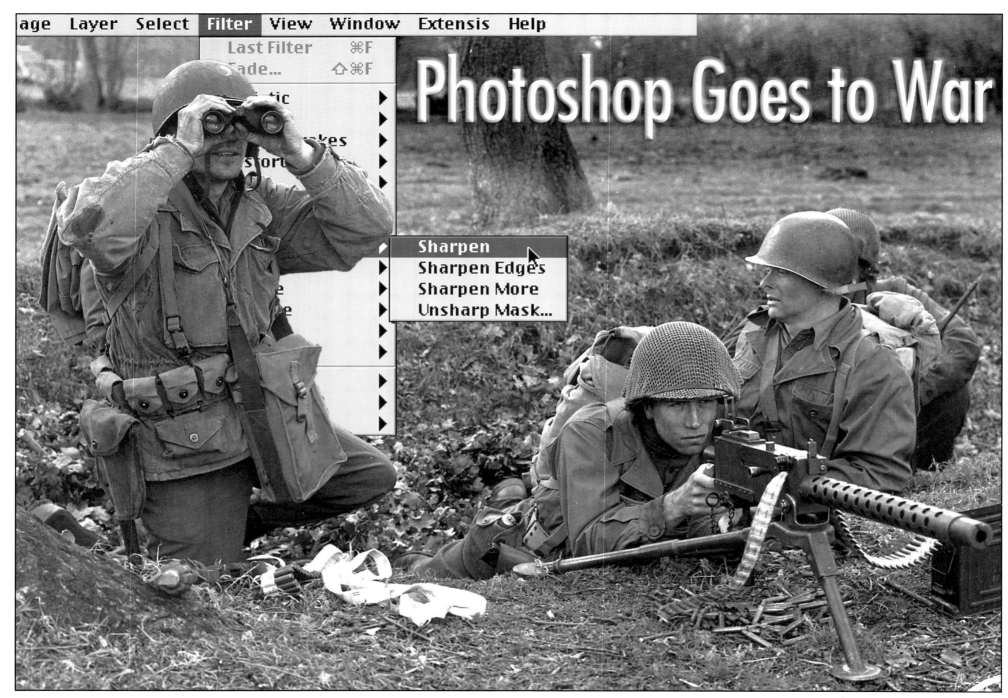

age   Layer   Select   **Filter**   View   Window   Extensis   Help

Last Filter   ⌘F
Fade...   ⇧⌘F

Photoshop Goes to War

Sharpen
Sharpen Edges
Sharpen More
Unsharp Mask...

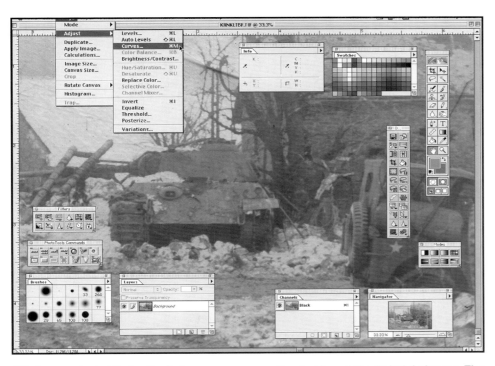

Window on the battle for the Ardennes, as seen on the desktop of the digital darkroom. The author utilised the digital standard for photograph manipulation and enhancement, Adobe Photoshop (Adobe Corporation, San Jose, CA, USA).

PHOTOSHOP GOES TO WAR:
In the service of history, the digital standard sharpens the focus on the past

Through the skillful and courageous work of German and American war photographers, the Battle of the Bulge has a richly documented photographic history. This is all the more remarkable given the atrocious conditions under which it was fought. Some of the most famous photographs of World War II were captured in the Ardennes under situations of duress and hardship. The composition and emotional range of these photographs speak to the photographer's eye at the moment; the US Army Signal Corps photographers in particular sought to capture the human element of fighting, reflected in the camaraderie and kinship which comes across in so many of their pictures. The German kriegsberichter (war reporters), given the nationalistic desperation of the Wehrmacht/SS counter-offensive, sought to sway opinion and boost morale, focusing skillfully on the polarisation of many aspects of the fighting: staged German 'attacks', armour rolling forward, scores of captured soldiers. The additional use of cinematic film sequences, many captured after the war, revealed the degree this propaganda played in their documentation.

The grainy, black-and-white nature of the wartime photographs in the Ardennes is a product of time, equipment, conditions and limitations. Colour film was rare and expensive at the time, and very seldom used in the field. By today's standards, its range and saturation was limited. Black-and-white film was the norm, though again, by today's standards, its performance was relatively fixed in terms of grain and speed. Photograph quality, needless to say, was also subject to virtual arctic conditions and harsh field realities. Storage conditions after the war, be they government archives or the desk drawers of war veterans, all took a further toll.

Until recently, photograph retouching was difficult and time consuming. The darkroom photographer's ability to either rescue damaged photos or enhance them was limited, and many of today's techniques were literally beyond the times and equipment of the past. When printed straight from damaged or sub-optimal negatives, the prints revealed their stressful lineage.

The last decade has witnessed the coming of the 'digital darkroom', through the dramatic acceleration of computing power and optical/digital techniques. What was once the purveyance of expensive, dedicated, chemically-based rooms can now be largely achieved on a reasonably-powerful desktop computer from a scanned photograph or negative. Yet even this last barrier of 'analog-to-digital' photography is falling: recent advances in digital cameras have broken the three-million-pixel level, yielding high resolutions on a reasonably-priced basis. It is now possible to go from camera to computer to high-end digital pre-press, all without the use of traditional film or developing.

This book was developed on a high-end Apple Macintosh blue-white, G3 PowerPC, running at 350 Mhz with 320 Mb of RAM. Twin studio display 17-inch monitors, each powered by separate RAGE 128 graphics cards, created a virtual, desktop surface almost a yard wide. Three internal hard drives, at 6.4 Gb each, resulted in 19.2 Gb on-board storage, supplemented by removable cartridges at 230 Mb each. Working chiefly from digitally-scanned photographs, virtually all of the pictures, both wartime photos and the author's modern comparisons, were reviewed and enhanced to eliminate damage, sub-optimal light levels, sharpness and balance. Since it also contains previously unpublished photos from the battle, these in particular needed careful attention to detail. Finally, in support of the 'then and now' format, the cropping sizes of each set was digitally matched to within a thousandth of an inch. The program of choice for all of these tasks and more was the latest version of the reigning digital standard, Adobe Photoshop. Used around the world by publishing and production houses of all kinds, this massively capable program can now serve wartime history, helping to bring the action of long ago into further relief and focus. Given its ground-breaking scope and future potential, some of its capabilities are illustrated here. By its very nature, the then and now photo format, seeking to reach across time by comparing scene locations, can benefit a great deal from these technologies. In the service of history, digital techniques can indeed sharpen the focus on the past.

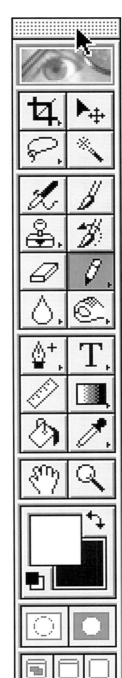

Tower of power. The main toolbox palette of Adobe Photoshop floating on the desktop. Each individual icon tab refers to the respective capabilities of each: pens, paintbrushes, cloning tools, eyedroppers, erasers, marquees, etc. In addition, each icon that bears a small triangle in its lower right-hand corner expands horizontally to reveal a further menu selection of similar types of tools. The three levels of boxes at the palette's bottom control foreground/background colours, masking tools and screen displays, respectively from top to bottom.

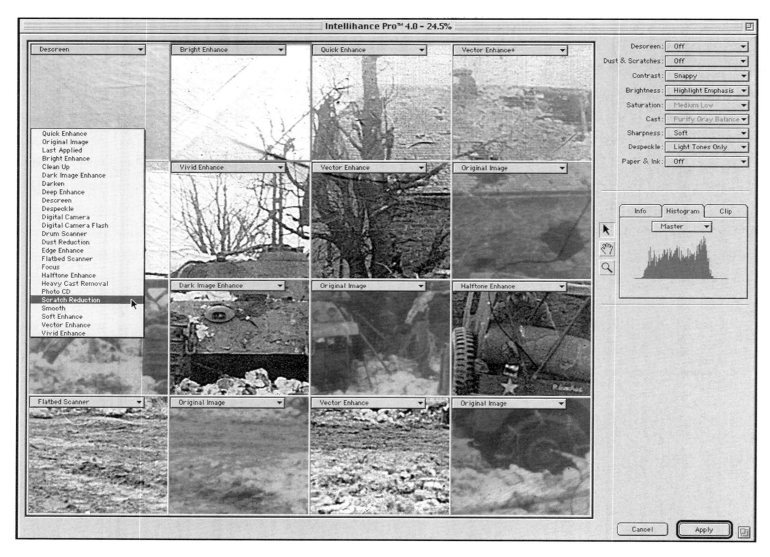

Intellihance Pro™ 4.0 - 24.5%

Descreen

Bright Enhance
Quick Enhance
Vector Enhance+

Quick Enhance
Original Image
Last Applied
Bright Enhance
Clean Up
Dark Image Enhance
Darken
Deep Enhance
Descreen
Despeckle
Digital Camera
Digital Camera Flash
Drum Scanner
Dust Reduction
Edge Enhance
Flatbed Scanner
Focus
Halftone Enhance
Heavy Cast Removal
Photo CD
Scratch Reduction
Smooth
Soft Enhance
Vector Enhance
Vivid Enhance

Vivid Enhance
Vector Enhance
Original Image

Dark Image Enhance
Original Image
Halftone Enhance

Flatbed Scanner
Original Image
Vector Enhance
Original Image

Descreen: Off
Dust & Scratches: Off
Contrast: Snappy
Brightness: Highlight Emphasis
Saturation: Medium Low
Cast: Purify Gray Balance
Sharpness: Soft
Despeckle: Light Tones Only
Paper & Ink: Off

Info   Histogram   Clip

Master

Cancel   Apply

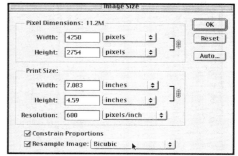

Size matters. Photoshop allows operators to set up basic settings such as height, width and pixel resolutions.

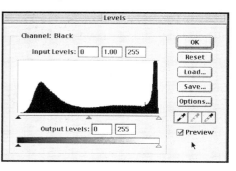

Shades of grey. Input and output brightness levels can be mapped to adjust contrast.

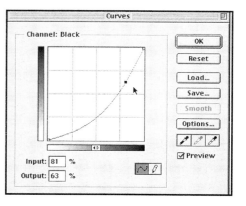

Curvilinear. Curves are used to more precisely map input and output brightness points.

The Battle of the Bulge, Through the Lens: 16 digital ones, to be precise. Adobe Photoshop code structure allows for third-party 'plug-in' programs to leverage its capabilities. One of the most popular and powerful is shown here, Intellihance Pro by Extensis (www.extensis.com) Intellihance allows the operator to view enhancement effects on a photograph in up to 25 separate pre-set windows at once, observing multiple effects in real time. Each window 'effects lense' can be selected through its own pull-down menu. Standard settings such as brightness, contrast, sharpness and despeckle can also be adjusted. Selected settings are then applied to the photograph. Finally, the effects of different types of ink and paper on print quality can be simulated to proof final output.

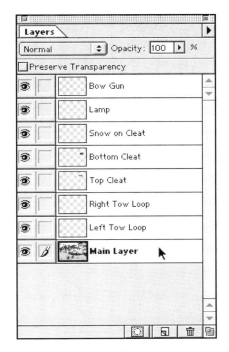

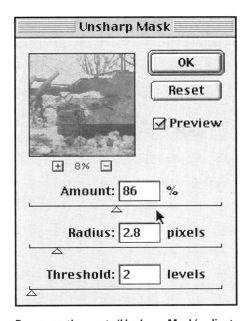

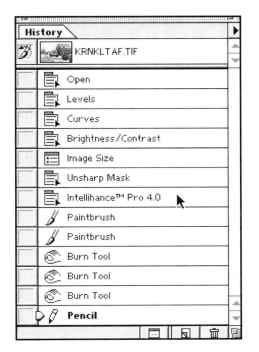

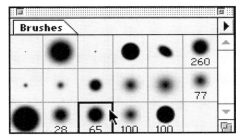

Quiver of brushes. This palette displays a pre-set collection of digital 'brush tips': size in pixels, hardness and spacing characteristics can all be modified and stored.

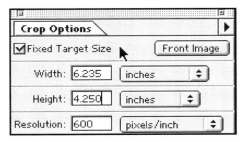

Layers upon layers. Effectively 'stacks of transparent work areas', each component or effect can be modified independently of the other, or layers and their effects can be linked.

Focus on the past. 'Unsharp Mask' adjusts pixel-level contrast of photo areas and/or edges. The degree of pixel-level sharpening can be adjusted and viewed in real time in a magnification window.

Going down in history. At any time or stage, the user can 'revert' back to a set point in the effects process, eliminating (un-doing) undesired effects.

Cut and wrap. A convenient crop-option palette lets the user match photo sizes precisely using a 'fixed size' crop tool.

Before: A previously unpublished photograph of a wartime scene in Krinkelt-Rocherath shows its age in terms of focus and light levels. The author has 'damaged' the photo even more for demonstration purposes. Correcting for anomalies such as scratches, marks, etc. would in no way detract from its authenticity and true composition.

After: With great care and respect for the original scene, the classic is enhanced and adjusted to remove visible flaws, and the reader comes just a little bit closer to history. (Photograph William C. C. Cavanagh Collection, courtesy Colonel Tom C. Morris)

AN HISTORIC FIND IN THE PRESENT-DAY ARDENNES

On December 27, 1998, in the low light of late afternoon, the culmination of four years of military research in the Ardennes yielded an incredible discovery. Approximately two kilometers south-south-west of the hamlet of La Vaulx-Richard, on a small, secluded farm, the author was absolutely astonished to find a completely intact King Tiger II, still in full battle regalia. Despite over 50 years of battlefield investigations by historians and amateurs of all types, a pristine example of the 'king of battle' itself still lay quietly undisturbed in a snowy field, adjacent to a fence on the corner of the farm. This incredible photo officially documents the existence of the proud historic beast as it was found around 3.15 p.m., after a clandestine tip from an aged local villager. If the author had not gazed upon it himself, he could scarcely have believed it was true. But there it sits today, resplendent in its original 'Wacht am Rhein' camouflage, still possessing its original bow machine gun, spare track links and front tow-hook loops; even its headlamp is still mounted on the glacis. The author quickly contacted the local authorities in the village, who agreed to watch over the field, as the author continued to contact the relevant officials in an attempt to impound the vehicle in the name of history and military study.

How could this historic, world-class find go completely unnoticed for all this time? By sheer serendipity, the author was investigating an SS unit action in the area, seeking the help of a local source in identifying the location of a particular wartime photograph. Upon recog-

nising the vehicle type in the photo, the local source told me that a tank very much like the one in my photo still lay resting in a farm field down the road, out of sight. I could scarcely believe my rudimentary French translation, yet set off at once. After visiting the farm, it quickly became apparent why this valuable find had remained hidden from the world for over 50 years. The farm, which for the time being will remain unidentified to protect the treasure which now resides therein, belonged to an old farmer of German extraction. Local legend had it that immediately after the war, this solitary figure took over the farm from its previous Belgian owners, who were killed in the battle which took place down the road. Some villagers went on to say that this figure was in fact a German officer from the unit which had swept through the village. Stricken with post-war remorse over what his unit had done, he had returned to the village to offer restitution. His subsequent assistance resulted in his running the farm in a most secretive manner until his death eight months previously at the age of 82. Until now, no one had been allowed onto the farm itself, and the villagers respected the reclusive visitor's solitary, secluded life. Upon clearing the house and its contents on his death, several of the villagers, walking the grounds for the first time since the war, discovered the armoured beast still sitting in a corner of the farm. Not wanting to draw attention to their village and the subsequent hordes of tourists, the secret was quietly kept to this day. Upon learning of this monumental historic discovery, and convincing the local villagers that the find would be treated with the utmost respect, the author was granted access to it, and the permission to finally tell the tale.

Preliminary research into the tank's original identity proceeded swiftly, thanks to its fantastic state of preservation. This superb relic is none other than the long-lost Tiger 211 of the schwere SS-Panzer-Abteilung 501, attached to the 1. SS-Panzer-Division. Careful investigation into the unit's activity on and around the evening of December 29, 1944 revealed tantalising yet mysterious references to the number of King Tigers used in the assault on the village. Interviews of the respective SS unit veterans 32 years after the war alluded to the activity of SS-Obersturmführer Rudolf Schmidt commanding a King Tiger which attacked the village from the east. In a brazen solitary move, SS-Obersturmführer Schmidt swept around the flank of the US 2nd Armored Division unit occupying the village centre (Task Force Brayer) and proceeded to eliminate no less than five Sherman M4A3 tanks, before losing contact with his unit. Veterans spoke of 'never hearing from Schmidt again'. Subsequent post-war salvage of the area failed to resolve the combat disappearance of the intrepid leader's vehicle of war. Analysis of the unit's hourly strength count, captured in Volume 2 of *Tigers in Battle* (Armor Review, Prescient Publications, 1972, Parkton, Maryland), makes only a single, cryptic reference to this anomaly: '... *on the evening of December 29, 1944, 501 unit strength had been reduced to three operational Tiger IIs by nightfall, as King Tiger 218 (Schwab) was disabled near the village bridge, and 211 (Schmidt) going unaccounted for in the heat of battle.*'

Today, the story has come full circle, and the pride of the unnamed village has at last been identified, along with its fateful history. Yet more historical discoveries await regarding this magnificent find, for first-hand examination by the author has found that the commander cupola's hatch is in fact still sealed from the inside. What treasures await its opening? In the very near future, this military time capsule will finally yield its secrets.

POSTSCRIPT: A PHOTOSHOP PHANTASY

What a dream! But alas, that is all it is . . . This composite photograph was the author's creation using Adobe Photoshop and a collection of close-up photographs taken by the author. First, a low-light photo of a snowy field was taken and chosen as the background setting. Armour aficionados will most likely recognise the tank itself as the specimen now residing in La Gleize, Belgium. However, this proud present-day survivor has well and truly been worked over by the author: original spotted Ardennes camouflage was added, as were the bow gun, tow-hook loops and glacis lamp (all borrowed from archive photos of Panthers in production). The spare tracks are in fact close-up photographs of Panther links from the surviving specimen at Houffalize. They have subsequently been cut out, weathered, transformed, scaled, distorted, and finally 'hung' on the original cleat brackets which still exist today on the La Gleize Tiger. The snow on the tank in the composite photo was also 'borrowed' from that in an author's photo of the Houffalize Panther; again, cut out, dimmed to match the low light and 'moulded' to fit the contour and crevices of the mysterious King Tiger 211. The snow stuck in its track cleats was painstakingly added by hand at the pixel level. The bow damage seen today on the La Gleize Tiger was easily removed (repaired!) by digital cloning, and the tank number itself changed from 213 to 211, also via cloning. Finally, to impart a feeling of location to No. 211, as it gradually sank in place under its own 67-ton weight, the snow and mud was digitally cloned and disturbed in a believable pattern. All told, 12 digital photo layers were used.

The true identity of the mysterious Tiger 211, once commanded by an enigmatic SS-Obersturmführer in defense of the Reich, is identified as the rare, restored, real-life mount of SS-Obersturmführer Rudolf Dollinger, attached to the 1. SS-Panzer Division 'Leibstandarte Adolf Hitler'. It now resides in the centre of La Gleize, Belgium, outside the December 1944 Museum. This photograph is the actual one used in the construction of the composite picture; the tank itself was masked out onto a layer, moved into the field, enlarged, scaled, painted, entrenched, weathered, outfitted and finally flattened.

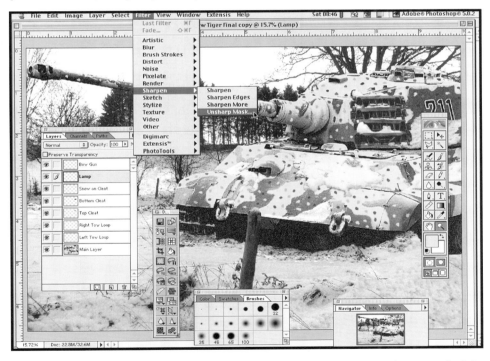

The 'historic' King Tiger No. 211, under construction. Transporting 67 tons of armoured might into a field was considerably easier with a Macintosh than a prime mover! 'Getting parts' for the tank's 'field upgrade' was a bit more difficult, though they were eventually secured and utilised. The camouflage pattern was studied from historic colour plates. Under the auspices of Adobe Photoshop, the king of battle once again assumes its rightful place in history.

A snowy field east of Nisramont, Belgium in January 1997 served as the 'corner of the farmer's field' where the historic discovery was made. The sun was indeed low in the sky that afternoon, yet Tiger 211 was nowhere to be found! It exists only in the mind of the author.

IN REPLY REFER TO:

Carpentier, Paul L.
PC-N ETO 004

19 April

Mr. Clarence R. Carpentier
410 East Swon Avenue
Webster Groves, Missouri

Dear Mr. Carpentier:

As promised you, I am writing again regarding your son, Private First Class Paul L. Carpentier, 37,605,665.

It has been my fervent hope that favorable information would be forthcoming so that you might be relieved from the great anxiety which you have borne during these months. It is therefore with deep regret that I must state that no further report in his case has been forwarded to the War Department.

I wish to again emphasize the fact that the Commanding Generals in all of our theaters of operations are making a continuous effort to establish the actual status of personnel who have been reported as missin